5

THE FEEL-GOOD CURRICULUM

The Dumbing-Down of America's Kids in the Name of Self-Esteem

MAUREEN STOUT, Ph.D.

PERSEUS PUBLISHING

Cambridge, Massachusetts

Many of the designations used by manufacturers and sellers to distinguish their products are claimed as trademarks. Where those designations appear in this book and Perseus Publishing was aware of a trademark claim, the designations have been printed in initial capital letters.

CIP information for this book is available from the Library of Congress.
ISBN: 0-7382-0435-8

Perseus Publishing is a member of the Perseus Books Group

Text design by Jeff Williams
Set in 11 point Minion by the Perseus Books Group

 2 3 4 5 6 7 8 9 10
First paperback printing, December 2000

Perseus Publishing books are available at special discounts for bulk purchases in the U.S. by corporations, institutions, and other organizations. For more information, please contact the Special Markets Department at HarperCollins Publishers, 10 East 53rd Street, New York, NY 10022, or call 1-212-207-7528.

Find us on the World Wide Web at http://www.perseuspublishing.com

To the memory of my father,
Dr. Terence David Stout (1917–1999),
who taught me the value of a good book.

Contents

Part III
Fighting Back: Challenging the
Consequences of Self-Esteem

Preface

Some years ago, after finishing a master's degree and feeling a little at loose ends, I took a part-time teaching job at a local university. I didn't know it at the time, but that job was to provide me not only direction for my future career but also provide inspiration for this book. I would be teaching an undergraduate course in the history of literacy to inmates in a medium-security men's prison. My students were considered the elite of the prison population, since all held high school diplomas and had proven their seriousness about their studies by paying a small sum out of their prison earnings for the privilege of working toward a university degree while behind bars.

My class numbered about ten students. I was aware that many of them had "graduated down" from maximum-security institutions and had therefore been convicted of very serious crimes. But there was an unstated agreement that they (with a few exceptions) didn't tell me about their criminal adventures, and I didn't ask. Perhaps my ignorance helped me get to know them as individuals and learn about the kind of upbringing each had experienced (mostly abusive) and what they expected to get out their education.

Of the group, a few stand out. There was Jeff, a thirty-something, fast-talking, would-be entrepreneur, who would tell me about his plans to go into banking when he got out. For him, getting a degree was a purely practical matter—it was going to help him in the business world. He was smart and funny and, as he admitted to me one day, knew something about banks (!). There was Bill, still in his early twenties. He was serious, hard-working, and eager to know more than I could ever teach him. He wanted to learn to improve his mind, since, according to his own admission, he hadn't paid much attention to his studies in high school. He asked me one day if I knew what it was like to be stopped by the police for walking home late at night "just 'cause you live in a crappy neighborhood." I had to tell him I didn't.

The student I remember best, however, is Richard, a native Canadian who had grown up moving from one foster home to another and had thus missed a lot of schooling. He was very shy and had the lowest level of achievement—and self-confidence—of all the students. Writing was a particular problem for him, as he had difficulty organizing and expressing his ideas. But underneath the bad writing I saw glimmers of ideas, of originality and creativity that could be developed. I knew I wouldn't be there long enough to help him improve very much, but I decided that, although he might very well fail the course, I would try to encourage him to continue to write. He persevered and with much effort improved his work considerably over the term, ending up with a C.

At the end of the term he came to me and said he never knew until now that he had the ability to achieve anything, since no one had ever expected anything of him. He was happy with the C, he said, since he had completed the course and had made progress and now felt that he maybe he did have the ability to write. It was the first time that I really understood what it meant to not have confidence in yourself, to believe that you are a failure.

I realized something more important, however: I could have told Richard a million times that he had potential and that he could succeed in school, but it wouldn't have made a particle of difference to him. He came to believe in his worth through his progress and achievement in the class. Nor did I give him a false sense of self-worth by giving him a grade he didn't deserve. He discovered his value through discovering his own imagination and creativity. His *self-esteem* came through success, not the other way around.

I decided that this teaching business could be a pretty satisfying way to earn a living, so after receiving my doctorate in education I began teaching future teachers. But something didn't seem right. Whereas my prison students had been eager to learn and clearly understood the benefits of a good education, many of these future teachers seemed apathetic, motivated not by the excitement of discovery but by grades that they seemed to think they deserved, whether or not they had earned them. These students seemed to think that they should get A's for effort rather than achievement, that high expectations were a form of oppression, and that they were entitled to good grades just for showing up in class. What was much more shocking, however, was where they said they picked up these ideas: from other teachers and from their professors of education.

Self-esteem, they had been told, was one of the main goals of public education. Creating a foundation of knowledge, producing informed citizens, or developing a moral sense were old hat: Feeling good about yourself is what school is for these days. These students had been indoctrinated by the prophets of self-esteem—their education professors—that the way to get kids to feel good about themselves is not by setting goals, striving for excellence, or helping others, but by telling them they're wonderful—whether they are or not.

Unfortunately, these fallacies promoted in the name of self-esteem—that low expectations are good, competition is bad, and school is for therapy—have damaged at least two generations of kids in the United States. And, in a sad irony, the students who are most hurt by these fallacies are those who were meant to most benefit from them: poor and minority kids, those who are most at risk for school failure. Dumbing down curricula in order to make kids feel good about themselves cheats them of the opportunity to develop their full potential and, in the process, develop *real* self-esteem—the self-confidence that comes only from success.

Success has moral as well as intellectual components, and in this book I propose that moral guidance, broadly defined, must be part of the foundation of public schooling. Research (and common sense) tells us that most parents want their kids to become good citizens and that virtues such as honesty, integrity, respect for others, and personal responsibility are concepts that we can all support. This discussion of moral education may not please either liberals or conservatives, since I am proposing a conception of moral education—and education in general—that does not fit neatly into a party political platform. Whether it pleases or not, however, if it engages participants on both sides of the education debates, it may help refocus the discussions on substance rather than rhetoric. What is at stake here is no less than the quality and future of children's lives, and that is something that is too big to be contained in any party slogan. That is what I learned from Richard and from many other students, who, like him, deserve better than what they've been getting for the past twenty-five years. They deserve an education.

If there is anger in this book, it is directed not at the kids but at the cynicism of some education professors who continue to promote ideas regarding self-esteem that do more harm than good. If there is passion, it is to get parents, teachers, and anyone else who is interested to understand how important it is to expect great things of all kids and to help them reach their goals. If there is hope, it is that those of us who have the luxury to debate these issues—the luxury of a good education—will come to realize that it shouldn't be a luxury but a right for all children.

Acknowledgments

I am very grateful for the encouragement given me by my friends and family throughout the writing of this book. I would also like to thank Frank Darmstadt for his help, Perseus Books, and my editor, Marnie Cochran, for her honesty, her critical eye, and her very good suggestions. And I must give a special thank-you to Edward Knappman, my agent, who took a chance on an unknown and has been unfailingly supportive. Thanks to all of you.

The Feel-Good Curriculum

Introduction

The False Prophet of Self-Esteem

If you think education is expensive, try ignorance.
—Derek Bok[1]

IT WAS CLEAR TO ME right away that I was in foreign territory. I had just started my first "real job" as a professor of education at a respected state university and was excited about the prospect of sharing what I had learned in graduate school with future teachers. I would be working in my areas of expertise—philosophy of education, educational foundations, and multiculturalism—teaching a required course to all teacher candidates. It would be rewarding, I said to myself, to be with people who saw teaching as an opportunity to develop children's minds and, like me, saw schools as the place where they develop intellect, character, integrity, decency—their hearts as well as their minds.

My first hint that perhaps not all my students shared my view of things came after I marked the first assignments. Students began trickling in to my office with the same comments and demands:

I need a better grade.
I deserve an A on this paper.
I *never* get B's.

These were not polite requests for me to review their work, to explain to them their grade and how they might have improved it. These thinly veiled threats meant: change the grade or else! The "or else," of course, to an assistant professor, can be quite terrifying: a complaint to the department chair, the dean, or—heaven forbid—the administration.

Along with those who clearly believed that they were entitled to an A, there were those who didn't think they needed to do any work and exhibited considerable surprise when they consequently failed the class. Then there were the more creative types who thought up some wonderful excuses for late work. (As others have remarked, it's amazing how many grandmothers pass away during exam time!) Taking a "necessary" vacation was a popular one. And then there were those who, in an apparent attempt to maximize the possibility of success, combined various excuses: One earnest young man told me that he had been obliged to accompany his wife to her grandmother's funeral but, perhaps sensing my suspicions, changed his story and confessed that the real reason for his absence was that he needed a vacation. And finally, there were those who just couldn't seem to follow directions. Despite detailed written and verbal instructions for every assignment, some people simply refused to do what was required of them. What I didn't realize at the time was that that was the crux of the problem: They didn't think that anything *should* be required of them.

I was mystified by these attitudes and behaviors, particularly as they came from people who were clearly eager to become teachers, who cared about kids, and who were obviously very dedicated to the profession. They seemed like nice people who happened to have some rather odd ideas about what being a student—and a teacher—is all about. What on earth was going on? Perhaps I wasn't explaining things clearly in class. So I tried to make my teaching style a little more "user friendly," so to speak, and against my better judgment modified (read: watered down) the curriculum in the hope of improving things. Although the students seemed to be enjoying the class more, they still came up with bizarre demands, rebelled against doing any actual work, and complained that I didn't give an A for effort.

After a couple of semesters I realized that my efforts were fruitless and decided to ask my colleagues about their experiences. Did they have these problems? If so, what did they do about them? While their responses to the first question reassured me and made me think that perhaps it wasn't just me, their answers to the second disturbed me. "Sure, everyone has those problems; that's just the way students are nowadays," said a few. "Students get bored easily and expect to be entertained," said another, "so you have to make the class as exciting as possible." "As far as following directions and handing work in on time—well, they're just not used to doing that, and it isn't important anyway, so don't worry about it. Oh, and if you want to avoid arguments about grades, just give most of them A's— that's what everyone else does."

There were only two possible explanations for my colleagues' rather shocking answers to my inquiries: Either they were so hardened by years of student demands that they had become cynical and expected nothing better from them, or they didn't see anything wrong with the behavior. I decided to explore the matter further and asked my colleagues why they thought our students expected and demanded good grades but didn't feel they should work for them. And did it concern them that many of our future teachers—no exaggeration here, I promise—couldn't write a coherent sentence, much less a research paper? Most of my colleagues agreed that these were, indeed, serious concerns. Almost everyone believed that future teachers should be literate, responsible students and should understand that grades are not just handed out like so much candy at Halloween. But, they said, it is a little late to be teaching people to write a five-paragraph essay in university. "It's not *our* problem if they can't write," said one. "The damage was done in high school. They were never expected to earn their grades." And, they added, these people are anxious to get out into the schools and start teaching, so it wouldn't be *nice* to fail them just because they haven't mastered some basic skills. It wouldn't be good for their *self-esteem*.

I started to remember other strange conversations with my colleagues. One of the more bizarre occurred at a faculty meeting at which we examined the results of a faculty survey on the purposes of public schooling. One faculty member had responded that schools should be like a womb for students. At first I thought this was a joke and, turning to my neighbor, was about to say what a good one that was when I stopped short. Rather than find this amusing, the group seemed to regard it as a profound statement regarding the public school, and all nodded grave agreement that schools should indeed be like a womb. You may well wonder what they meant by that. Well, a womb is a warm, secure, and insulated environment. The unborn child is protected and nourished until she is ready to face the world and, perhaps most important, no demands are made on her.

This is what professors of education believe schools should be like: places in which children are insulated from the outside world and emotionally—not intellectually—nourished. We should expect nothing of them but give everything to them; they should be cared for, counseled, and analyzed, and the whole school environment should be centered on their needs. Schools are no longer for learning essential skills or acquiring knowledge but for cultivating what Daniel Goleman calls "emotional intelligence": the ability to get along with others, understand one's feelings and one's emotional hang-ups, and generally figure out how to deal with others effectively.[2] This attitude explains why my colleagues always referred to the importance of making kids feel good about themselves but rarely, if ever, spoke of achievement, ideals, goals, character, or decency. It was all about *feelings*. It was all about *self-esteem*.

Now while I'm just as in favor of self-esteem as the next girl, I had always labored under the assumption that feeling good about oneself—the essence of self-esteem—was, or should be, the consequence of hard work, achievement, learning from one's mistakes, giving to others, trying to be a better person, or other similar endeavors. It had never occurred to me that I could bypass all that and just wake up and decide unilaterally (or with the help of my teachers) that I was a superb human being. I didn't realize that just by being in the world I was special, special enough to deserve grades, respect, and opportunities without ever having to earn them. But this is the dominant view among not only professors of education, but their students—our children's future teachers.

Every semester when I would ask my students what they believed the role of a teacher should be, the replies would be the same:

To be a student's friend.
To get the students to feel good about themselves.
To get them to see me as one of their peers.

They would also, with chilling predictability, express in different forms the following beliefs. First, children shouldn't be challenged to try something that others in the class are not ready for, since that would promote competition, and competition is bad for self-esteem. Second, grading should be avoided if at all possible but, if absolutely necessary, should be done in a way that avoids any indication that Johnny is anything less than a stellar pupil. In other words, grading should reveal only strengths, not weaknesses, and if there are no strengths, then we should make some up. Third, effort, not achievement, is what counts, and grades should reflect that. Fourth, discipline, when necessary, should take the form of "mediation" and "peer counseling"; that way the student never has to acknowledge or obey the authority of the teacher and the teacher can avoid any responsibility for her students' behavior. And, fifth, any discussion of morality, character, or virtue is to be avoided at all costs because, after all, everyone has his or her own view of right and wrong, and all must be respected—whether they merit it or not.

What astonished me was the consistency of these responses. With few exceptions, all my students, every year, expressed the same views on education. Although some felt more strongly about certain issues than others and expressed several variations on the theme, the core beliefs were the same. Schooling should be for, above all, developing, promoting, and protecting student self-esteem. Developing intellect and character were of secondary importance and, to some, seemed of no interest at all. But I realized that these teachers were only echoing what their professors—my colleagues—had taught them and what they had been taught by their teachers in school: that we all deserve high self-esteem, irrespective of our true worth to ourselves or others. Feeling good about oneself is all that counts.

The End of Ideals and the Birth of Self-Esteem

How did we get here? When did the purpose of schooling become to discover oneself rather than discover the world? When did we begin to replace the historic purposes of the common school—teaching a core of knowledge, preparing citizens to be active participants in the democratic process, providing a skilled workforce—with the ideology of the self-esteem movement? Although it was probably always understood that a positive side effect of education is having an educated citizenry capable of making rational educational, employment, and personal choices, the public school was never intended to serve the personal whims of each individual. Indeed it cannot do so, since a public school, by definition, must provide the education that the public as a whole—not as individuals—wants. One of the reasons the public school is constantly under fire, of course, is that the public can rarely agree on just what that education should be and thus schools are constantly trying to balance conflicting political, social, and educational interests. But what is clear is that the cultivation of self-esteem was never an overriding interest and was only considered (if it was considered at all) a consequence of achievement, hard work, and responsibility. Only recently in the history of American schooling has self-esteem become the primary goal of education.

This book tells the story of the self-esteem movement—its effects on our schools and society, and, most important, how we can fix what has gone wrong. Our current addiction to self-esteem grew from the increasing influence of the therapy movement in schools and in society over the last seventy-five years. That movement, in turn, has fed off the anti-rationalism and anti-intellectualism that characterize contemporary post-modern culture, itself a result of a collective disillusionment with the ideals of classical liberalism that have historically grounded both our schools and our society.

Until the twentieth century, Americans believed in the Enlightenment doctrines of progress, rationality, and man's increasing control over his political, social, economic, and physical world. Individual (and social) progress is of course the heart of the American Dream, and schools are where we prepare the hearts and minds of another generation to adopt it as their own. Teaching American history and the core subjects, reciting the Pledge of Allegiance, and engaging in team sports promote citizenship and a collective understanding of this uniquely American value while acquiring the basic skills and knowledge of a liberal education provides each student with the tools to pursue the dream in his or her own way.

But throughout this century, and particularly over the last thirty years, Americans have been losing their faith in the classical liberal ideals of social justice and progress and have turned to the new science of psychology for answers. Scarred by the national experience in Vietnam and wrenched apart by continuing racial divisions—and also perhaps because of a history of political isolationism and individualism—Americans turned inward for answers. And when they were offered something that claimed to help them feel good about themselves again, they embraced it wholeheartedly. Psychology was already becoming an important area of social science and by the 1940s was exerting considerable influence over educational theory and practice. By the 1960s the language of psychology began to infiltrate popular culture. The self-help industry was born.

The popularity of psychology was boosted by the disillusionment of intellectuals with the ideals of the Enlightenment and the concept of progress, which many were beginning to view as a myth built on the back of the slavery and colonialism that masked the grim realities of postindustrial capitalist economies that perpetuated economic and racial inequalities. So the optimism of modernism began to be replaced (in academic circles at least) by the cynicism of postmodernism and poststructuralism. And in many ways the idea of self-esteem is the perfect icon for a postmodern world: entirely self-referential, highly relative, ill defined, totally individualized, and deliberately ignorant of either the concept of community or the ideal of progress. If acquiring high self-esteem has replaced the ideals of creating a civil society, ensuring social justice, or developing character and intellect, we have truly fulfilled the gloomy destiny of postmodernism by replacing those ideals with new ideologies: narcissism, separatism, emotivism, and cynicism. The idolization of the self is the ultimate consequence not of modernism but of our failure to preserve its promise.

If It's Broke, Why Not Fix It?

As I explain throughout the book, the concept of self-esteem has become so entrenched in the national psyche that dislodging it is going to take considerable time and effort. But in Part 3 I provide practical suggestions on how we can all fight our collective addiction to self-esteem and how we might replace these very destructive ideologies with ideals of empathy, connectedness, rationality, morality, skepticism, and hope and thus begin the next century with a philosophy of education that will help sustain it into the new millennium. This new philosophy must be something formed from public debate, not handed down from on high by academics or policymakers. And the foundation for this new philosophy must be grounded in ideals, not ideologies, and in commonsense practices, not educational fads that change from one year to the next.

Instead of narcissism, we need empathy—the ability and desire to enter into and understand the experiences, ideas, and feelings of others. This will help us with our second task: replacing the separatist tendencies that the self-esteem movement has produced with a sense of connectedness, both between individuals and between ethnic and racial groups, because we live in communities, neighborhoods, towns, and cities, and we create meaning in our lives largely through our interactions with others. The story of the human experience is in many ways the story of a search for personal happiness and fulfillment, but since the origins of man that search has been collective, not solitary.

Emotivism, the third ideology or "symptom" of our addiction to self-esteem, is the absence or deliberate denial of rationality. Emotivists act on their feelings and emotions and in the process undermine the importance and necessity of rationality in creating good students, good schools, and a civil society. It is also amoral, since being a moral person requires one to also be a thinking person. We need to resurrect rationality, teach our kids to be critical thinkers, and show them how to be decent and thoughtful individuals. And finally, skepticism and hope must replace the rampant cynicism that we see in young people today. Cynicism is perhaps the most pervasive and most pernicious effect of the self-esteem movement and is the perfect icon of a postmodern society. It is very fashionable to downplay idealism and claim that everyone is only out for oneself and that there's nothing left to believe in. But if we have indeed created a society in which each of us only looks out for number one, we can also re-create a society in which we care for each other and in which children still dream of a better future and, most important, are given the skills they need to make those dreams come true.

What philosophers call "living the good life" depends upon building a good society, and that society can only be built by individuals working together, not working on themselves. This does not mean that we must all share the same view of how society should be constructed or even the values it expresses, nor does it mean subsuming our needs to those of others. It does mean that our journey to self-discovery should be marked by the occasional stop to see how others are faring and to ask them if they would like to ride along with us for a while. And on that journey the ideology of self-esteem will only lead us astray, because although it promises fulfillment it only increases our mutual alienation. And there's no self-help manual for that.

PART ONE

Creating a Culture of Therapy

How We Got Here from There

1

What Is School For, Anyway?

I read Shakespeare and the Bible, and I can shoot dice.
That's what I call a liberal education.
—Tallulah Bankhead[1]

HISTORICALLY, PUBLIC SCHOOLING HAS SERVED both the public interest of creating good citizens as well as educating individuals, providing them with a solid foundation of skills and knowledge. Despite research indicating that most parents still support these purposes, the prevailing wisdom among professors of education seems to be that schools should be redirected to cater to children's emotional and psychological needs. Preparing them to enter society or giving them a classical liberal education is seen as considerably less important. In fact, the ideology of the self-esteem movement poses a serious threat to the ideals of liberal education and is threatening to replace them as the core purposes of public education. But before examining the traditional purposes of schooling and the effects of the self-esteem movement on them, we need to gain an understanding of what this movement is all about.

Question: What Does It Mean? Answer: Not Much

Despite the enormous amount of writing on the subject of self-esteem, both in the popular press and in academia, few self-esteem advocates appear to feel the need to establish a generally acceptable working definition of it. But definitions are important because they indicate how a particular concept is used and reveal one's worldview. Some observers regard self-esteem as the value we put on characteristics that differentiate us from others[2] while others equate self-esteem with self-respect, arguing that it should not be a reward for stacking up well to others in some area but should be a basic right of an individual in a just society.[3] The current definition of self-esteem used by educators and psychologists seems to be what we might call an "entitlement" view of the self: feeling good about oneself irrespective of individual or social attributes or characteristics.

If self-esteem refers to the value that we put on ourselves, the current notion seems to be that we should all put a high value on ourselves, whether we deserve it or not. Put crudely, this view of self-esteem means *feeling good for no good reason*. It is entirely divorced from any concept of merit; the idea is that we are all entitled to feel good about ourselves, no matter what others think or whether we have done or said anything to warrant it. This way, of course, all of us can have high self-esteem because there are no criteria for it. All we need to do is claim it for ourselves and we have it. Self-esteem advocates Matthew McKay and Patrick Fanning write that "the problem of self-esteem is this human capacity for judgment."[4] In other words, self-esteem may be damaged by judgment (by oneself or by others), which must therefore be avoided at all costs.

Typically, self-esteem is not defined at all in self-help books or teacher manuals, but one gets a good feel for the current thinking about it by its associated words and phrases: working on the "inner light,"[5] thinking positive thoughts, rejecting the negative, self-love, positive self-talk, and so on. John P. Hewitt in *The Myth of Self-Esteem* describes the "conventional wisdom"[6] about self-esteem, noting that today people relate self-esteem to many different aspects of their lives, from how they view themselves physically to their success in business to how they raise their children. He contrasts the current wisdom on self-esteem—that it's something we can and should control individually—with what he terms the "old-fashioned" view on self-esteem: that it should be something that is earned. The latter view constitutes true self-confidence, which I propose in this book. I believe that self-esteem is not something that we are entitled to simply by existing. It should be based on some idea of competence; that we merit self-esteem and, perhaps more important, the esteem of others because we have done something to deserve it.

Hewitt does not try to arbitrate between these two perspectives, since his interest is primarily in how and why members of a culture choose to believe in a particular concept and not specifically whether or not the concept can be proved or disproved with evidence. But my concern is with precisely this issue. All observers, whether promoters or critics of self-esteem, agree that it has become one of the most important concepts in American life, and it clearly exerts profound influence over virtually all school policy and practice. But surely, if we are going to decide what and how our children learn, how we raise our children, and how we interact with one another based on the idea of self-esteem, we need to be sure that the concept is useful, meaningful, and definable. If it is going to be what the California Task Force on Self-Esteem envisioned it, the "unifying concept to reframe American problem solving,"[7] we need to be pretty confident that we are basing our decisionmaking, policymaking, and problem solving on something reliable. This book examines the reality of self-esteem and how the public has been tragically misled by academics, policymakers, and educators into believing in a concept that is not only empty but very dangerous.

In fact, the absence of a clear definition of self-esteem is one of the most dangerous aspects of our addiction to it. Teachers and professors of education refer to it as if we all know what we are talking about, but we don't really understand what it means until it is too late, when we see its effects: grade inflation, lowered expectations, and social promotion, among other things. No one bothered to tell parents that education researchers in their wisdom decided that giving Johnny the C he earned would be bad for his self-esteem and that they decided he should get the A he didn't earn instead. What they also didn't tell them—or Johnny, for that matter—was that as a result of this practice, Johnny will not be aware of what he hasn't learned until it is too late, when he graduates from high school and finds out that he really doesn't know very much of anything at all. Then just how good is he going to feel about himself? But no one wants to answer that question. As one observer puts it, "If self-esteem is our goal, we're making our kids feel terrific about doing less and less."[8]

I suggest, then, that meaningful self-esteem (or self-confidence), in addition to being based on competence, should also have moral dimensions; that we should be judged by others and judge ourselves on how we treat others and how we conduct ourselves in the world. This is in direct contradiction to the prevailing view of self-esteem, which claims that positive feelings of self-worth are necessary *before* we can achieve anything worthwhile in life and, moreover, that we should never judge others. But anyone who has ever given something to another without any expectation of reward or recompense will say that the reason they feel good about themselves is precisely because they have given something to another, and in the act of giving have discovered something good in themselves. In fact almost any activity that requires an investment of the mind, body, or soul and leads to self-improvement or the betterment of others is an activity that will naturally lead to feelings of self-worth. That is meaningful self-esteem: feeling good about oneself because of intentional effort aimed at improvement and accomplishment.

These criteria seem to me to be reasonable and indeed "reasonableness" should be the principal criterion of appropriate self-esteem, according to one observer, Richard Keshen. In *Reasonable Self-Esteem* he identifies six guidelines for reasonableness, all of which are markers to which the reasonable person would refer when deciding just how good about herself she should feel: weighting, adequacy and truthfulness, consistency, sincere assent, universalizability, and harmonization.[9] The first three refer to the individual's willingness to be as accurate and honest as possible when determining her self-worth. The "sincere assent" guideline is particularly important, since it says that a reasonable person will revise a reason for self-esteem if, upon reflection, she finds that it was unjustified. The "universalizability" guideline is also important, since it suggests that a person should hold the same standards of worth in others' attributes as in her own. And, finally, the "harmonization" guideline says that the reasonable person will ensure that her sense of self-esteem is consistent with her overall value system.

Although we are unlikely to take the time to go over each of these guidelines every time we happen to feel good about ourselves, they do provide a very useful grounding for a commonsense notion of self-esteem that is based on *something:* competence, honesty in self-evaluation, respect for others, or other similar notions. Keshen's discussion tells us that, contrary to the prevailing dogma, it is not reasonable for each of us to decide, quite arbitrarily and with disregard for any objective criteria, that we should feel good about ourselves. There must be reasons for our self-esteem—good reasons—and we must be honest enough to admit to ourselves and others when we have been puffing ourselves up with no reason at all.

The Attraction of Self-Esteem

The goal of the self-esteem movement is, of course, high self-esteem: we all want to feel good about ourselves. The idea is simple: Each of us must work on loving ourselves. We must accept ourselves and others for who and what we are. Tolerance is important. We must not judge ourselves or others, nor demand much of anyone. Children, especially, are to be accepted nonjudgmentally and must not be challenged academically or disciplined, since that might make a dent in their self-concept. It is the "I'm OK, you're OK" view of the world.

This is a very seductive notion. Who among us likes to be judged? We all crave acceptance. So for many the self-esteem movement doubtless seems like a wonderful guide for life because it does not include the demands made by, for example, organized religion. Most religions require that man admit his imperfections and spend his life trying to become a better person. This means, if not following specific religious teachings, at least generally adhering to some basic rules of civilized conduct. But the self-esteem movement says that we are all just fine the way we are and that the only conduct we need concern ourselves with is our own. In the language of self-esteem, we need only "discover" ourselves; get to know "who we are" in order to be self-sufficient. We don't have to explain ourselves to anyone else, apologize for, or even admit to, bad behavior, or follow anyone else's rules, since we answer only to ourselves. Why look to religion for emotional and spiritual sustenance when you just have to look in the mirror and find it? Why look for a god elsewhere when you have one right in front of you?

Whereas religion and society try to constrain us and demand that we conform to rules and accept our social obligations, the self-esteem movement promises us the opposite: liberation from all constraints. To many Americans who believe their liberties are being slowly eroded by the state or by corporate or other interests, this is a very appealing idea. The self-esteem movement has in fact given new ammunition to civil libertarians, who fight any attempt to modify rights with responsibilities, while fostering what Christopher Lasch identified twenty years ago as a culture of narcissism.[10] And the very strong individualism that characterizes much of American culture no doubt explains why the self-esteem movement has become more popular here than anywhere else in the world.

The idea of self-esteem also appeals to Americans because it refers to the concept of self-reliance, which is the underlying principle of the American Dream: study hard, work hard, pull yourself up by your bootstraps, and you too can be a success. It is the perfect expression of "life, liberty, and the pursuit of happiness." Of course, as Thurgood Marshall once pointed out, "None of us got where we are solely by pulling ourselves up by our bootstraps. We got here because somebody . . . bent down and helped us pick up our boots."[11] Nevertheless, the dream and the faith in self-reliance persist. Finally we have a religion that doesn't tell us we're sinners and a god that accepts us as we are. This must be nirvana. But the relationship experts have this right, at least: If it seems too good to be true, it probably is.

Addiction and Its Effects

The self-esteem movement is the original naked emperor, promising much but, when unclothed, revealing itself as a false god. Religious doctrine can be used to manipulate, alienate, and control people rather than enlighten them, and the doctrines of self-esteem are no different. In fact the self-esteem movement is probably a greater threat to our intellectual freedom than more visible fringe religions or cults because it is insidious. It is represented by no church, mosque, or synagogue, yet its doctrines are well-known; it does not often appear as the subject on a course syllabus in colleges of teacher education, yet it pervades all subjects. It is not a formal part of the curriculum in public schools, yet its effects are seen in the attitudes, behaviors, and skill levels of children from public schools across the country. There is no accredited school or formal training for self-esteem (apart from various self-help workshops) yet thousands have set themselves up as "experts" in it and sell us books on how to get it for ourselves.

But what do we learn from these books? Sadly, we learn very little, but their authors and the self-help industry in general gain a lot from us, the unwitting consumers. The movement creates a dependence on self-help books, which feed off our endless insecurities and personal traumas but promise that if we read just one more we'll be thin enough, smart enough, and "emotionally intelligent" enough to get through life intact. The trick here of course is that if the road to salvation lies in "knowing yourself," that is very likely a never ending process, so people buy countless books on how to become happy but never actually reach that state, for two reasons: first, because absolute happiness is probably impossible to achieve, and second, even if were possible, it would be unlikely to come about through endless navel gazing.

The self-esteem movement also creates a permanent state of victimization. The student is inadequate—a victim of bad parents or mean teachers and an uncaring society—and must be "cured" by a variety of therapeutic practices and teaching methods designed to foster self-esteem. This is particularly evident with kids who fall outside our expectations of what is "normal" either intellectually or behaviorally. They are immediately identified as "learning disabled" (so the special education teachers have something to do) or are diagnosed as having attention deficit disorder and put on a variety of medications whose long-term effects on children are unknown. In a tragically self-fulfilling prophecy, these kids will only achieve what is expected of them: very little. They are likely to begin thinking of themselves as victims, which they are: not of imagined illnesses but of the self-esteem movement.

This sense of entitlement and victimhood extends into society, as well. After the Enlightenment man exchanged religious worship for the ideals of progress and liberalism. But these gods, their image now tarnished, have themselves been replaced. Man now worships himself. But we also have a concept of civil society, a social compact, in which individual rights and liberties are balanced with individual responsibilities. We have a shared understanding of, if not a common good, at least how to peacefully coexist. It seemed that man had finally learned that unfettered individual or social excesses threaten the social contract and the happiness of each individual who shares in it.

But the self-esteem movement has spawned a new kind of barbarism. As anyone who has been the victim of road rage—or the latest, air rage—can attest, there is an increasing sense of entitlement permeating society at large. The idea is, sadly, already familiar to us: I want to do what I want, how I want and when I want, and nothing and no one is going to stop me. The self-esteem movement has given us a new golden rule. No longer is it "Do unto others as you would have them do unto to you" but "Do it to others before they do it to you"!

Self-Esteem in Schools

One need only pick up a local or national paper to get a (bad) taste of the current state of America's public schools. Just glancing through some of the research on schools I find the following: Only nineteen states require students to pass state tests to graduate from high school and only six have laws that will link students' promotion to test results in the future.[12] No states are truly holding teachers accountable for their performance by either rewarding or sanctioning them based on how well their students perform on tests.[13] In a recent survey of incoming college freshmen conducted by the Higher Education Research Institute at UCLA only about 33 percent of freshmen reported doing more than six hours of homework per week, down more than 10 percent from a decade earlier.[14] And the achievement gap that exists between whites and minorities in higher education, as well as K–12 education, continues. In the academic year 1994–1995 of a total of 1.16 million bachelor's degrees awarded, only 54,000 went to Hispanics and 87,000 to blacks, whereas 913,000 were awarded to whites.[15]

From teacher quality to national standards to funding and minority issues, the state of public education leaves a lot to be desired. One could go
on forever citing the ills that plague contemporary American schools. But
there is also a lot to cheer about in America's public schools. Schools today
educate a vastly more linguistically, culturally, racially, and economically
diverse population than anyone could have imagined when the first common schools opened in the early nineteenth century. For example, in the
city of New York there are about 120 different languages spoken and in
Los Angeles there are at least 90. Despite this diversity, the national
dropout rate is less than 10 percent, although it is much higher among
some racial groups than others. And for the first time, the percentage of
black students earning a high school diploma equals that of white students, according to a recent report by the U.S. Census Bureau on educational attainment.[16] Since 1990, six states have shown improvement in
fourth and eighth grade mathematics scores on the National Assessment
of Educational Progress.[17] And in 1999 twenty-three states provided financial assistance to teachers seeking national board certification, up from
only thirteen in 1998.[18]

Schools also provide basic health and welfare services that would otherwise simply not be available to some children, although, as I discuss in the
next chapter, providing these services may be putting an unnecessary
strain on the school system. We are also educating more adult learners
and new immigrants to help those who did not profit from their formal
education or who were educated elsewhere to become literate, acquire a
high school diploma, and gain the skills they need to become full participants in American life.

Clearly it is a mixed bag. The bad news—and the embarrassing truth—
about many of our current school problems is that they are consequences
of the self-esteem movement. The movement's practices and methods do
nothing to foster authentic self-esteem—the confidence that arises from
achievement—but rob children of a real education and make a mockery
of the school system in the process. Until very recently, words like "standards" and "achievement" were virtually taboo because the education establishment views them as "uncaring"—the most damning word in the
self-esteem lexicon. The good news, as I explain throughout this book, is
that many of the movement's negative effects can be easily remedied by
getting rid of its more dangerous practices and replacing them with
proven, commonsense policies, methods, and practices.

And the best news of all is that the tide is turning. Since I began re-
searching this book about three years ago, I have witnessed two dramatic
changes. The first is that the public—particularly parents—have become

more vocal about their dissatisfaction with what their kids are (or are not) learning in school. Parents cannot understand why little Johnny and Janie can't read in the third, fourth, or fifth grade; why they frequently don't have homework; why they don't have any grades on their report cards (if they receive report cards at all); and why the teacher insists that everything is fine. One thing that educators have gotten right over the years is that when parents become actively involved in their children's education, everyone wins. And as parental participation has grown, parents have become better consumers of education, have gained more knowledge about school policies and practices, and feel more confident about speaking up when they see things that concern them.

Second, and in large measure in response to parental criticism, education professors, teachers, and policymakers have begun to take another look at the practices invented with self-esteem in mind, and many are finding them lacking. Whole language learning and Ebonics, two pet projects of self-esteem promoters, are coming under serious scrutiny. Whole language learning is the brilliant idea of teaching reading to young children by, in essence, avoiding teaching them at all. Children are given "literature"—that is, books that they do not yet have the skills to decipher—and are allowed to "explore" these books to see what sense, if any, they can make of them. The result of this immoral experiment, which I examine in Chapter 5, is at least two generations of kids, now adults, who read poorly (if at all), dislike reading, and probably have a justified mistrust of educators. Forget hooked on phonics. We're hooked on therapy. But fortunately, many teachers across the country are dusting off their phonics books and are returning to actually *teaching* reading—something that had quite gone out of style.

Ebonics (from "phonics" and "ebony"), which I also discuss in Chapter 5, is a more insidious reading fad because it targets only black Americans. Ebonics is using the black vernacular, or "street talk," in schools to teach black children, in order to get them to feel good about themselves and the way they talk. They are only to be exposed to the presumed trauma of learning correct English when they appear psychologically prepared for it. It takes little imagination to see that, if it were to be implemented on a wide scale, the consequences would be similar to those of whole language learning: a lowering of skill levels and attainment, and an increased alienation from school generally.

"Behavior modification" and "mediation," rather than simple discipline, are also being reevaluated because teachers are beginning to understand that children need clear boundaries and that negotiating everything is not necessarily in the best interests of the student or the teacher. Another practice that has recently come under fire from academics, teachers, and even President Clinton is social promotion. This refers to passing students on to the next grade whether or not they have mastered required material. It is defended by self-esteem advocates who argue that "success builds self-esteem. It works well every time, and best when the line of successes remains continuous and unbroken."[19] But to enjoy self-esteem, one needs to experience *real* success, not the false sense of success that comes from social promotion. Self-esteem advocates contend that children might suffer if they are held back, but the real suffering comes after their public schooling. After twelve years of social promotion, how high will their self-esteem be when they graduate from high school functionally illiterate?

I believe that we are witnessing the beginning of a return to commonsense practices in school. Nevertheless, over the past century the self-esteem movement has immensely influenced curricula, teaching methods, and evaluative practices. This brings up some important questions: What should we teach in schools, anyway? What do we expect students to know when they finish school? And how has the influence of the self-esteem movement changed the purposes of the American public school?

The Common School and Its Goals

Today's public school developed from the "common school," so named because it was created to teach all children in one schoolhouse rather than in the church schools, charity schools, and boarding schools that had educated the nation's youth up until the early to middle nineteenth century. Horace Mann, a nineteenth-century educational leader from Massachusetts and the so-called "father of the common school" believed that universal education was the key to improving society and that the common school would serve as an equalizing influence in American life. Mann's vision was a publicly funded school open to all children, irrespective of class or social standing. But common schools were not invented simply to provide students with knowledge and skills for their personal enhancement. On the contrary, they were primarily seen as a tool to educate a citizenry into the dominant social, political, and moral values.

Schools were seen as a way to improve society through promoting common bonds while providing equality of opportunity for individuals. Here we come to a classic dilemma of public schooling: How do we teach children to become independent, thinking adults while ensuring that they adopt society's values? This is a particularly urgent question today, given our emphasis on teaching about ethnic and cultural diversity. As I discuss at more length in Chapter 7, identity is seen as essential in the development of self-esteem, and ethnicity is considered the root of identity, so teaching about one's ethnic heritage is today a core purpose of public education, whereas teaching "common values" is politically charged and highly controversial. Whose values are we talking about? Are they really common? Today's multiculturalists contend that political conservatives are only interested in promoting their views of education and society, whereas conservatives argue that those on the left are only interested in promoting theirs.

Both, of course, are right. Public schooling in America has never been, nor will it ever be, politically neutral. Public schools are institutions of the state, and reflect in their curricula, teaching methods, and textbooks the dominant political ideologies as well as the special interests of any given era. But they are not simply institutions invented to serve government; they were invented to serve the people, and the individual, and individuals can, therefore, have great influence over what goes on in schools. It is at once the biggest strength and the biggest weakness of the public school, since it means that parents really do have the power, if they wish to exercise it, to ensure that schools are educating their children as they would wish. The other side, of course, is that anyone with a particular ideological agenda—creationists, school prayer advocates, or multiculturalists—can exert considerable influence over school policy and practice.

But in the early days of the public school, emphasizing cultural difference through multiculturalism was not an issue; schools taught the presumed "common heritage" and common political values so that children would grow up to be responsible citizens. Advocates of the common school believed that an educated citizenry was essential to sustain democracy and protect the integrity of American public institutions. It was, and is, the most enduring goal of public schooling: to develop a citizenry that participates actively in public life, for that participation is the foundation of democracy.

So along with political and moral unity, cultural unity was seen as another desirable goal of the public school. This new common school was seen as the ideal place to teach the common language, culture, and heritage of the United States. As the current debates over bilingual education illustrate, language is considered the vehicle through which all aspects of culture are transmitted. How or if it is taught symbolizes its importance in society. In the early days of the public school, the idea of teaching different languages to allow students to learn about their heritage was unknown; the goal, on the contrary, was to "Americanize" students. Schools were not for teaching about different cultures but for teaching people to share one culture and know one heritage. This was before the days of the "mosaic" or "salad bowl." These were the days of the "melting pot." By molding like-minded individuals, early supporters of the common school hoped to prevent or at least mediate social problems like crime and violence. Since everyone (in principle) attended school, inequalities caused by poverty or other social ills would be attenuated not only in school but in society as well. Public schools were given the burden of fixing what was wrong in society; a burden that it still carries today, and one made even heavier by the self-esteem movement.

Schools were also meant to train future workers who would help sustain the national economy and were thus seen as the perfect place to instruct children in the Protestant ethic of hard work and obedience. And finally, schools were to provide a moral foundation of Christian ethics that would develop God-fearing individuals who respected their government, their elders, and their community, and who would lead decent, productive lives. With the exception of the now very contentious goal of promoting cultural unity, these original purposes of the public school have changed very little since the invention of the common school. We still believe that creating an educated populace is essential to preserve a democratic system; we still want (or say we want) to promote equality and we still need productive workers. And despite our arguments over what we mean by a "common culture" most people probably still believe that we have some things in common, even if we're not entirely sure what they are.

The American public school was based on a very simple and very logical premise: Teaching children to reason, providing them a core knowledge base, and giving them solid moral instruction would enable them to live decent, useful lives. Their education would prepare them to search for what philosophers call "the good life." As I discuss in later chapters, this goal has been appropriated by the self-esteem movement and has now overtaken all others in the public school. But before they became distorted by self-esteem, these purposes provided the foundation for what we call a classical liberal education.

Liberal Education for a Civil Society

Modern and contemporary views of education grew out of the Enlightenment, when philosophers told us that our salvation lay in reason, not religion, and that we should use that reason in our search for truth and in our pursuit of progress. Education was seen as an essential tool in that pursuit, since schools are where reason and the importance of truth are taught. That education is called a "liberal education" not because it embodies what we today call "liberal" politics (referring to those on the political left) but because it reflects the classical liberal *philosophical* ideals that underlie virtually all American political, economic, and social institutions: freedom, democracy, and individual rights and liberties. (In fact political conservatives today are rather more likely to defend the concept of liberal education than political liberals, many of whom view it as an outdated and oppressive idea.)

A liberal education is meant to foster these ideals and empower students to become independent thinkers or, as Charles W. Anderson notes in *Prescribing the Life of the Mind,* "shake them out of the dogmatic slumbers of inherited belief or unexamined presupposition."[20] Thus a liberal education means more than simply teaching random bits of knowledge: it means teaching them in a way that cultivates the mind. In fact, the traditional idea of liberal education is that the mind can *only* be properly cultivated if the student is taught certain core courses, particularly the humanities and literature classics—what has come to be known as the Western canon. These form part of a basic curriculum that includes mathematics, biology, physics, and chemistry; social studies, which comprises history and geography; English language and literature; foreign languages; physical education; art; and music.

The central purpose of liberal education is to teach the individual how to reason, what we refer to today as "critical thinking." This phrase requires clarification, since it has been grossly corrupted by the self-esteem movement to refer to students talking about how they *feel.* The real meaning of critical thinking is the ability to hypothesize about something, examine arguments and weigh evidence concerning that something, and come to defensible conclusions regarding it. Critical thinking is the ability to view ourselves and the world as objectively as possible because it requires us to transcend our own narrow perception of things and examine the world from a variety of perspectives.

Another purpose of liberal education is to provide the student with a body of knowledge that, along with her ability to reason, gives her the tools to pursue further learning and generally lead a productive life. But the most important benefit of liberal education for the individual is the development of metacognition: the ability to analyze one's own thinking processes and learn how to learn. Metacognition is the ability to become aware of one's own actions and perceptions in the world, to escape, if only momentarily, from the prison of our emotions. It is in fact the only true antidote to the narcissism and anti-rationalism of the self-esteem movement, for it demands that we try to see the world as it really is—neither how we would like it to be nor how we *feel* it to be.

Critics point out that we can never acquire an entirely objective perspective of anything, that we are always in some sense prisoners of our own worldview. That is true. But it is that very effort to examine the world clearly, reflect on one's own biases and prejudices, and recognize the moral weight of democratic principles that makes reason, progress, and civil society possible. That is why a liberal education is so important—it is where we learn what reason, democracy, and social justice are all about.

It is reason that has permitted man to create civil societies and live with others, if not in harmony, then at least with some understanding of the necessity of what we know as the social compact: the rules, obligations, and responsibilities that govern our collective lives. Although today those of us who have grown up in democratic societies might challenge Hobbes's notion that the sovereign of a state should be absolute, history shows us that his contention that man's desire for power leads to a life that is "solitary, poor, nasty, brutish, and short" is true.[21] It is our reason that led us to understand the need for the social contract, and it is only that contract that prevents us from retreating into barbarism.

But as I discuss in more detail in the last chapter, by telling us to focus on our emotions, educators—the handmaidens of the self-esteem movement—are undermining that contract, denying the possibility of progress and threatening to return humanity to the days when power was the only universally understood political currency. The only difference is that emotion has replaced power as the dominant force in society. But the two function very similarly. Emotion, like power, recognizes only itself; it cannot be reasoned with and is defined unilaterally by the person experiencing it. This is why it is so dangerous. Most of us believe that schools should be organized rationally, that teaching should be based on proven methods, and that education is for developing the mind, body, and soul. However, today's educators—and their students—do not recognize the importance of reason. They only recognize their own emotions. But this is truly the road to barbarism. We need reason to help us make sense of emotion. Emotion, like power, needs to be tamed; it needs to be civilized, and it can only be civilized through rational means.

This is why we need to preserve liberal education against the encroachment of the self-esteem movement: because it defends against the dangers of self-esteem that I discussed in the Introduction. We must recognize, of course, that there are different approaches to liberal education. Political liberals and political conservatives, who probably agree that children need some kind of knowledge base, disagree on just what that base should consist of, how we should teach it, and why. Liberals believe that the curriculum should be made "relevant" to students; schools should educate "the whole child" and not just teach the basics. Developing what Daniel Goleman calls "emotional intelligence" is at least as important as developing the intellect.[22] Liberals regard the public school as a place where individuals learn about themselves, primarily through multicultural and bilingual education, which is intended to give students not only linguistic and cultural skills but also high self-esteem.

Conservatives, on the other hand, defend the original idea of a liberal education: that the intellect can only be properly developed if children are taught the core curriculum, and not what Arthur Schlesinger Jr. calls a "sanitized," "feel-good" history of ethnic studies classes. There is, he argues, no evidence to indicate that they promote self-esteem.[23] Conservatives contend that reason can only be developed through study of the "great books" and generally regard multiculturalism and bilingual education with distaste, since their inclusion in the curriculum may precipitate the removal of the "core" courses and thus threaten the educative process. Self-knowledge and examination of feelings are not of significant interest to conservatives, since they represent the opposite of what they contend a liberal education is about: getting outside ourselves and exploring the world around us.

But both liberals and conservatives believe in the importance of acquiring *some* body of knowledge; both support the development of critical thinking and both believe that the knowledge and skills that children acquire in school should in some way prepare them for higher education or employment. Thus despite some important political differences, there are threads of a common philosophy of education that most people, irrespective of political affiliation, share. Indeed, it is crucial that we try to forge such a philosophy, for the following reasons.

First, without any common understanding of what it means to be educated it is impossible to implement school reform that has any chance of success. Second, it only makes sense to have some agreement on what education is before condemning our public schools for not providing it! And third, if we have some agreement on what education is, or should be, we then have a starting point from which we can measure the effects of the self-esteem movement on it. But first we need to define just what it means to be educated.

Who's Educated, Anyway?

We have discussed the original purposes of the public school: creating an informed citizenry, teaching a common culture, preparing students for employment, and so on, but surely the central purpose of public schools should be to educate. But what exactly are the criteria for being educated? Can we say that twelve years of public school education is sufficient to create an educated citizenry? And are schools really educating or are they performing other functions?

The first point that comes to mind here is that if we *had* been properly educating people in schools, we would never have become drawn into the self-esteem movement because our common sense—the everyday expression of critical thinking—would have told us how wrong it is. But I'll leave that for now. The first thing to note is that just as our political perspectives color our view of public schooling, they also affect what we think it means to be educated. For example, a liberal would likely contend that an educated person must be tolerant and must have an understanding and appreciation of different races and ethnicities. She might also say that an educated person feels good about herself, is concerned about racial and economic inequality, and supports measures designed to alleviate them, such as multicultural education. But she would probably also say that educated people must have mastery of some body of knowledge and are critical thinkers.

Conservatives would define the educated person somewhat differently. Like liberals, they believe that mastery over a body of knowledge is essential to being educated, but it must be mastery over a very *specific* body of knowledge: the Western canon. The conservative might say that an educated person defends the notions of freedom and individual rights, is a critical thinker, and is a patriot. But again, there is overlap between the two positions. Both sides would no doubt agree that education takes place not only within schools but outside of them. Talking with different people, traveling, working, pursuing leisure activities, reading, and even— dare I say it—watching television can all be educative activities. But whether we learn anything from these experiences depends upon what we do with them.

For example, traveling allows us to experience other cultures, languages, and customs and can provide us a wealth of knowledge—if we are ready to accept it. Some people are not, of course, because the farther away they get from home the more obnoxious they become. We have all had the unique privilege of being near the tourist in the fluorescent jogging suit who screeches loud enough for anyone within a three-mile radius to hear: "Where's the McDonald's?!! This isn't like at home!!" or even better, "Doesn't anyone here speak English?!!?" Of course, the point of traveling is seeing what *isn't* like home and learning at least a little of *someone else's* language, something that some people never figure out. Thus whether our life experiences are educational or not depends upon whether we use them to further our understanding of ourselves and the world around us or to reinforce our own (false) sense of cultural superiority. Our experiences should cause us not just to think but to think carefully and critically, for as William James once pointed out: "[Thinking is] what a great many people think they are doing when they are merely rearranging their prejudices."[24] Finally, and perhaps most important, we should be changed because of our experiences and our outlook should be transformed, even if only a little. After all, becoming educated should be about trying to become something better than we are and thereby making the world just a little better as well.

If we think about the people we know, we will probably find some who have a lot of formal schooling, but whom we do not necessarily consider educated. The professor ensconced in his ivory tower, unable to converse with the outside world or use his knowledge in a practical way, is a classic example. If he has a lot of "book learning" but no social skills, is he educated? It is debatable. On the other hand, we also know people who have little formal schooling but whom we would consider educated. I had a friend many years ago whom I met in Italy and whom I will call Carlo, who fell into this last category. He was a high school dropout who made his living selling sweaters fashioned by local women in a street market in Florence. He had inherited the stand from his father, as is the tradition, and made a decent living, dependent though it was on the summer tourist season.

He was a friendly and witty fellow who spoke very good English—better than my Italian, which I had learned at university. As I got to know him, I became increasingly impressed with him. Not only did he speak several languages very well, but he traveled widely throughout the world during the winter months when there was little work, and returned from these trips with not only anecdotes and souvenirs but also a deep understanding and appreciation of different peoples and their traditions. Carlo was thoughtful, reflective, and curious—clearly a critical thinker. He read a great deal of literature and history, and his bookshelves were filled with classics in English as well as Italian. He was also a music lover and had a collection that included Basie as well as Bach, Ella as well as Elgar. I learned much from my conversations with him, and although I had far more formal schooling than he did, I would say without a doubt that he was by far the more educated.

Clearly education takes place not only in schools, but outside schools as well. Even those who have little formal schooling can become very educated persons. Now this is not meant as a recommendation that kids drop out of school because formal schooling is (or should be) a great foundation for becoming educated. The point is rather that even those who have not had the benefit of much formal schooling can, if they are literate, curious, and self-motivated, educate themselves. The second main point, then, is that becoming educated is a lifelong experience. We do not wake up one day and say, "Finally! I'm now an educated person." Nor is it a label or badge we wear to show that we are better than anyone else. Becoming educated is a continual process of acquiring knowledge, testing beliefs, examining presuppositions, and using reason to make sense of our lives. Indeed, when we start thinking that we're educated, it is a sure sign that we're not! My favorite description of it is the following: "To be educated is not to have arrived at a destination; it is to travel with a different view."[25]

The third point is that becoming educated must involve some development of the intellect. Whether that development takes place primarily in the school or in the home, the development of logical and analytical reasoning—critical thinking—is essential. But of course we don't just think in a vacuum (ever try to think about nothing?); we need something to think about; some subject matter to chew over; some body of knowledge that will put our brains to work. Critical thinking is like reading and writing: you can talk about it all day, but in the end you learn to do it by just doing it. So fourth, we need to learn some body of knowledge.

So far, then, we can say that the educated person knows something about a variety of core subjects, can analyze them, and uses his reason—not his emotions—to negotiate his way through life. We might add additional criteria, some of which my students have suggested over the years: that an educated person understands his or her intellectual and moral limitations and works to improve them; that he can put his knowledge to practical use; that he is someone who knows how to learn and is, like my Italian friend, intrinsically, rather than extrinsically motivated.

One criterion I haven't mentioned is self-esteem. It is striking that not once, in all the years I asked students to define an educated person, did any of them define an educated person as someone with high self-esteem. Now it is quite likely that, in the process of becoming educated, and as a result of our achievements, we begin to feel confidence in ourselves, and if so, so much the better. But self-confidence is a natural development of the educative process and cannot be instilled artificially, independent of achievement or learning. A liberal education can and should help children develop a real self-confidence, but the currently popular idea of self-esteem—feeling good for no good reason—is neither a criterion of being educated nor a consequence of it. It makes one wonder, then, why we are spending so much time and energy promoting it in schools.

Whether or not graduation from high school makes someone educated depends upon two things. First, it's a good start. Most of us are not as motivated as my Italian friend and need some external stimulus and the company of others to help us learn. So both the organization and the duration of schooling provide a good foundation for becoming educated. Second, while some young people may be sufficiently motivated, learned, and wise by the end of high school to be considered educated, for most of us it is only the first stage of a lifelong journey. Most of us are only beginning to have a glimmer of who we are and what the world is about, and we only begin to understand some of that through experiences we have after high school and college. So the most important thing we can do in school, apart from providing the foundation, is to nurture and develop the spark of excitement in learning, for that is what gives kids the drive to continue their journey of discovery long after they leave school.

And for each of us the journey is a little different. I remember very clearly after graduating from high school how much I did *not* want to go immediately to college. I knew I would go but not until I had done some other things (I wasn't quite sure what). So while all my close friends went on to university, I worked in an office for a year. Deciding that was not for me, I saved some money and arranged to go to England to attend university the next fall. One week before leaving, I ran into a good friend from high school who mentioned that she was also going to Europe the following week to travel with two girlfriends. Well, in less than twenty-four hours I had decided that college could wait another year, gave my parents back the money they had given me for school, and announced I would be touring Europe instead.

Although they didn't try to stop me, my parents were not too keen on this idea, fearing that I had given up college for good. Off we went and discovered that although my friend and I were compatible, four was too big a group. So we split up, and my friend and I went on our way, traveling throughout Europe for four months. It was, without a doubt, the best thing I ever did for my education, for it opened up a whole new world and whetted my appetite for more learning. When I started college the next fall, I was ready to learn. And after eleven years of university my parents stopped asking me if I was ever going to go to college!

And You Thought Schools Were for Educating

Becoming educated is thus an exciting and mysterious process that only begins in school. In fact, schools do much more than educate our kids. Most of what our children acquire in school is socialization and training. Socialization refers to the processes through which people adopt certain values, habits, ways of thinking, or behavior. We are all being socialized all the time in schools, at work, in the home, and elsewhere. Socialization is thus a process of culturization or habituation: learning how to function in a variety of contexts. It is never a value-free exercise, though, since in each environment we are learning different behaviors and customs.

The cliques that we see in schools are the result of socialization. Kids join up with others who are like them or are what they want to be like, and they develop their own miniculture within the school. Each group distinguishes itself from the others through its dress or speech and by other factors, whether it's the athletic types (the jocks), the smart kids (the nerds), and so on. Gang affiliation is just another type of socialization, attracting kids who typically do not have a stable home environment so feel a need to strongly identify with other kids, often by exhibiting antisocial and violent behavior. The more extreme the behavior, the stronger the identity statement.

Parents and teachers need to be vigilant about what group and what values kids are being socialized into, because socialization can have very negative or very positive influences on children. For example, schools have rules on dress, behavior, and academic requirements that are intended to socialize children into the values that the adults have decided are appropriate, such as respect for one's elders, punctuality, the importance of hard work, and so on. Schools have always performed this very positive function, and for some kids provide the only stable environment they will ever experience. Although parents and teachers may think the kinds of groups that kids socialize themselves into are weird or undesirable, most are harmless expressions of individual identity and the very normal need to rebel against the overarching socialization of the school culture.

Until recently, then, socialization patterns were pretty easy to identify. Parents and teachers tried to socialize kids into the "right" values, customs, and habits, and kids tested them by rejecting those values and acting out. It is a tug-of-war that is particularly evident in the middle school and early high school years, but most kids, even those who act out, know right from wrong, understand the importance of an education, and do in fact respect the adults in their lives. And by the time they leave school as young adults, most have the moral and intellectual foundation to begin their lives. The self-esteem movement has changed all that, however, so that no one knows anymore just what the rules are or, more important, what they should be.

Over the last thirty years, the self-esteem movement has so permeated the school culture that the traditional roles of teacher and student have been completely transformed. The authority that the teacher once symbolized has been almost entirely demolished. Teachers today are not considered intellectual leaders but servants and counselors whose sole function is to serve the every whim of their students. Students learn that they do not need to respect their teachers or earn their grades, so they begin to believe that they are entitled to grades, respect, or anything else for that matter just for the asking. Almost any behavior, short of killing a fellow student or the teacher, is acceptable and may go unpunished, so if they're not being taught them in the home, kids do not learn basic codes of civil conduct. This of course encourages self-centered behavior and attitudes, as I discuss a little later, but it does something else, too.

When there is a recognizable structure of authority around them, kids have a sense of security, knowing what they can refer to or whom they can turn to when they need help. They also know what they are rebelling against. When that structure is removed and the people who used to represent it lose their authority, those boundaries crumble. With no moral, academic, or behavioral reference points, kids turn to their peers for support and create their own societies and their own structures, which, without adult guidance, often take very destructive forms like gangs. The frustrating part about all this is that parents, teachers, and even kids know how important guidelines and boundaries are. But we have become so taken in by the promises of the self-esteem movement that we disregard both the evidence and our common sense.

To make things more confusing, self-esteem literature so emphasizes the best interests of the children that parents and teachers are fooled into thinking that making children believe they are the center of the universe is doing something good for them. As I explain throughout the book, we are actually cheating kids of a real education and depriving them of the cultural and moral constraints that they need to develop into mature, responsible adults. And perhaps worst of all, the school practices intended to promote self-esteem—grade inflation, cooperative learning, social promotion, ungraded report cards, and so on—not only fail to do what they are intended to do but actually undermine children's respect for the educative process. Our task as educators and parents, therefore, is to end the indoctrination into self-esteem ideology and return some structure to kids' lives.

Along with socialization comes training. Training involves teaching someone how to do something—learning a specific skill that has a practical application. We train kids all the time in school, when we ask them to put their names at the top of their papers, when we teach them how to spell (because you can't always explain *why* a word is spelled the way it is—it just is) or when we tell them how to behave or walk down the hall in an orderly fashion. These are all forms of training. Education, however, is a much broader and more complex enterprise, involving not only knowing how to do things but, more important, why we do them and what they mean.

Training is an important part of education because we want children to be able to actually use their knowledge and skills when they graduate from high school. But it should only be one aspect of education. Like socialization, however, it has virtually taken over the school curriculum. The danger of this is that unless one has had the benefit of a real education and not just training, one does not know how valuable it is. So kids are often excited about the training they get in driver's ed or woodworking class, but they may not feel quite as excited about learning the complexities of twentieth-century history. That is because they can readily see the relevance of the former but not the latter. But distinguishing what is relevant from what is not is something that one only begins to understand with time, and with education. This is one reason why it is so important to limit the latitude that children have in choosing their classes in school: because they haven't learned enough yet to know what they need to know.

Socialization and training go hand in hand; the former is learning about different mores and customs and the latter is learning how to put them into action. Again, having real education somewhere in here is essential. For example, while it is always interesting to examine with a high school class the reasons why some of their peers join gangs, we don't want them to just go off and join a gang because they heard about it in class. What intervenes here is critical thinking. If kids know how to analyze an issue and talk about it rationally, they will be able to evaluate it and then make a reasonable judgment about it. They will be able to separate the emotional attraction of a gang from the real problems it might create for them and for society in the long term. But the self-esteem movement's emphasis on emotions rather than intellect prevents kids from developing the skills that allow them to resist socialization into undesirable kinds of life. They become attracted to a variety of forms of training or socialization but fail to see the importance of getting an education. The self-esteem movement itself promotes training, rather than education, because it is anti-intellectual, focusing on individual emotions rather than universal truths or ideas.

Training primarily involves the acquisition of a specific skill for a specific purpose, whereas education is about developing the mind so that one can acquire the intellectual (and practical) skills necessary to function effectively in a variety of contexts. A major difference between being trained and being educated lies in one's ability to problem-solve. A friend told me something he had observed one day with his employees that perfectly described the difference. He owned a sound studio in which he produced music for television and movies. When a project came in, he hired contract workers for the job and, as there was a sound engineering school down the street, he would often hire someone who had recently graduated from the school.

Naturally, some people he hired were better at the job than others, just as some people are more congenial than others, or work harder. But after several months and as many projects, he saw that the workers fell into two groups: those who were problem solvers and those who were not. Sound engineering is a relatively complicated business; unexpected problems arise all the time for which there may be no obvious answer. What my friend discovered was that the workers who had gone to a college or university and had a general, liberal education were almost invariably the ones who were able to use their critical thinking skills to analyze the problem, hypothesize as to its causes, and propose possible solutions. Those who had only been trained, not educated, got stuck when faced with the problem and would run to him with every glitch, asking him to fix it. They were not able to generalize from a particular problem to a more global one, nor transfer knowledge from one area to another.

While training can be a part of schooling, it should not be the most important part, nor its sole purpose. Schools should educate individuals; liberate them, so they can choose their future from the many opportunities available. Unfortunately, under the influence of the self-esteem movement we are doing quite the opposite. Our addiction to self-esteem is producing some alarming symptoms that undermine the entire educative process. The first and most obvious of these is narcissism.

The Four Symptoms of Our Addiction

Narcissism

Perhaps nowhere in the developed world has individualism taken such hold as in America. Things that in other countries are considered privileges or responsibilities Americans consider rights, such as owning a gun, driving a car, or owning property. However, many people are beginning to question whether the concept of individual rights has gone too far, and whether it may be time to reconsider the state of the social compact in America. They point to Western Europe and Canada, where issues like gun control and health care are seen quite differently than they are in the United States. Many Americans believe that the right to carry a gun is enshrined in the Second Amendment to the Constitution, despite wording that refers not to individuals but to "the people" and a "well regulated Militia." In the United States, carrying a gun is a right. But in Canada, for example, carrying a gun is considered a responsibility, and there is a general social pressure for individuals *not* to own or carry weapons other than for law enforcement or hunting.

Access to health care is another issue on which Americans differ from their Western European and Canadian counterparts, who consider free or low-cost health care a right. It is society's responsibility to provide that care for all its citizens. Many Americans, however, consider health care more of a luxury or a very personal right: If you can afford it, you are entitled to it; if you can't, you aren't. The failure of the Clinton administration's efforts to establish some sort of national health care program or guidelines, despite the reality that 40 million Americans do not have access to health care, is ample evidence of how entrenched this perspective really is.

The "social democracies," Britain, Canada, France, Norway, and Sweden, to name a few, subscribe to a definition of the social compact, and the rights and responsibilities of the individual in it, that is somewhat different from the definition subscribed to by the United States, which might most accurately be called a highly individualistic democracy. When Americans debate important issues such as gun control or health care, the scales are typically weighted in favor of what best serves the individual. So carrying a gun, for example, does not entail significant public or personal investment, although it does have, as we know, enormous social costs. Carrying a gun is considered a right. Universal health care, on the other hand, would require significant public monies, funds which come, of course, from individual taxes, and taxes, for many Americans, are the symbol and substance of government interference in individual lives. Thus publicly funded health care is considered a restriction on individual liberty, whereas access to firearms is viewed as its ultimate expression.

There are, of course, benefits to a strong sense of individualism, primarily the protection of individual rights. But it also provides fertile ground for radical individualistic and narcissistic movements, of which the self-esteem movement is the paradigmatic example. This may explain why the self-esteem movement has prospered in this country more than any other: because Americans are naturally drawn to ideas and theories that emphasize individual rather than collective concerns. Narcissism is a very common syndrome that has probably afflicted most of us at one time or another. The social pressure, for example, on women to be thin and on men to be muscular only exacerbates this tendency. Narcissus, you will recall, was the youth who rejected the love of the nymph Echo and was punished by Nemesis, who made him fall in love with his own reflection in the water. Absorbed with self-admiration, he fell into the lake and drowned. The term "narcissist" thus refers to someone who indulges in self-worship or is in some way excessively self-absorbed.

Narcissism in regard to appearance is rampant. We are no longer interested in just following a healthy lifestyle or improving our looks. Physical perfection is the goal. I recall a conversation I had several years ago with a friend who was about to go to Cannes for five weeks for the film festival. While I was thrilled for him (and a little jealous), rather than be excited about the prospect, he was terrified that he would get fat, since he wouldn't be able to go to the gym during the five weeks. Narcissism had eaten away any pleasure he might have had in the experience. And a quick visit to the local gym will confirm that he is not the exception, but rather the rule.

But this, what I call superficial narcissism—being obsessed with one's physical appearance—is harmful primarily to oneself and can be regarded as just another unfortunate personality trait. It is when the obsession with self leads to an inability to recognize the needs and rights of others that it becomes a problem for all of us. Just as overexercising one muscle can be damaging to the physical body, overindulging in self-love harms the body politic. This is deep narcissism and, like a cancer infecting the tissues of the body, it is a malignancy that destroys the social, political, and moral tissues that connect us to one another. As Christopher Lasch notes, narcissism is the logical consequence of extreme individualism.[26] When self-love becomes the goal of every individual, it undermines the social compact, which, like the Golden Rule, only works if we love one another as well as ourselves (or at least act as if we do).

That may mean giving up something we want because it's in someone else's interest and not always demanding that our needs be fulfilled before everyone else's. This is anathema to self-esteem experts, who tell us that we must always put ourselves first, even with our children. Matthew McKay and Patrick Fanning, authors of a popular book on self-esteem, warn parents that "when you put yourself last, when you chronically sacrifice for your kids, you teach them that a person is only worthy insofar as he or she is of service to others. You teach them to use you and make it likely that later on they will be used."[27] Being a considerate, giving person is not seen as something valuable but is equated with being used.

And in fact the narcissism that is taught in schools is the most damaging, for children who are not taught to empathize with or respect others at an early age are unlikely to develop these capacities on their own. Until age three or four children are naturally egoistic, recognizing only their own needs. But by the time they enter school, they are beginning to understand that others have needs too, and one of the tasks of schools should be to nurture recognition of the rights of others. Instead, however, we have created schools that are child-centered in the extreme, where every aspect of schooling is organized around—and this is the important point—what *children* want and perceive to be in their best interests and not what is in reality the best for them.

The good news is that jettisoning narcissism requires neither great acts of courage or heroism nor a total denial of one's own needs and wants, but a simple recognition that others exist. Creating a civil society requires acknowledgment of that fact. Giving the other guy the parking place, waiting your turn in the grocery, or asking your neighbor how you can help her out when she's sick are all examples of the simple acts of decency and empathy that make life with others bearable. A little giving goes a long way. The antidote to narcissism is thus very simple: empathy. Empathy is the ability and willingness to share in the emotions of another. It is not hard to exercise because we all know what it is to fear, to love, to be angry, or to rejoice. These are universal human emotions that cut through all racial, class, or national borders. Empathy, then, involves the recognition that we are all connected by our humanity. Although we may express it, define it, or talk about it in different ways, each of us shares with others the gifts and challenges that are part of being human. But recognizing this involves fighting the second symptom of our addiction to self-esteem: separatism.

Separatism

Despite the official desegregation of schools as a result of the *Brown* decision in 1954 and the introduction of multicultural and ethnic education, racism is alive and well in America. Years of injustice are now well rooted in the collective memory and African Americans, Hispanic or Latino Americans, Native Americans, and, to a lesser extent, Asian Americans are retreating into the familiarity and cultural safety of their own communities, saying to white America: "We don't need you; we don't want you; we just want to stay with our own group."

White American liberals, in particular, find this confusing because they thought that the whole purpose of desegregation and multiculturalism in schools was to help us all understand each other. After all, it was a black man, himself the object of white racist violence—Rodney King—who asked, "Can't we all just get along?" But many minorities now see multiculturalism in a different way. Their daily experience tells them that they are still not viewed as equals of white Americans. White is still, unfortunately, considered "normal" and anything else is "different." Even in multicultural studies, nonwhites are called "different" and books on counseling minorities have titles like *Counseling the Culturally Different.* For nonwhites, then, multicultural curricula and ethnic studies are a way to affirm that "difference" but in a more positive way. Instead of allowing Anglo Americans to define their difference, many minority groups are now emphasizing their unique cultures and histories, celebrating them by emphasizing their positive and not their negative attributes. It is one way to regain control of their identity.

For many years, minorities have had their identities either completely negated or defined wholly in terms of the "norm" of the white man. Thus it is hardly surprising if black Americans and other groups wish to capitalize on the idea of being outside the mainstream and redefine themselves as positively distinct. This is one kind of separatism seen in schools that is clearly a legacy of racism and institutional discrimination. But it is inflamed and exacerbated by the self-esteem movement, which defines identity primarily in terms of ethnicity, although, as I discuss in Chapter 7, identity is really multidimensional, not unidimensional. But the prevailing wisdom is that knowing who you are and feeling good about yourself means feeling good about your ethnicity. Here the self-esteem movements and the multicultural movements coalesce. High self-esteem is considered important, and we get high self-esteem by "knowing ourselves." In the contemporary climate "knowing yourself" means knowing your ethnicity and feeling good about it. So making schooling multicultural or introducing ethnic studies in high school or university is considered the best way to foster high self-esteem.

Emphasizing identity has become an issue for girls, too, because feminist theory of the last thirty years has taken the same separatist route as cultural theory. Until very recently the dominant view among feminist scholars was that girls and women have been oppressed in schools and in society (which in many ways they have) and that the way to address this oppression is to segregate girls into separate classes so they don't feel that they have to compete with the boys. This strategy can be quite successful in math and science classes, but people are now beginning to realize that as a whole it leaves much to be desired.

Segregating students, whether on the basis of race or gender, even for apparently defensible and educational reasons, is not a long-term solution to the difficulties that minorities or girls face in school. It suggests that there is something wrong with these students, and I don't believe that is the message we want to send to our young people. I have observed the same attitudes being expressed by foundations that claim to be supportive of women and give grants for women doing research. One of the most well-known of these explicitly states that it only supports women doing research *on women's issues*, as if that is all that is relevant to women. What about women studying political issues, men's issues, or animal issues? Aren't these just as worthy? This sort of narrow-minded, head-in-the-sand approach only serves to marginalize women even more.

A dispute once occurred at a university over an advertisement for a faculty position that identified one of the desirable qualities of the candidate as "dynamic." Women on the faculty and elsewhere vehemently objected to this word, saying that seeking a "dynamic" candidate was implicitly discriminatory against women. The reasoning here fails me. Can't women be just as dynamic as men? And the strange part about these kinds of discussions is that these objections are always made by self-described feminists who claim to be acting in the best interests of women and are supposed to believe in equality. It seems to me, however, that arguing that women are somehow deficient in dynamism or any other attribute, for that matter, is hardly the way to promote equity. So rather than segregate female students, suggesting they need "special help," we need to fix the school culture. The kids don't need to be "fixed" but the schools—and our attitudes about minorities and women—probably do.

Although this insistence on "difference" can thus be seen as a natural consequence of the minority experience in the United States and may be a necessary stage in the continuing struggle for equal rights, the consequences if it persists may be nothing short of apocalyptic. Rodney King's rather plaintive question struck a chord with everyone not only because it was remarkably gracious, given what he had endured, but because it represented how many of us feel, black and white: We acknowledge the differences between us, but we really would like to understand and accept each other—just "get along."

It may be natural for us to create mini societies with those we identify with most closely, whether it be on the basis of gender, sexual orientation, culture, class, or race, but it does not create a healthy society. A collection of ghettoes does not a community make. Living in ghettoes, we live in ignorance—of ourselves as well as others. And it is ignorance that leads to prejudice, and prejudice to racism. The decision in *Brown v. Board of Education* was supposed to make it clear to all Americans that separate but equal is a bankrupt concept. It is more than ironic—it is tragic—that the idea that provided an excuse for institutionalized racism against black Americans is now being held up by some as an ideal. Separate but equal cannot be defended on any basis of social justice or equality. If, as I argue throughout this book, most Americans want a civil society and schools that truly offer equal educational opportunity, they must reject the notion that the inhabitants of such a society can live equal—but separate—lives.

Perhaps, as Robert Bellah and his colleagues write in *The Good Society*, Americans find the notion of social and political interdependence problematic, given their history of individualism (although the kind of communitarianism he and others like Amitai Etzioni propose is also problematic).[28] Although technological inventions like the Internet are supposedly making the "global village" even smaller and more intimate, I wonder whether the interactions we have with one another via phone, fax, and modem qualify as meaningful in any human way or whether they are simply ways to interact while avoiding the messiness of intimacy. But if we are growing more, rather than less, alienated from one another as a result of our increasing dependence on new technologies, we have even more of a reason to make the effort to talk to one another: man to woman, black to white, Asian to Latino. And is working with one another, rather than against one another, really so difficult? Are there no ties that bind, no common values, no shared hopes or dreams? Of course there are, for they are what make society possible.

These common political and moral values such as a belief in democracy and equal rights and freedoms, a belief in hard work, respect for persons, tolerance, honesty, integrity, and so on—can bridge the cultural divide. Just as justice is sometimes only evident when injustice is apparent, these bonds may become visible only in times of crisis, when people are so distraught by events that their distress overrides other differences. But the bonds are no less real for that. When we witness the horrors of the Oklahoma City bombing or the seemingly endless spate of school shootings, we do not stop to think how many whites or how many blacks are among the dead; how many rich or how many poor. We grieve equally for all.

But we are not just united through tragedy, but through the common political values that sustain civil society in America. By emphasizing these values we can replace a sense of alienation with a sense of understanding; reject separatism and replace it with connectedness. It is the classic case of the glass being half empty or half full. Although there are ways in which we are different, there are also many ways in which we are connected, so why not capitalize on them? In schools that means teaching about similarities as well as differences, expanding children's minds by teaching them about foreign cultures, and using the multicultural curriculum to foster understanding of ourselves and others, not perpetuating ignorance by glorifying difference.

Emotivism

One of the principal purposes of a classical liberal education is to teach critical thinking. Being able to think critically means being able to examine ideas, evaluate arguments, and recognize the existence of other points of view than our own. It also means understanding the process of learning—acquiring what is called "metacognition": put very simply, the ability to examine one's own thinking processes and evaluate them. Critical thinking is probably the most important skill that children can learn in school, since it is what allows them to explore the world.

When children begin school at age six, they are beginning to emerge from an egocentric view of the world and suddenly see that it is full of things independent of themselves. They are excited about learning and eager to know everything they can about this unfolding universe. This is when critical thinking can begin, through science experiments, studying characters in stories, reading about history, or looking at maps of the world and seeing how other people live. By looking at the world around them, evaluating what is good and bad about it, and examining their role in it, children start to emerge from their egocentrism and begin to develop their rationality. Critical thinking is thus the first step toward developing reason.

Without rationality, we could not create laws or even determine what is right or wrong, since doing so depends upon evaluation of various claims and arguments. That evaluation, whether it be regarding justice, politics, or morality, is the foundation of a civil society. One of the most important roles of the school, therefore, is to develop these thinking skills. The self-esteem movement has, however, successfully transformed schools from places where children acquire knowledge and develop critical thinking to places where they explore their feelings. Rational thinking is no longer seen as necessary, desirable, or even possible. "How I feel" has replaced "how I think."

This is part of what we call emotivism. Philosopher Alasdair MacIntyre defines emotivism as "the doctrine that all evaluative judgments and more specifically all moral judgments are nothing but expressions of preference, expressions of attitude or feeling, insofar as they are moral or evaluative in character."[29] Emotivism is the view that there is no rational or moral framework, and no set of rules, that can help us decide which moral perspective is better than another. Everything is just opinion; there's no real "truth" out there, and everyone's view is just as good as everyone else's.

What this means is that no one can ever convince anyone else through rational argument that his or her perspective is better than another's. So if two people disagree about some social or philosophical issue, they just agree to disagree, and pretty much give up the notion that one of them may be more right than the other. This may sound at first quite reasonable. After all, most of us were brought up to respect other people's opinions. But if we really believe that there is no better definition of justice, of truth, of decency, or any other important concept, we begin to slide down the slippery slope of relativism. Tolerance and mutual respect are fine, but if we do not hold on to the idea that some notions are better than others, some actions better than others, or that some acts are criminal, then anything goes. This is what is known as relativism, which judges every idea relative to other ideas but not to some objective standard. When we embrace relativism, we become unable to identify right from wrong, and worse, we no longer care which is which.

Thus teachers may think they are doing students a favor by downplaying individual critical thinking skills to promote activities and games designed to promote self-esteem, but they are in fact doing them a great disservice. One of the themes of this book is that self-confidence is important but it must be authentic. Authentic self-confidence develops from intellectual, physical, and moral effort and achievement, and can come as much from lessons learned from failure as from success. Children develop strength from experience—the good, the bad, *and* the ugly.

Rationality is not hard to teach and from it, morality follows. All we have to do is nurture kids' natural curiosity and not deaden it by asking them how they are feeling every minute of the day. Now one may well ask: What is wrong with expressing feelings? Nothing at all, within limits. Feelings are very important, but they need to be balanced with reason. When we are in the grip of very powerful emotions, we are likely to be quite unable to view the world in any kind of objective light. That is why reason and critical thinking are so important: They help protect us from our own and others' prejudices and idiosyncrasies. Emotion without reason is narcissism and it leads to barbarism.

As philosopher of education Harvey Siegel points out, critical thinking allows a child to become self-sufficient through his ability to make rational, independent judgments about the world.[30] So if we really want to "empower" children, as self-esteem advocates claim, then we need to give them the tools to help them do that. Becoming a critical thinker is empowering because it liberates the mind; becoming a moral person liberates the soul.

Cynicism

Of the four symptoms of our addiction to the self-esteem movement—narcissism, separatism, emotivism, and cynicism—it is perhaps cynicism that poses the greatest threat to our children and our society because it threatens to stifle the one thing that keeps us all going, even in our bleakest moments: hope. It is particularly painful to see children who seem to have lost hope and faith in life because it is one thing that children normally possess. They view life in relatively simple terms and (at least until adolescence hits) are naturally optimistic. When they experience good and bad, they expect good to prevail, even when their experience tells them otherwise.

For example, children who have been abused frequently refuse to condemn their abusers, not only for fear of reprisals or of not being believed but because they have a fundamental need to be loved and believe that people are basically good. What happens to these children when they grow up, however, is that they become adults who may have difficulty accepting, expressing, or understanding real love in mature relationships. They have the need for love but, sadly, are cynical about it, having lost their faith that such a thing exists. This is cynicism: a loss of faith and hope in something or in someone. And the more important that something is to the person, the stronger the cynicism about it when he or she experiences the loss.

It is important to understand here the difference between skepticism and cynicism. Skepticism, along with hope, is the antidote to cynicism. Philosophers define skepticism as a belief that sure knowledge of how things really are may be sought but cannot be found.[31] I would define a skeptic as someone who believes that there are truths in life, and ideals, and therefore something to believe in, but that it may be difficult to positively identify them or pin them down. Skeptics use reason to try to reach the truth and do not accept anecdotal evidence or "feelings" as proof of its existence. They demand evidence. They want to believe in good things, but they don't just accept any idea that comes along. A skeptic is a rational optimist.

Cynics, on the other hand, do not believe in anything. Most of us probably know a few. They're the people who are not only very critical of everyone and everything but also seem very unhappy. They are unhappy because they have no ideals. They believe that all ideals are myths; people are only out for themselves, and you have to be on your guard at all times not to be taken in. When we look at what is wrong with contemporary society with its violence, corrupt politicians, and apparently irremediable social issues, we may tend to agree with this. Yet most of us still cling to hope, believing that some good remains in our public servants, that violence can be ameliorated, and that society's inequities can be addressed. That is part of what life in a civil society is all about: examining its problems and figuring out how to fix them. A skeptic will examine the realities and then figure out a practical way to remedy them, but the cynic will just point to society's problems and say, "See? I told you. Everything's rotten." The cynic has lost hope and faith.

The life of the cynic, then, is one of pure narcissism, since there is nothing worthwhile in life other than satisfying one's own desires. And ironically, it is the self-esteem movement that is largely responsible for the loss of faith and hope that we see in some of our young people. Although at first it would seem that feeling good about yourself would help combat cynicism, in fact the opposite is true. Faith and hope and ideals come from exploring our abilities and learning about the world around us, envisioning possibilities in the future, not endlessly examining and reliving how we felt when someone was mean to us or why we "feel" we're not good in math. At least on one point the self-esteem movement has it right: The worst psychological event that can happen to any person, but particularly a child, is a loss of faith in oneself. But faith in oneself and self-confidence are meaningless and illusory unless they are based on something, for if there is anything more damaging than losing faith in oneself it is finding out that that faith was misplaced. And, ironically, that is just what the self-esteem movement has done.

For example, according to a recent study by the Higher Education Research Institute at UCLA, 53.6 percent of college students reported a strong sense of intellectual self-confidence (compared to 34.8 percent in 1971) and 69 percent of freshmen expect to earn a bachelor's degree, compared to 58.7 percent in 1974. Unfortunately, the reality for most of these young people falls far short of their expectations. In 1995 just 28 percent of high school graduates between the ages of 25 and 34 had completed four or more years of college.[32] Instead of ensuring that kids have a strong foundation of knowledge, today we ensure that they have very high self-esteem. We have traded substance for image. Consequently, these young people believe in a future that they will never realize. They have been praised to the skies by well-meaning parents and teachers and thus have a very high—and very illusory—sense of their self-worth. They have been given grades they did not earn and think they are prepared for college, whereas in fact they are not. According to the U.S. Department of Education, nationally about 30 percent of all college students take at least one remedial course, and at my university, for example, over half the students require remedial help.[33] The self-esteem movement has given false expectations to our children and has thereby deprived them of real hope. Realizing they were cheated, is it any wonder they become cynics?

Kids need something outside themselves to believe in: another person, an idea, or a goal. They need hope in the world. Americans are not by nature a cynical people but, like everyone else, they are influenced by their environment and need to see something they can feel optimistic about. The generation born in the 1960s or later—the tail end of the baby boomers—had little to put their faith in. The bad politics (and bad music!) of the 1970s, together with the greed and excesses of the 1980s, certainly didn't provide much inspiration. That generation and those that followed, the so-called Generation X and now the "baby boom echo," have been called spoiled because materially they have it pretty good. But they will likely never have the buying power of their parents, and when they are eligible to draw from their social security benefits the economists tell us that they will find that the well has dried up.

They may also have missed out on something more important: character. Their parents and grandparents acquired strength from having survived the Depression and the Second World War, and older siblings might have been active in the civil rights or women's movements. But these kids grew up with little to fight for or even feel passionate about. They have been infected with what Peter Sacks in *Generation X Goes to College* calls the "cancer" of postmodern public schools and universities.[34] Characterized themselves by mediocrity, they foster the same in their students, who expect much but expect to give very little to get it.

It is trite, but nonetheless true, that suffering creates character. I am not suggesting that children should suffer, but today's kids, for all that they may have been indulged, have been deprived of the privilege of being challenged. If they are indeed a "me" generation, it is primarily because their faith has been questioned by the cynicism of the self-esteem movement, their intellects left unused, and their curiosity dulled. All they need to right this situation are schools that challenge and excite them, parents who are involved with them, and a society that welcomes and values them. But before we talk about fixing things, we need a better understanding of how we got here. Where exactly does the buck stop? With teachers and with *their* teachers, professors of education.

2

Inside the Ed School

The Politics of Teacher Education

A gentle, unintellectual, saccharine, and
well-meaning . . . bumbling doctor of undiagnosable ills,
harmless if morosely defensive. He is either a mechanic . . .
or he is the flatulent promoter of irrelevant trivia.
—Arthur Powell and Theodore Sizer[1]

WHOM DO THESE WORDS DESCRIBE, and to whom can they be attributed? They describe the typical education professor and they were written, not, as one might imagine, by a news reporter nor a former student with an ax to grind, but by Arthur Powell and Theodore Sizer, at the time former dean and associate dean, respectively, of the Harvard School of Education. One may well wonder what would provoke respected members of the profession to refer to their colleagues in this way. A look inside colleges of education and the process of teacher education will explain it.

When I began my university teaching career, I was shocked by my students' behavior. Somewhat naively, I had expected eager faces and curious intellects, but what I frequently encountered was bored looks and a distinct lack of curiosity about almost everything. It wasn't that the students were not interested in becoming teachers; after all, they had chosen this career voluntarily. And it wasn't that they had no interest in children; they were all looking forward to getting into the classroom and seemed very dedicated to their chosen profession. They just didn't believe that they needed much in the way of teacher education before doing so.

One of the reasons many of them had this attitude is that about two-thirds of them were already teaching in public schools. What the public—

and parents—may not realize is that in many states anyone who has a bachelor's degree and has passed a minimum competency exam can begin teaching, as long as they are concurrently enrolled in a teacher education program. Although some of the students in my classes were not yet teaching or were just starting their credential program, many had been already working for several years on an emergency credential. Perhaps it is not surprising, then, if some had little patience for their coursework, feeling that they had already mastered the necessary skills in the classroom.

The content of my course is a particular frustration for some of these students. Since they feel they already know what they are doing, they seem eager to take only courses that help them in very practical ways: how to discipline, how to organize a roll sheet, how to deal with the politics of the institution, and how to teach specific courses. What I teach doesn't give them any of that. It is a course in the sociology and philosophy of education that deals with the social, political, and economic conditions in which schools operate as well as the kinds of questions that I addressed in the first chapter: what it means to be educated, the difference between education and training, and related issues.

Some students enjoy the course material but others find it irrelevant. For them, what is relevant is what can be put to immediate practice in the classroom. Studying the context of schooling; considering the confluence of race, class, and gender and their effect on learning; and examining one's own philosophy of teaching are not considered "relevant" to the practice of teaching. "Reflective practice" is the ideal of teacher education, and my course is supposed to teach the reflection part. Unfortunately, most students seem to want the practice but not the reflection. For example, many students write in their course evaluations that the research assignments are not useful: "How does all the material help me as a teacher?" It helps, of course, by prodding students to think more carefully about their practice and about the practice of teaching in general.

Curiously, however, there is a distinct division within each class between those who find it useful and stimulating, and those who bemoan its irrelevance. This division does not fall, by and large, on ethnic, class, or gender lines. It is generational. Students who are in their mid-thirties or older are almost invariably interested, curious, hard-working, and polite, quite unlike their younger colleagues, who frequently exhibit narcissistic, anti-intellectual, and anti-school attitudes. They have an attitude of entitlement.

Of course, the older students are more mature and most have had other careers. Thus they are highly focused on their studies and know how to conduct themselves in public and in a classroom. But there is another reason for this division. Adults in their thirties and beyond had the good fortune to go through school before the self-esteem movement completely took it over and thus they escaped the worst of it. They are less likely to assume the attitudes and behaviors it fosters.

Of course not all rude behavior or self-centeredness can be blamed on the school system. Parents must assume the greater responsibility for child rearing, and adults must be held responsible for their own actions. But years ago students who didn't have parents who taught them how to be principled, mannerly individuals were nevertheless generally expected to behave properly at school, work for their grades, take responsibility for their failures, and learn from them. Neither students nor teachers had been completely indoctrinated by the self-esteem movement.

So complaints that "other professors don't care what our writing is like" and "other professors don't care if we hand things in on time" and "other professors don't care about critical thinking" come almost invariably from the younger students. But they are also expressing a truth: that with some exceptions, most of their professors do not care about those things. The vast majority of education professors have bought into the ideology of self-esteem and support it fervently.

Disturbingly, most professors of education seem to really believe that promoting self-esteem is what school is for, and in good faith they indoctrinate teachers to believe likewise. As Professors Powell and Sizer noted, if education professors are anything, it is well-meaning. If there were ever a case of good intentions leading to hell, this is surely it. Now there may be some who understand the dangers of the self-esteem movement but put ethics aside and go along with it to protect their careers. But whether self-esteem dogma is taught naively or cynically, the effects on our children are the same: devastating.

Thus before we jump on teachers' backs and blame them for the sorry state of the nation's schools, we must remember that most teachers going into the field today got it from both ends. They are themselves products of the self-esteem movement in schools. They were taught that effort, not achievement, is what counts; that they are entitled to grades on demand; that they need not master course material to be passed to the next grade; that they won't be punished for bad behavior but rather sent to "anger management" classes or be told they are sick and given a pill. Sick indeed: not the students, but their ideas, which have been reinforced by their professors in their teacher education courses. So if you have ever wondered where teachers get their weird ideas, read on.

Inside the Madhouse: The Politics of Education

The public often perceives university professors as having a pretty cushy life. In some ways it is, but the reality is considerably more complex than that. It is true that once a professor has been awarded tenure it is notoriously difficult to get rid of him or her—for any reason. But the road to tenure is a long one and is really about politics much more than teaching or research.

Like public schools, universities are small worlds in themselves, and each department has its own society and politics. The ed school is populated with the usual variety of misfits, miscreants, and misogynists as well as (thankfully) a sprinkling of relatively normal, bright, and honest individuals. People form cliques, usually on the basis of shared research or teaching interests, and departments are typically characterized by a lot of misunderstanding, envy, and jealousy among these groups. Professors are very protective of what they perceive to be "their" teaching and research domains and defend them at all costs.

Although we like to think that ed schools are first and foremost about education, much of the faculty and administration spend a great deal of time and effort on fund-raising (euphemistically called "development"), soliciting both research funds and individual and corporate donations. Currently, the most popular form of moneymaking involves "developing" grants to improve school/university/community partnerships—one of the major trends in school reform. There is a lot of interest in philanthropic circles as well as in the federal government regarding these good works, and consequently a lot of money around for schools of education to get their hands on.

The College of Education at my university is involved in a variety of projects, and one day I decided to try to find out more about one of them. The words "stakeholders," "partnerships," "team leaders," and "needs assessment" were bandied about with great enthusiasm, but somehow I had never been able to get a clear picture of the program. So at a presentation by the "team leaders" one day of one of these programs, I asked what I was sure was going to be a silly question: "What exactly do you intend to accomplish in this project, and how?" Rather than look at me pityingly, as I frankly expected, the two professors seemed confused and a little flustered. They explained that they were going to be promoting school–university cooperation and collaboration. "Great," I replied. After all, who could be against that? "But collaboration for what? To achieve what?" "Well, collaboration, you know, to improve schools."

This went on for some time, but I never did figure out just what the project was for. The reason for my confusion was kindly explained to me later by another colleague. Getting grants is a competitive business and the trick, he said, was to secure the money first by writing a slick proposal. Worrying about how to spend it came later. Naively, I had assumed that one would have to identify a real need in public schools, formulate a specific plan to address it and *then* look for money to implement it. I guess this was my education in "development" issues. This is not to say that schools do not benefit in any way from these projects but that their needs are secondary to the university's political interests. And people have few qualms, apparently, regarding the source of the money. A notorious former "junk bond king" has close ties to the College of Education, and I recall a picture of him and the former dean smiling together at some college function. Sometimes a picture really does say a lot more than words could ever tell.

What concerns me most about the politics in the field of education is the very fact that it *is* no better than politics in other fields. While I have never been under the illusion that professors of education were any better than anyone else, it seems to me that they have an obligation to set a high standard of learning and ethics. There are undoubtedly many professors who sincerely make students' interests their priority, but, unfortunately, they are often the ones most vulnerable to the lure of the self-esteem movement, precisely because they are so well-meaning. In their strong desire to *do* good they focus primarily on helping students *feel* good but miss out on the opportunity to encourage teachers to *be* good—to become better persons. Others will simply go to any lengths to achieve their ends, and ethical concerns do not seem to give them much pause. This was brought home to me forcibly in graduate school.

The chair of my department took an interest in my work, encouraged me to present papers at conferences, and took me with him to a local symposium on an area of mutual interest. He seemed a decent fellow, was generally well-liked, and I thought highly of him. When I wrote a paper for his class, I received an A, and he wrote that it was "a good paper, at least the part I understood"(?!). He told me that he was writing a paper on a similar topic and, being interested in it, I naturally asked if I could have a look at it. He refused and I thought no more about it until I heard him speak at a conference.

His paper was on a similar topic but with a different slant. I listened with interest until I heard a paragraph that I immediately recognized. He had taken a few words directly from a paragraph in my paper and paraphrased the rest of the paragraph. It was shocking and very upsetting, but it got worse. Several months later I had the dubious pleasure of seeing my words in print, under his name, as president of a prestigious association, in the association's journal. Maybe that was his version of collaboration. Some time later when he asked me if I was still doing the topic I had originally chosen for my dissertation, I was relieved to be able to say that I wasn't and decided not to share with him my new area of interest, in case he felt like collaborating on that one too!

A senior colleague witnessed the whole episode and encouraged me to complain. To this day I have not (although I guess now the cat is more or less out of the bag), knowing that if I were to ever need anything from my alma mater it would be very difficult if I had publicly exposed a very senior faculty member. The politics and power relations at schools of education, and indeed throughout the university as a whole, discourage graduate students, including teachers in training, from speaking up when they are harassed, oppressed, exploited, or otherwise abused. They know that if they do, they may find life at the institution unbearable. This may be one reason, in fact, that the self-esteem movement has flourished in schools of education: Even if some future teachers (and junior professors) can see it for what it is, they are unlikely to challenge the dominant ideology, knowing that doing so could very likely damage their academic and professional careers. The message graduate students and indeed junior professors receive is patently clear: Don't rock the boat or you'll be thrown out of it.

Psychology Rules

I have often wondered what makes the doctrine of self-esteem so enticing to some professors of education and so uninteresting to the rest of us. Disciplinary background seems to have a lot to do with it. It is important to understand that schools of education are dominated by the field of educational psychology, a specialty that permeates research and practice in several other fields: special education, elementary education, secondary education, educational psychology and counseling, and deaf education. The only area that does not rely heavily on psychological theory or practice is social and philosophical foundations of education, which includes courses on the history, politics, and economics of education as well as other issues, such as public policy and multiculturalism.

Teachers need both psychology and philosophy. They need to know basic principles of cognitive and emotional development as well as the social

and political context in which students learn. But because teacher education programs are so heavy in psychological theory, it is especially important that future teachers take some sociology and political theory to
balance it out, in order to gain some understanding of the complex political, economic, and racial aspects of teaching in the public schools. Indeed,
I often tell my students (only half-jokingly) that my course is the antidote
to all the psychology they get.

Unfortunately, due to the increasing influence of the self-esteem movement, psychology is becoming even more dominant in teacher education,
and courses that address the nonpsychological issues are being slowly
weeded out. Whereas the 1960s saw a growth nationally and internationally in philosophy and foundations of education, since the late 1970s the
ideas of self-esteem have grown in popularity and philosophical concerns
in education have taken a back seat. Teacher education programs focus on
methods (how to teach something), cultural diversity (from a psychological standpoint), and curriculum content. At my institution, for example,
the larger issues are addressed in only one course. Master's degree candidates focus on one of the principal specialties mentioned above and can
usually complete a degree without ever having to take courses in the social
or philosophical foundations of education.

As the only remaining faculty member in philosophy of education at
my institution, I have heard the following question repeated endlessly:
"What use is all that philosophy, anyway?" "These kids just need to know
how to teach." "You have their head in the clouds; we have their feet on
the ground." Neither the faculty nor the students, by and large, see the
value in asking the big questions: What are schools for? What skills or
knowledge should students have when they graduate? Are we really educating children in school or are we just helping them feel good about
themselves?

These questions are just too thorny to deal with, apparently because
they actually require us to think. Whether they like it or not, future teachers need to be acquainted with the purposes of public schooling, which
have little to do with psychology and everything to do with philosophy
and politics. Without these courses, future teachers will have little or no
understanding of what schools, writ large, are all about. The view that
teacher education, like public education, should be all methods and practice and should involve no actual thinking has some of its roots in the
general anti-intellectualism of American society that originated, at least in
part, in colleges of education. If professors of education do not consider
critical thinking worthwhile, it is hardly surprising that their students—
our children's future teachers—share that view. In other words, if those

who educate the educators do not believe in the ideals of a liberal education, who will?

The implications of this perspective are very serious indeed. We expect
teachers to uphold the ideals that have guided public education in North
America since its inception. But in order to uphold them, they have to be
taught them. The reason that the purposes of schooling are being undermined, replaced, and forgotten is that professors of education don't think
they are *practical* or *relevant* and because they support the ideology of the
self-esteem movement. (The two are linked, of course; one cannot logically support the idea that schooling is solely for emotional development
and also believe in the ideals of liberal education, since these two concepts
are diametrically opposed.) Public schooling now resembles training
more than education, in the way I defined it in the first chapter, because
professors want it that way. But if training rather than educating
schoolkids is dangerous, training rather than educating their teachers is
ultimately much more serious, simply because of the number of children
an educator influences throughout his or her career.

Why Teacher *Training* Must Become Teacher *Education*

Colleges of education are charged with imparting what might be called
the science of teaching: the knowledge, skills, and practical strategies that
teachers need in order to function effectively in a classroom. The first requirement for teachers is a solid command of their subject matter. In order to enter a teacher education program candidates must normally have
at least a bachelor's degree, preferably in the subject matter they will be
teaching (in the case of high school) or in liberal studies (if they intend to
go into elementary education). Second, they need to understand the socioeconomic context of schooling. Third, they need to know how to teach.
The last two areas form the body of their teacher education. Although
programs of teacher education vary from state to state and even within
states, at reputable institutions future teachers can expect to take more or
less the same kinds of courses.

Teacher education programs normally take two years after the degree,
although there are respectable one-year programs. Many students and
professors think two years is an inordinate amount of time to spend
learning *just* to become a teacher, and academics frequently discuss how
to make teacher education shorter and more "user friendly." One of the
more popular ideas is to have future teachers enter an undergraduate de-

gree program in education upon entering college, so that when they graduate they have both a bachelor's degree and a teaching credential. The obvious advantage of this idea from a student's perspective is that the time required to get a teaching credential is shortened.

But we should be examining this from the perspective of the best interests of their future pupils. Since many teacher education candidates who already have degrees exhibit such low levels of literacy and basic knowledge, removing the requirement of an undergraduate degree would only ensure that those levels drop even further. It also raises the question of whether teachers need a solid foundation of knowledge to be able to teach it to their students. In other words, which is more important: to know how to teach or to know the subject one is teaching?

The answer should be obvious. Teachers need both, and candidates who graduate from accredited teacher education programs should have both solid subject-matter knowledge and effective teaching skills. But given the paucity of core knowledge that students demonstrate, it is absolutely critical that teachers have respectable depth and breadth of knowledge in the liberal arts and sciences before going into a teacher education program, for the simple reason that that knowledge is itself the essence of what children should be learning in schools. Teachers who don't have the necessary foundation cannot possibly share it with others.

The ideal of a classical liberal education is founded on that knowledge, which is shared with the student through the intermediary of the teacher. Allowing teachers to bypass it means reducing the role of teacher as educator to teacher as technician. Public school teachers should be the true intellectual leaders of our society, since they have the responsibility for shaping generations of minds. When I tell my students this, they look at me in considerable consternation, realizing the burden that is placed upon them. It is indeed an enormous responsibility. But it is also a privilege, for apart from ensuring basic health and welfare needs, what is more important than educating our youth?

The very dangerous part of training instead of educating teachers is that it prevents teachers from developing the intellectual tools, the experience, or the conceptual understanding to differentiate between the two ideas. The differences between teacher education and training parallel the differences between child education and training. Teacher training involves "methods" courses that include such subjects as how to teach reading to third graders or how to teach social studies to middle school kids. In these courses students might also learn how to put together a lesson plan as well as the basics of classroom management, organization, and discipline.

These courses are indeed necessary because without them new teachers would enter a classroom without any practical idea of how to proceed. But training in how to do things is simply not enough. Teachers need metacognition, an understanding of how to learn and how to help their students learn. They also need to know the kinds of "big" ideas that differentiate the educated teacher from the trained teacher: how material in different subject areas or domains interconnect; the ways in which the world itself is increasingly interconnected yet still balkanized, or the implications of schools' increasing dependence on technology.

Training in discrete activities or methods reduces the process of teacher education to a series of "how to" courses without any comprehensive overview of why they are doing what they are doing. It is the lack of a guiding philosophy of teaching that would never be permissible in other professions. For example, we would never allow someone who has only a couple of years of college science and training in the use of power tools to operate on our brain! We require them to have a foundational knowledge of anatomy and physiology, as well as many other areas, before obtaining the specialized training and internship required for neurosurgery. It would be ludicrous to have it any other way because people's lives would be in danger.

Simple "training" of teachers is no less dangerous. Although the danger may seem more remote and the effects less obvious, they are no less serious. Allowing children to be taught by teachers who are themselves not properly educated is just as unethical as allowing a technician to operate on their brains. Death from the latter is likely to be dramatic and immediate, but children who are taught by poorly educated teachers also die, but it is a slow, agonizing death, characterized by the loss of curiosity, the decline of critical thinking, an increase in apathy, and, finally and most tragically, the death of hope.

To compound matters further, if teachers are trained, rather than educated, neither they nor their future students will ever know what they are missing. Thus we must convince future teachers, who have grown up with the idea that self-esteem and training are what schools are for, that schools should educate *because becoming an educated person is a good thing in and of itself*, irrespective of any practical skill or job that may result from it. One of the most wonderful gifts that an educated teacher can give her students is help them experience those "aha!" moments that are what becoming educated is all about. Perhaps it is not until we experience those moments ourselves that we realize how education can transform our lives.

I had one of those "aha" moment in my third year at university. I was an English major, and taking a course called "Victorian Novel," which I would have enjoyed but for an instructor who hated women and spent half of her time flirting with the men and the other half telling us about her cats. I was also taking advanced Italian language, as well as an Italian film and literature course, political theory, and a wonderful survey course in the history of Western art.

I think the art course was the catalyst for this transforming experience. Although it was a class of over two hundred students, and a survey course to boot, in a year we learned a lot about Western art. What made it so enthralling was not only the instructor's youth, energy, and excitement but his ability to describe the art in aesthetic terms and also situate it in the political, social, and economic climate of the day. Paintings that I had viewed before as interesting, but nothing more, suddenly took on a whole new significance and told me about an entire culture and way of life. This, in turn, made my political theory courses, which were a little on the dry side, much more meaningful, and my language and literature courses added another element to the picture.

I felt as if I had been given a gift: the ability to see the growth and development of different cultures and to understand how politics affects social class; to see how the role of women varied from one culture to another and yet evolved in a similar pattern over time; to see how the role of the artist depended on the political and economic fortunes of the ruling class, and many other concepts. I learned a number of things, but the understanding of the overall picture was the most important of them. That understanding is the beginning of the sense of connectedness that educators should promote: between our place in history and other eras, between ourselves and other people, and between ourselves and the physical, social, and intellectual worlds.

I began to see what lies at the heart of becoming educated. I saw that art, politics, sex, war, family life, the class system, and economics are all related and that a big part of understanding life is about understanding society in all its complexity. I also saw that although we teach subjects as if they were discrete categories of information, they are in fact masses of information that we have organized in certain ways in order to make sense of them. It is necessary to organize knowledge in order to teach it, but the organization is largely arbitrary, since knowledge can be packaged in a variety of ways.

Gaining an understanding of the big picture is not confined to higher education. Children also get those moments of understanding. Their experiences may be simpler, but they are just as important. Understanding photosynthesis for the first time gives children an insight into the growth and development of plant life as a whole and can make them look at a garden or a forest in a whole new way. Following the development of a character in a book can help them see how others experience the same things they do, and they begin to see the connections between themselves and others. Learning a second language not only allows them to communicate with people who speak that language but opens a door onto a whole variety of cultural experiences. Recognition of those connections is the real evidence that something truly educative is going on. And teachers need to understand the importance of that kind of synthesis, and need to have experienced it for themselves, in order to be able to help their students know the thrill of "getting it." That is what we might call the art of teaching.

The Art of Teaching

Professors of education can teach the "science" of teaching to their students: subject matter knowledge, teaching methods, behavior management techniques, child psychology, and so forth, but the art of teaching is something that each teacher must develop on her own. The interpretation of ideas, the performance part of teaching, and the creative ways teachers get their students interested in the material are all part of the indefinable art of teaching. But as philosopher of education Elliot Eisner writes about teaching, "When it is sensitive, intelligent, and creative—those qualities that confer upon it the status of an art—it should, in my view, not be regarded, as it so often is by some, as an expression of unfathomable talent or luck but as an example of humans exercising the highest levels of their intelligence."[2] The art of teaching is not talent alone, then, but the intelligent use of one's creative resources, married with one's "scientific" knowledge about teaching.

But unless the person has a chance to explore and demonstrate his or her talent, it may lie dormant and unrecognized. I remember one student who perfectly exemplified this. She was a pleasant young woman and a very bright student, who did well on all her assignments. She almost never spoke in class, however, and seemed quite shy. Like everyone else, she was part of a group of five or six students who were responsible for presenting and analyzing some of the class readings. Her group's presentation was on the subject of teacher education, as it happens, and she was the first in her group to go.

Her talk was on the frustrations that teachers experience in the classroom, the reasons why they burn out, and what they can do to stay motivated and happy in their profession. She came into the class carrying a beaker of beans floating in water. Some of the beans stayed on the bottom of the beaker, some hovered around in the middle, and some floated to the top. We were a little baffled by this, but we were also very interested to see what the beans were for. Everyone was looking expectantly at the student. She had captured everyone's attention before ever saying a word.

She explained the existence of the beaker. As a science teacher, she frequently used visuals along with hands-on exercises to help explain scientific phenomena to her students, so she thought she would try the same with us. She explained that the beans on the bottom represented teachers who had complete burnout and had given up on teaching. Those in the middle were experiencing some stress but were still treading water, as it were. And the beans on top represented teachers who had learned through a variety of measures to deal with the stresses of teaching and had thus risen above them.

Not only did her visuals make us all giggle (since some of the beans didn't seem quite happy with their assigned status and rebelliously wandered about in every direction) but, more importantly, they got everyone involved in the material. From there she used a variety of visuals and challenging questions for the class that kept them engaged for the duration of the presentation. Although the presentation was itself impressive, it was actually the transformation in this student that had all of us literally sitting with our mouths hanging open. She was engaging, funny, smart, ironic, well-informed, and interested in her colleagues' viewpoints—all marks of a good teacher. When she stepped in front of a class—here a class of her peers—she came alive, and all the intelligence and wit that she had displayed on paper was now evident in person. When she finished, we all clapped and cheered, and I thought how privileged we were to have witnessed some truly great teaching.

Are We Expecting Too Much from Our Ed Schools?

Like all academics, professors of education must make a name for themselves in order to survive professionally. As well as teaching, they must publish articles in their area of interest as evidence of their research. But education professors have a special interest in the relationship between teaching and research, simply because teaching *is* their field of research. Thus they have the additional burden of proving to their colleagues in other university departments that the work they perform in schools qualifies as research and should be taken seriously. Education professors also have a special responsibility, since their research is actually "tried out" on public school students, who are the unfortunate guinea pigs for every new educational fad.

Where colleges of education differ from other departments, however, is that they have a special responsibility to the public as well as a more immediate relationship with them. We expect departments like colleges of engineering, physical education, or mathematics, to contribute in some way to the improvement of society. But, with the exception of medicine and the biological sciences, we don't depend on them for our immediate survival and well-being.

But we do expect immediate results from colleges of education. We expect them to turn out well-prepared and responsible teachers who are able to deal with the complex problems of contemporary public schools. And we look to professors of education to lead the way in developing research that will improve student learning and achievement in practical, measurable ways. What that means, particularly with the rise of the self-esteem movement, is that the public has to be vigilant about staying on top of educational research. It doesn't just "trickle down" in a few years into the public consciousness but is directly injected via teachers into the public schools, usually before the public has a chance to sample the idea, chew on it, and digest it for itself.

This is an unfortunate aspect of the relationship between teacher education and the public schools because it means that parents have no chance to halt a program before the damage is done. Academics may have many years of formal schooling, but the public has common sense on its side. It is a sure bet that if the public had known in advance that we were going to be teaching kids to read by not teaching them and disciplining them by requesting that they agree to "mediation," there would have been an outcry, and many of these fads would have been stopped before they gathered momentum.

Society's expectations can be unfair when it expects teachers and their professors to accept burdens that they cannot possibly bear. Because all of us have gone to school, few of us think that teaching is a very difficult job. We all know the saying "If you can't do, teach; if you can't teach, teach teachers." "How hard can it be?" we ask ourselves. "Why can't teachers get Johnny to read, or even behave?" One of the principal reasons is the subject of this book: the self-esteem movement. By focusing almost exclusively on self-esteem in teacher education, we have effectively undermined teachers' ability to teach and have brainwashed future teachers into believing that high self-esteem as it is currently understood—feeling good for no good reason—is one of the most important (if not *the* most important) things students can acquire in schools.

This attitude was evident in a recent survey I gave to teacher education students on the origins, importance, and meaning of self-esteem in teacher education programs and in the public schools. Sixty-nine percent of respondents believed that social or emotional intelligence (i.e., getting along well with others or being in touch with their feelings) was a more important skill for success in life than academic or intellectual intelligence (only 19 percent supported the latter). Sixty-eight percent believed that teachers should learn about self-esteem in order to teach it to their students in public schools and 73 percent believed that schools should try to encourage high self-esteem in children. And when asked to identify which characteristics define self-esteem, 50 percent of respondents identified "feeling good about yourself," and 31 percent responded with "self-acceptance." Not one of the respondents identified "working on self-improvement" as a relevant criterion for self-esteem. Again, the prevailing wisdom seems to be that one does not need to justify one's feelings of self-worth either to oneself or to others.

Another reason for many children's failure to achieve or behave according to our expectations is our often unrealistic expectations of public schools. Americans have always had great faith in their public schools to serve the purposes for which they were invented: educate the citizenry, turn out productive workers, and promote social equality. This faith is very important and may well prove critical to our success in overthrowing the self-esteem movement. If one thing is clear about public education, it is that Americans understand its importance and want the best for their children. The downside of that faith is that it tends to place burdens on the public schools that should be borne by other public or private institutions.

For example, we expect schools to provide basic health and welfare needs that should be the responsibility of parents or, if the parent is absent or neglectful, health care agencies, social services, or child welfare agencies. These misplaced expectations have two sources, one of which is the self-esteem movement. As I discuss in more detail in the next chapter, the self-esteem movement, with its ideas of "treating" the "whole child," along with the influence of the progressive movement in education, has effectively transformed the role of the public school from academics to caretaking.

The second source comes from the simple fact that many of this society's social needs are not taken care of by other institutions. Since there is no form of national health care and since everyone attends school, schools have been required to assume responsibility for immunizations, identifying and preventing child abuse, and basic nutritional and health issues. In *It Takes a Village and Other Lessons Children Teach Us* Hillary Clinton ex-

plains how children need not only the care of loving parents but community support in many forms, whether it be preschool, Head Start programs, or prenatal care.[3] We speak often enough of "wards of the state,"
but children today are becoming wards of the school system, a place where
they can be warehoused, since we either can't or don't want to deal with
them. Morally, schools have little choice but to step up to the plate, given
the paucity of government services in these areas, but they are forced to
assume an unnecessary financial and political burden, leaving fewer resources (including precious time) for what should be the real purpose of
schools—educating.

The situation is no different when it comes to violence. Despite a national decrease in violent crime (down to 1.59 million incidents in 1997
from a recent high of 1.93 million in 1992[4]) and increasing cooperation in
many urban areas between the police and school districts, schools still
have the major responsibility of keeping criminals out of schools, preventing crime among their own student populations, and protecting students from the overall influence of a violent society. Again, these are
public responsibilities that should be assumed by parents and communities, as well as law enforcement agencies.

One obvious effect of these pressures is that, clearly, schools can never
measure up. If we now expect public schools to feed and clothe our children, provide them with medical care, give them psychological counseling, and shield them from violence, they will have precious little time left
for academic instruction. Schools are neither organized nor equipped to
serve these functions. The public is upset that children are not being educated and blame it on the teachers. Meanwhile, teachers are confused as to
what their job is, having received different messages from their education
professors and from the public. The public says, "Educate our children!"
while their professors tell them their real job is protecting children's self-
esteem.

Not surprisingly, professors of education, like teachers, often feel be-
sieged by the public's demands on education and become defensive. Because the public expectations of our schools are so high and the media
portrayal of them is so low, many professors of education whom I have
encountered exhibit an extraordinary degree of paranoia, convinced that
the press is out to get them and that the public just doesn't understand
what education is all about. To make matters worse, colleges of education
are considered the low man on the professional totem pole in universities,
below colleges of engineering, medicine, law, or management. They are
not even listed among the professions in the *Princeton Review* of U.S. professional schools. The guide for college entrance in 1999 published in

Time magazine includes all the professions listed above but not education, although a brief section on education is included in *U.S. News and World Report's* equivalent "best graduate schools."

This may explain some of the egomania of education professors. An exaggerated sense of self-importance is by no means confined to teacher educators, but ed schools do seem to be small worlds inhabited by large egos. The bad press just compounds professors' insecurity about not doing "real" or "serious" research like their colleagues in the biological or physical sciences (as I discuss in Chapter 9, these fears may in fact be justified). And since educational research has always been perceived as being less rigorous and less "objective," professors feel compelled to defend their work at all costs.

As a result, when education professors are confronted with the latest salvo from the press regarding the sad state of schooling and teacher education, we tend to react badly. In faculty meetings the reaction is not a serious examination of the pressing issues but almost invariably condescending self-defensiveness: "Those people don't understand the real problems!" "They're just out to make us look bad!" "They don't even understand what whole language learning is all about!" Not once have I ever heard a faculty member say something like, "The writer makes some provocative points in the article. Let's talk about them." Never.

What we may be witnessing is the ultimate irony—a serious self-esteem problem among professors of education. Academics in general are not generally known for their good looks, stylish dressing, or witty dinner conversation, education professors included. This, compounded with the pressures I have described and the defensiveness they exhibit, suggests a low level of self-confidence. If this is true, they have put themselves in a prison to which only they hold the key. If they stopped adopting the kinds of silly and dangerous ideas that the self-esteem movement promotes, they would be taken much more seriously by their fellow academics as well as the public, and no doubt begin to earn the respect they feel they deserve. (I wonder if there's a group for that?)

Now I Know How Alice Must Have Felt

The obsession with self-esteem combined with professorial insecurity results in some pretty weird "research" and some unusual academic experiences. At a recent national conference on education, I had the opportunity to experience the absurdity firsthand. I attended a presentation by a number of respected professors from the United States, Canada, Norway, and

Japan on cooperative learning. Cooperative learning is the K–12 version of collaboration, and it is one of the centerpieces of the self-esteem movement. It essentially involves grouping children of different abilities together in the classroom and encouraging them to work together on projects. The idea is that the brighter students will help the slower ones and that all the students will learn the value of collaborative versus competitive effort. It bears repeating that self-esteem advocates see competition as nothing less than the devil's work.

I arrived a little late and thus missed the introduction by the moderator, which would no doubt have tipped me off as to what I was in for. After being ushered into the only remaining seat in the room, I saw there was little chance to escape, except out the window. As the presentations commenced, I realized that the audience was not to be treated to a serious analysis of the pros and cons of cooperative learning, but rather a series of brief sermons on its virtues. Oh well, I thought, I'll just tune out.

No such luck. As the first presenter ended and responded to questions, the moderator jumped up and said, "Now, everyone, get up out of your chairs and turn to your neighbor, and share with him or her what you learned from this presentation." I had grossly miscalculated. The moderator, along with the panel, was plainly not going to let us out of the room unless we had ourselves experienced what we would be teaching our students. This is a typical strategy when teaching teachers: make them demonstrate the kinds of teaching strategies they will be using in the classroom in order to see how they work in practice. A fine idea in its way, but unnecessary and distracting at a conference.

I glanced furtively at the man on my right and then the one on my left and breathed a sigh of relief. They were both pretty crusty-looking old-timers, one of whom smelled very strongly of beer. I was pretty sure that they were not going to stand for this nonsense, so I settled back into my seat and perused the program, seeing what other interesting panels were on offer. However, I was clearly too quick to judge. The man on the left turned to me and asked me what I had learned. In a slight panic, I mumbled something inaudible to both of us and said boldly that I wasn't all that crazy about these audience-participation tactics. He smiled kindly, and I thought for a moment that he might pat me on the head as one would a confused child. But he apparently thought better of it and leaned across me to chat with the barfly to my right. Every time madam said "jump" they jumped and obediently "shared" what they had learned. I sat on my chair, holding my breath and desperately trying to figure out how to make a dash for it, all the while feeling distinctly like Alice in Wonderland, alone amongst a very odd crew.

What if we all rebelled, I thought? What would the moderator do then? It would be an interesting psychosocial experiment, and I glanced around to see if there were any likely candidates to join in a mutiny, but it was clear there was to be no revolution that day. Teacher educators, not given anyway to highly original thinking, apparently act like everyone else when they are herded together: compliant—even bovine. Deciding it would be too uncouth—not to say plain rude—to just jump up and run out, I concentrated on the presentations themselves, thinking that I would undoubtedly pick up some gems of wisdom.

I did learn quite a bit, but what I learned profoundly disturbed me. Each of the five panelists had developed a different study to examine the effectiveness of cooperative learning on achievement and behavior. As advocates of this teaching strategy, they hoped to demonstrate that cooperative learning improved achievement for some, if not all, students and resulted in improved behavior across the board. Sadly, this was not to be. Each panelist reported that the children in the cooperative groups neither raised their achievement levels nor improved their behavior. The advanced students were frustrated and bored, resenting the fact that they had to teach the slower students, and the slower students felt intimidated and depressed at always having to be coached by others. Although some of the students enjoyed the group work, many reported feeling angry because some members did not pull their weight or annoyed that they were forced to work with others much of the time rather than work independently.

The presenters deserve credit for having the honesty to discuss their findings in a straightforward fashion, but the conclusions that they unanimously drew from their research were astonishing. Without exception, each stressed that, just because the research illustrated the failure of cooperative learning in the two areas where it was supposed to be effective did not mean that there is anything wrong with the idea. The problem is with the students and with society.

According to the panelists, students just need to be taught that working together is better than working alone, despite the fact that society largely rewards individual effort and achievement, not group work. Although learning to work with others is a necessary skill in the workplace, when it comes to the crunch, it is individuals, not groups, who get fired or promoted and individuals, not groups, who must earn a high school diploma or college degree. And no matter how much researchers would like to think that one survives or fails in society based on his or her cooperative skills, all the evidence, for better or for worse, points the other way. Schools—and professors—have an obligation to prepare students for the reality, not the fantasy.

Despite unequivocal evidence that their ideas made no sense, these professors would not abandon them, no matter what the costs to public school children. This story illustrates not only the defensive egomania of some education professors but also the death grip that self-esteem has on the education establishment. Cooperative learning is considered so central to developing high self-esteem that professors continue to support it despite all evidence to the contrary. The fact that students are not to be allowed to learn in the way that suits them the best but indoctrinated into the belief that cooperation is always better than competition is a frightening indication of the lengths to which professors and teachers will go to protect their beliefs. When they then turn around and say that what they are doing is in the students' best interests, as they did in this case, it is not only stupid and dangerous, it is the utmost in hypocrisy. How ironic that those who claim to be so concerned with students' welfare will go to any lengths to indoctrinate them into something that may well do them more harm than good!

At the end of this little flight of fancy, I decided to ask the obvious question of one of the presenters. "Why do you not at least look at cooperative learning a little more critically, after the results you show? How can you continue to support it unconditionally, when it appears, at least from this research, to be an abject failure?" Although I parsed my questions in somewhat more conciliatory terms than that, I did not get very far. The presenter tried to explain that it was a great idea anyway and that perhaps I didn't understand it properly. When he turned from being patiently patronizing to clearly annoyed, I decided it was time to fold my tent and go home. But the day was not a complete loss. We had agreed on one thing, at least: It is certain that I don't understand cooperative learning the way he and his colleagues do, and I think I prefer to keep it that way.

One thing is always true about academic conferences: contrary to what one might think, they're never dull. There's always something new and interesting to learn (whether one wants to learn it or not!). The most important education conference worldwide is probably the AERA (American Educational Research Association) annual meeting, at which all the fields of educational research are represented and which is attended by about 10,000 people from around the world. The session I attended on cooperative learning was one of the more "tame" offerings at the conference, which has gotten considerably more bizarre as the self-esteem movement has taken hold.

In a symposium called the Archeology of Social Justice one presenter offered a paper entitled "The Maternal Nurturance Trap: Discursive Practices of 'Social Justice' in Gender Equity Pedagogy in a Swedish Compulsory School." In a session on the ever popular topic of collaboration, one paper was entitled "Close to You: Up Close, Safe (But in Your Face) Research and Teaching Relations in a Feminist Classroom" while another proposed "Changing Our Minds, Changing Our Bodies: Power as Embodied in Research Relations." In a roundtable called Taking Teaching Seriously in Teacher Education: Five Self-Studies one presenter shared with the group "The Paradox and Pathos in Attempting to Fail a Student Teacher" (pathos indeed!) while a session under the heading "Explorations of Gender, Culture, and Freedom: Education in a (PC) Postmodern Moment" offered us, among other things, "Spear Fishing in Wisconsin: Critical Multiculturalism and Teacher Education" (your guess is as good as mine); "Sexuality, Teachers, and the Sexual Culture of the Secondary School," and "PC (Politically Correct) Multicultural Education." Incomprehensible, maybe; irrelevant, perhaps, and pompous—but not boring.

While it is amusing to examine the unusual offerings at these kinds of events, it is also instructive. An analysis of the paper topics tells us that the ideas of the self-esteem movement are not limited to one university, one state, or one specific area of research. They infuse almost all the principal research areas in Canada as well as the United States, including discipline; evaluation and assessment; standards; policy studies; early childhood development; primary and secondary language acquisition; multiculturalism; curriculum theory and content; and so on. Even educational technology, which might be considered the least likely candidate for recruitment into the self-esteem movement, is caught up in its web, as the following paper titles illustrate: "Collaborative Reasoning Around African American Literacy Texts Using a Multimedia Software Tool," "Enhancing Biliterary and Biculturalism Through 'Live Chats'" (biliterary what, by the way?), and "Perspectives on Learner-Centered Technologies: Taking Curriculum Integration Seriously."

A quick look in the local college bookstore gives us another way to gauge the prevalence of certain ideas or trends in teacher education, and these days, self-esteem is everywhere. The following titles I found in the bookstore of the University of British Columbia, a highly respected research institution in Vancouver, Canada. The subject headings in the bookstore under teacher education shared the focus of those in the United States: inclusion, multiculturalism, counseling, psychological foundations and (naturally) cooperative discipline. Some of the titles are intriguing, to say the least: "Creative Mathematics" (as opposed to dull and boring math, I guess), which includes "non-traditional math assessment" figured prominently in one section, while in the section on counseling psychology "Becoming an Agent" caught my eye. This was not, disappointingly, a tome telling the reader how to break into the field of espionage, but one explaining how one can empower oneself and take control of one's life. (The fact that "agency" really refers to someone acting on someone else's behalf is presumably beside the point.) And "Authentic Assessment for English Learners" tells the reader how to evaluate students by any means other than testing while in the counseling section the reader is informed about "Counselling the Culturally Different."

Teacher Education: The Short Course

Not all of the books about teacher education are as silly as these, however. Many tomes have been written over the years about the problems in teacher education and how best to remedy them. One of the most important early works was written in the 1960s by James D. Koerner, called *The Miseducation of American Teachers*. Koerner discusses the development of the field of teacher education, quality of instruction, state requirements and other important issues. Although some of the numbers, in terms of student populations, ed schools, and so on, are out of date, his essential analysis of the field of teacher education is very contemporary. He writes that, with a few exceptions, educational journals are "especially depressing," "ill-conceived, ill-written, and ill-edited."[5] He notes that "educationists as a group are near the bottom of the academic ladder"[6] and that "weak students gravitate to weak faculties, thus compounding the problem of inferior personnel in Education."[7]

Even educators are forced to agree with some of this. A recent paper by the Association of Teacher Educators on reforming teacher education notes that "for years teacher preparation has had the image of being accessible and accommodating—that is, easy to enter, relatively brief in nature, convenient to academic programs in the major, lacking in academic challenge, inexpensive, and nonexclusive."[8] They also note that "the quality of teacher preparation across institutions is clearly uneven. Among these institutions, instances of best practice, instances of questionable practice, and unfortunately, instances of indefensible practice can be found."[9] Although the report issues a number of recommendations to strengthen preservice teacher education, suggestions for raising standards for entrants are conspicuously absent, and nowhere is the issue of self-esteem addressed.

However, the education establishment is beginning to realize that teacher education is indeed in a sorry state. New York recently adopted stricter teacher education standards and will require higher education institutions to obtain accreditation for their teacher education programs by

December 31, 2004.[10] Similar steps are being taken in California, Georgia, Massachusetts, and New Hampshire, as states try to improve the quality of candidates coming into the field, establish higher standards for teacher preparation and certification, develop new content standards in schools, and ensure that schools of education are accredited by the National Council for Accreditation of Teacher Education.[11] Even the American Federation of Teachers, one of the two national teachers' unions, is joining in the debate. The president of the AFT, Sandra Feldman, recently wrote that "we have to insist that the people in charge don't allow (just) anyone to teach our children. It doesn't take an Einstein to see the wisdom of that."[12]

But we are making progress. Koerner, despite his criticisms, noted that at the time he was writing things had improved considerably from previous decades. Although teacher-training institutions historically admitted "virtually anyone," some had begun to raise admissions standards and by the early 1960s required an average of C or a little better for acceptance.[13] This is still the common standard for admission to teacher education programs in Canada as well as in the United States. For example, at the University of British Columbia, students are required to show a C+, or 65 percent, as a baseline grade average, and at my institution in California the baseline GPA standards for new admissions in the 1998–1999 academic year ranged from 2.28 for undeclared majors to 2.88 for physical education majors. Currently there is no standard GPA required for all applicants.

This would seem frustrating to the aspiring teacher, not knowing whether or not she has met the admissions requirements, but there appear to be two reasons for the policy. First, some majors are considered more academically rigorous than others, so those in physics, math, business, and chemistry, for example, are likely to be let in to the program with a lower GPA than those in art, music, or theater. Second, there is a critical shortage of credentialed teachers in California, and if the institution were to insist on a specific standard for admission (unless it were lowered to a C), then it would not be able to admit as many candidates as are required. In other words, a fluid standard allows the College of Education to admit those who have less than a C+ average if they are needed. Standards thus become a casualty of demand, and our children end up with teachers who probably should not be there at all.

Surveys of student teachers disclose that, despite the generally low level of applicants, they frequently refer to their education classes as irrelevant and less than challenging.[14] Teaching is (erroneously) not seen as intellectually challenging, so brighter students choose another career. (One wonders how *they* would perceive education classes.) Consequently, the public does not consider teaching prestigious and some people question whether it really is a profession. Although salaries vary widely, in general teachers do not earn a salary comparable to that of other professionals. So those expecting to earn a middle-class or upper-middle-class salary do not even consider teaching as a career possibility.

There is a clearly delineated structure to teacher education, at least at respected institutions. All programs include some variation of the same core courses, typically elementary education and secondary education, and sometimes a middle years education program. In Canada a specialty in French immersion or French as an additional language is often an option; in parts of the United States, particularly Texas and California, the language concentration is Spanish. Coursework includes the same essential topics: curriculum theory and practice, measurement and testing, instruction in the subject areas (language arts, math, social studies, etc.), teaching methods, developmental theory, behavior management, and courses on special education, which focus on the needs of learning disabled or gifted students. Courses in multiculturalism or bilingualism are often included somewhere in the program as well. Finally, there is an extended practicum, in which students put theory into practice by working as teachers or apprentice teachers in public schools.

Indeed, teacher education varies somewhat at each institution, but the basic core of courses is represented in some fashion. Nonetheless, Koerner states unequivocally that the field of education should recognize that "its record has been more one of promise than performance" and "ought to reconstruct itself as an academic enterprise, bringing its claims to power and authority into reasonable relation to its demonstrated virtues and improv(e) its standards at every point in the system."[15] That was over thirty years ago and we are only now beginning to seriously address the question of standards.

The Sins of the Fathers

A much more recent study of the state of teacher education is Rita Kramer's 1991 book, *Ed School Follies*, itself subtitled *The Miseducation of America's Teachers*. Kramer traveled across the country visiting a number of well-known and lesser-known teacher colleges, and came up with some devastating results. She separated the country into several geographical areas and visited a couple of colleges in each area. What is striking is that despite differences in geography, student population and ethnicity or college philosophy, one thing unites them: the unwavering belief that school-ing is primarily about feelings and self-esteem.

Kramer describes a motto displayed on a wall in a classroom at the State University of New York: "We Choose to Feel Special and Worthwhile No Matter What." "Loving kids" is seen as the proper motive for choosing teaching as a career and the objective in assessment is not, Kramer tells us, "on any objective goal but on the well-being of the individual student."[16] This was all too familiar to me. Countless students have told me that lov-ing kids makes a successful teacher; no one has ever said anything about loving school or loving learning.

Kramer also describes a children's literature course at Eastern Michigan University, in which the professor urges her students not to read the books (children's books) for the exam, just their notes. The professor tells them what to memorize, gives a sample question, explains the question, and summarizes the story.[17] Once more, déjà vu. Against my better judgment, I have resorted to summarizing course material before an exam, hoping that at least some students will study it. Without it, there is no hope be-cause they do not possess the skills to organize, memorize, or synthesize a term's worth of material. Even if they did, they wouldn't use those skills because they think they deserve to get the questions in advance. That is where I draw the line. Clearly the students and I both have high expecta-tions. Unfortunately, they differ widely. Students write in their course evaluations that they expect a "cushion of bonus points to boost the midterm or group presentation grade" and demand to know "how to get an A on papers," as if there were some kind of magic formula.

Kramer describes the idyllic scene at the University of California at Los Angeles. I received my Ph.D. from UCLA but knew little about its teacher education programs, which are entirely separate from the doctoral pro-gram, so I read this section with considerable interest. In a class on teach-ing bilingual reading the professor tells the students that it is more important to create a positive atmosphere than to correct mistakes,[18] as does the professor in charge of the class on teaching poetry, who also stresses that getting kids to do poetry is far more important than teaching anything about it.[19] If this seems odd, it isn't, if you follow the dubious logic of the self-esteem movement: Correcting mistakes or telling children that they are wrong is detrimental to their self-esteem.

From my present institution, which Kramer also visited (before I was there), she provided examples of more of the same kind of attitude. In one class, after viewing a video on the dropout problem in Los Angeles, stu-dents offered their opinions on the reasons for problems in schools. One student, also a mother, claimed that the problems in schools were due to too much competition and said that her daughter's self-esteem had suffered because she was put in a low reading group (although it was not labeled as such).[20] And, indeed, my survey of student teachers indicated that cooperation and mediation get high marks as practices that help foster high self-esteem, whereas competition is downplayed as antithetical to its development or, at the very least, unimportant.

While this may sound odd, again it is no surprise to those of us who spend our days in the field of teacher education. I recall one student presentation on the purposes of public schooling, in which the student unwittingly encapsulated some of the main ideas of the self-esteem movement in a few brief sentences. Schools, she said confidently, were to foster high achievement through constructivist teaching (more on constructivism in Chapter 9); administrative decisions were to be taken through consensus; discipline was to be achieved through conflict resolution; and learning must be democratic and student centered, achieved through student empowerment. As with any fad, students quickly learn the jargon from their professors but spend little time analyzing what they are saying and what, if anything, it means.

There may be some hope, however, in the fact that student teachers seem somewhat ambivalent about these received notions of schooling, although they are usually unaware of that ambivalence. I recall in particular two students who expressed views that directly contrasted with their behavior. They were both mature students who, as is frequently the case, took their studies a little more seriously than their younger classmates. One day we were discussing why public school students seem to have difficulty following basic directions when given an assignment.

These two students asserted that kids felt entitled to do what they want (as a result of the self-esteem movement) and did not demonstrate sufficient respect for their teachers. They claimed that in their classrooms, they always expected directions to be followed. I was pleased to hear this, since the majority of the class seemed to think otherwise, but I was confused when it came time to hand in the next assignment. Despite very detailed written instructions, a verbal explanation, and several reminders, neither student handed in the assignment on time, and when it was handed in, it was not at all what I had requested. When I quietly spoke to one of them, she admitted that she had, in her words, "dropped the ball." But couldn't I make an exception for her? I asked whether she gave exceptions in her class. "No," she replied. "Only if there are extenuating circumstances." "Well, same here," I responded and, to give her credit, she responded philosophically, accepting my judgment as fair.

There are students, then, future teachers, who do have what we might call "the right stuff" and who haven't quite accepted all this self-esteem nonsense. In fact, some of the results from my student teacher surveys are quite heartening. When given a list of attributes of teachers and asked to choose which of those attributes best described the kind of teacher they wanted to be, twice as many chose "demanding" over "caring" (44 percent to 22 percent), although caring was the second most popular answer. They reject the notion that maintaining high standards damages student self-esteem and believe that social promotion, the very popular practice of passing students to the next grade irrespective of achievement, is actually damaging to self-esteem (contrary to the prevailing wisdom in self-esteem circles). Although 39 percent believe that teaching self-esteem is *as* important as teaching subject matter, 44 percent believe that teaching academics (subject matter) is *more* important than teaching self-esteem. So there is reason to be optimistic: not all of our future teachers have been so completely indoctrinated into the self-esteem movement that they cannot evaluate it objectively.

It is also gratifying to meet former students who tell me that although the stuff they learned about "positive discipline," child-centered classrooms, and massaging students' egos seemed great in theory, it either doesn't work or is actually counterproductive to the learning process. Many students have told me that they felt very nervous about asserting authority in their classrooms, fearing (as they had been told) that doing so would damage students' self-esteem. What they discovered, of course, was that they needed to exercise their authority in order to gain the students' respect and to keep order in the classroom. But this did not prevent them from being caring, interested, and involved teachers. Many teachers really do want to be something other than caretaker, counselor, or best friend to their students. They want to be intellectual leaders and take their students on what can and should be a wonderful journey. And the job of the professor of education should be to prepare them to pursue that goal.

Unfortunately, only some teachers have the wherewithal to withstand the all-pervasive influence of self-esteem. They, as well as the ones who are not so strong, deserve our support, for it really is a case of the sins of the fathers being visited upon the sons (and daughters). Clearly, if the buck stops anywhere, it must be with the professors, but solving the problem of poorly educated teachers is not easy. Since the self-esteem movement has been part of schooling since the 1960s, the teachers who are now in training were themselves victims of the movement (if they attended public schools). They are thus disadvantaged both by their early educational experiences as well as by their teacher education. Their experience in school taught them that effort is what counts, spelling is unimportant, and schooling is for learning about oneself.

This explains the utter confusion of many of my students when I explain that I would be thrilled if everyone got an A but it has to be earned. I am there to help, but they are ultimately responsible for their learning and their grades. As bizarre as it sounds, these kinds of demands seem to them very unfair because they are unlike anything they have yet encountered. Consequently, when they begin their teacher education program, it is an uphill battle for those of us who are trying to teach ethics and responsibility along with subject matter, but for those preaching self-esteem, it's a breeze, because the students are primed for it. They don't have to be convinced of the rightness of the self-esteem movement because they have already accepted it. In his book *Generation X Goes to College* Peter Sacks exposes the depths of this culture of entitlement. As a college journalism instructor, he tried out what he calls "the sandbox experiment" in which he catered to his students' every whim to see what would happen. He became a very popular teacher and was awarded tenure. His story shows us the extent to which institutions of higher learning are being increasingly ruled by students, who, as he says, "have a hard time getting out of bed to get to class, or trouble distinguishing a comma from a semi-colon in written English."[21]

That last statement really struck a chord with me. I estimate that about 70 percent of my students (remember, they all have bachelor's degrees) do not understand the difference in spelling or meaning between "principle" and "principal"—a particularly distressing error given their chosen profession! They frequently use the former when referring to the head of a school and just as often correct me when I write something like "the principal problems of schools are." Once, after correcting the error in almost all the class papers, I asked one of the brighter students, who seemed unsure of the usage, why she thought the word in my phrase above should be spelled "principle." She replied that she had asked another education professor and he had told her so. I have seen this error many times on a number of handouts from colleagues, so I am no longer surprised.

Of course illiteracy is not solely the fault of the self-esteem movement, nor of professors of education. If today's student teachers were not read to in the home when they were young or later encouraged to read independently, we should not wonder at their poor skills. Nevertheless, it is shocking to see teacher trainees who do not know the difference between possessives and plurals (a common error is "the teacher's walk down the road"), or possessives and contractions (its and it's, for example) or between such common words as "effect" and "affect," "then" and "than," "whose" and "who's," and "their," "they're," and "there."

These are grade school errors that could have been prevented by early childhood reading but should have been corrected well before middle school, let alone college. The good news for the instructor is that the annoyance of correcting these kinds of errors is alleviated by the occasional challenge of interpreting some of the more imaginative spellings, such as "emencly" ("immensely") and "biest" ("biased"). The faculty, of course, claim that literacy is a big concern. Yes, it is a problem, yes we need to do something about it, but no, no one ever actually does anything about it. When I finally asked my colleagues why we couldn't just raise entrance requirements or improve the required writing test for teachers, I was told that it wasn't that simple and, anyway, they (the professors) would feel bad if too many people failed. This absurdity aside, they are right that it is not that simple. The primary reason for teachers' inability to write or spell is social promotion. When they were in school, they were not required to demonstrate competency before being advanced to the next grade.

Indeed, some people are always imaginative enough to find ways to thwart any legitimate efforts to raise the status or standards of the teaching profession. An example of this was the recent fight over testing for emergency credentialed teachers in California. Because of the demand for teachers in public schools, in that state, as in about thirty others,[22] anyone with a bachelor's degree who has passed a basic skills test, the CBEST, can acquire an emergency credential and teach in schools, as long as he or she is also taking classes toward a formal teaching credential. The CBEST has always been described as a basic skills test that comprises reading, math, and writing sections designed at an eighth to tenth grade level.

In 1996, a lawsuit, considered the nation's biggest employment discrimination case, went to trial, with lawyers arguing that the CBEST discriminated against Latinos, African Americans, and Asian Americans who were unable to pass the test. Although 80 percent of white applicants pass the test on their first try, the rate goes down for other groups: 53 percent for Asian Americans, 49 percent for Latinos, and 38 percent for African Americans.[23] The plaintiff's attorneys contended that these figures demonstrate that the test is biased against minorities while the defense argued that the results simply reflected candidates' backgrounds. The test had earlier been found discriminatory by the U.S. Equal Employment Opportunities Commission, but the state was not required to take action as a result of that finding.[24]

In this instance, however, the judge ruled against the plaintiffs and in his ruling wrote: "The state is entitled to ensure that teachers and others who work in public schools possess a minimal level of competency in basic reading, writing, and math skills before they are entrusted with the education of our children."[25] If minority candidates are failing this basic test in great numbers, it does indeed indicate discrimination: not in the test but in our school system, which is failing to provide minority students the education they deserve. It is important to note that this case was brought on a watered-down version of the test: A couple of years earlier, the California Commission on Teacher Credentialing had modified it, removing some of the more difficult geometry and algebra questions and extending the time allowed to complete it.[26] In addition, there are no limits on the number of times an individual can take the test.

Fortunately, the judge saw that state had the right and, more important, the responsibility to ensure that children are taught by adequately prepared teachers. But these teachers did not see it that way. They apparently thought that they had a *right* to teach, and no test—however basic—was going to stand in their way. It is just another depressing example of the view that each of us is entitled to what we want, whether we merit it or not. If the candidates had truly had children's interests at heart, they would have worked at improving their skills rather than try to eliminate or dumb down through litigation an already dumbed-down test. This judgment reminds us that teaching is not a right. It is a privilege and a responsibility.

•   •   •

As a professor of education I am frequently the unwitting recipient of promotional educational materials and magazines. Many of these contain gift ideas for teachers and students, including everything from watches with smiley faces on them to sweatshirts with saccharine sayings about how wonderful it is to be a teacher. I usually pay little attention to them, since they are almost invariably useless as well as tacky. One day, however, I was perusing one of these catalogs with a kind of depressed fascination when I came upon a really useful item (that the manufacturer made certain to describe as a "humorous" gift just in case anyone got any ideas): a small urn with the words "Ashes of Problem Students" written on it. I wonder if there's a discount for ordering in bulk. . . .

What's So Progressive About This?

Child-Centered Education and the Transformation of the American Public School

We teachers can only help the work going on,
as servants wait upon a master.
—Maria Montessori[1]

IT IS DIFFICULT, IF NOT IMPOSSIBLE, to know if a statement like Montessori's is intended to be understood literally. Unfortunately for all of us, self-esteem promoters seem to have taken Montessori's words literally and run with them. As a general principle, centering education around a child's needs is a worthwhile idea, but under the aegis of the self-esteem movement it has been taken to its most absurd limits. Although it is quite reasonable to argue for considering students' cognitive, physical, moral, and even emotional needs when teaching, we must remember that teachers still are—or should be—the authorities in the learning process.

Teachers have a responsibility to provide knowledge to their students that, particularly in the early grades, is absolutely essential for the students' success in later grades. Elementary schools should be providing the DNA of education: the building blocks of knowledge upon which all further knowledge is based, what we usually refer to as the three Rs. Teachers are also responsible for providing sufficient structure and organization in the classroom so that material can be presented in a progressive, incremental fashion. In addition, they need to ensure that basic rules of behavior are followed so that every child can benefit equally from the learning environment. Learning appropriate behavior, including manners and a basic moral code, is important per se but is also essential to ensure that some students are not disadvantaged because of a classmate's misdemeanors.

In fact, it is both impractical and illogical to try to tailor schooling to each individual's needs, simply because schools must answer to policymakers, the judiciary, and, most important, the public, all of whom have an investment in the education of our youth. Although teachers clearly have a duty to their pupils, both individually and as a group, they also have a public duty to provide instruction in those areas that the public has deemed important. There is no question that balancing students' needs with public demands is a difficult role, one exacerbated by the expectation of the self-esteem movement that teachers add counselor and therapist to their job description. The self-esteem movement is, in fact, the most recent and most powerful expression of the idea of child-centered education, which began not, as one might imagine, in the 1960s, but in the early part of the twentieth century.

An Educational Revolution: The Birth of Progressive Education

In the first chapter of *Experience and Education,* originally published in 1938, philosopher of education John Dewey wrote that "mankind likes to think in terms of extreme opposites. It is given to formulating its beliefs in terms of Either-Ors, between which it recognizes no intermediate possibilities."[2] Dewey was specifically referring to the debate over the relative merits of "traditional" versus "progressive" education, and the polarization he identified still exists. Those who support the former, he said, believe that education involves information and skills that must be transmitted to students. Traditional schooling also involves teaching standards of conduct and moral training and is characterized by a highly regimented organization.[3]

"Progressive education" on the other hand, Dewey argued, is characterized by cultivation of individuality, free activity as opposed to external discipline, learning from experience rather than from texts and teachers, acquiring skills that are deemed relevant to the individual at the present time rather than preparing for some unknown future, and becoming acquainted with the world rather than learning through static aims and old materials.[4] Progressive education was more than just a narrow educational reform. Educational historian Lawrence Cremin describes it as "a vast humanitarian effort to apply the promise of American life, the ideal of government by, of and for the people" to the new urban civilization of the latter half of the nineteenth century.[5] It was a broad effort to improve education through improving people's lives and vice versa.

Francis W. Parker, a superintendent of the Quincy, Massachusetts, public schools in the late 1800s, is considered the "father" of the progressive school movement.[6] At that time, schools were typically dominated by the "traditional" approach to schooling, characterized by rigid lockstep instruction, heavy reliance on textbooks, and drill and memorization exercises. These were teacher-centered schools. Parker proposed instead child-centered schools in which magazines or other materials would be used to supplement existing curricula and children would learn at their own pace. They would learn through experience—by doing things—not by rote memorization.

There were three main philosophical strands within progressive education. Parker and his colleagues represented one strand, the "pedagogical" or "child-centered" progressives.[7] Their focus was primarily on the individual child's learning experience. Very simply, this meant tailoring instruction in schools to the needs of all children, an idea that Jean-Jacques Rousseau expressed in his classic work *Émile*. The second strand was populated by the "social progressives."[8] Their interest was more in the role that schools might have in improving society along progressive lines, as well as transforming the traditional role of the school from simply educative to include concern for vocational issues, health, family, and community life. They were the reformers. The third strand included the "administrative progressives," who sought to use the new research in psychology and the social sciences to make schools more efficient and, by implication, better for each individual.[9] This is also called the "scientific" strand. All three strands have influenced contemporary education in important ways. The idea that schools should be vehicles for social reconstruction is still very much with us, as is the idea that schools should be laboratories in which researchers "try out" their latest findings. But it is the child-centered strand that has had the most influence and has been a continuing thread in public schooling through the self-esteem education of today.

The ideals of child-centered education—having schools care for the whole child rather than just educate his intellect and tailoring curriculum to the child's needs—are still attractive to most teachers, who are typically

very caring individuals. "Loving kids" is a fine idea, but the intellect seems
to have little place under the umbrella of caring. In terms of where this
idea of education as "caring" started, it is difficult to say which is the
chicken and which is the egg. Did the progressive movement promote this
view of education in which the self—and self-esteem—is paramount, or
was the movement an outgrowth of a tendency that already existed? Probably both. "Child-study," a reform movement that lasted from the late
1880s through about 1910, helped provide an ideological foundation for
the child-centered strand of progressivism.[10] Child-study reformers argued
that curricula and schools should be child-oriented rather than organized
around traditional subject matter, like Latin and Greek.[11] Thus incipient
strands of child-centered thought were developing both in academia and
in the common schools by the time progressivism got under way.

One thing is certain: Progressivism must have seemed like a breath of
fresh air at the time. By the end of the nineteenth century, schools had become very bureaucratic institutions characterized by a rigid administrative hierarchy, regular progression from one grade to another, a graded
course of study for all schools to help ensure uniformity in teaching and
grading, and an emphasis on planning, order, and punctuality.[12] This emphasis on efficiency and rationality was seen as necessary simply in order
to deal with the numbers of students coming into schools during the first
decades of this century: enrollments in secondary education, for example,
rose from 4.8 million in 1929–1930 to 7.1 million in 1939–1940.[13] It was
believed that instruction should be delivered in the most efficient way, in a
well-planned and strictly controlled learning and administrative environment. This environment was considered optimal for inculcating middle-
class values and socializing individuals for entry into the culture of an
industrial workplace. Schools thus mirrored the industry models of the
time, which needed well-trained and punctual workers to keep the facto-
ries working.

Efficiency is certainly an important educational value, but a focus on efficiency above all else is likely to be counterproductive and is certainly not
in the best interests of the student. In these tightly controlled schools, students were passive recipients of knowledge, which was parceled out in dis-
connected pieces that, even for the most motivated student, was often
hard to digest. It is as if the students are passengers on a schooling train
that just goes along with or without them, without any necessary direction or philosophy. But perhaps more damaging than the obsession with
rationality and control was that traditional education and traditional educationists did not deal with students as people coming from complex social and economic environments but as isolated and passive objects.

Decades of experience and research—as well as common sense—tell us that this is neither ethical nor effective teaching.

By the late 1930s the progressive movement in education had transformed itself from a radical movement to a respected mainstream ideology in education. A statement by the Progressive Education Association gives us a very clear indication of the group's mind-set, which seems to have been assumed by today's self-esteem promoters. They noted in 1937 that "to 'experiment' with children, to 'experiment with taxpayers' money' are not the crimes they used to be."[14] Pity.

Progressive educators recognized that the community from which children come has a significant effect on their learning, and they made efforts to include that community in the educative process. They also viewed students as members of an integrated community within the school. Rather than teach children in isolation from each other, which emphasizes the separation between teacher and student and between teacher and administrator, progressive schools believed in teaching children as members of a society to which everyone in the school belonged. Whereas traditional schools emphasized social and intellectual control, the new schools emphasized freedom of thought and movement. Students were no longer required to sit unmoving in their chairs but were encouraged to contribute to the learning process and unleash their creativity.

In progressive schools students were required to learn some basics but were also encouraged to do work that fulfilled their individual needs, and thus each child would likely be doing something different from the others. Considerable time was spent practicing student self-government, attending assemblies, and doing student group work. Teachers worked with their pupils on an individual or small-group basis, since they were no longer required to stand and deliver a lesson from the front of the class. When students finished a section of work, they requested a test from the teacher. If they succeeded at the test, they went on, and if they didn't, they worked on areas of weakness and took the test again. No one failed.[15]

It is not difficult to see how the progressive movement gave ideology and energy to what we now know as the self-esteem movement. The idea of authority being taken from the teacher and given to the child; the notion that no one should fail a test; the emphasis on personal creativity and collaborative group work—these are all hallmarks of the current self-esteem movement as well as the progressive movement of the 1930s and 1940s. And it was undoubtedly with the progressive movement that the idea of educating the "whole child" was invented, which is the very core of the self-esteem movement. And, sadly, the idea that it is quite acceptable to use children as guinea pigs for educational experimentation persists.

But if the characteristics of the progressive movement presaged those of the self-esteem movement, so did its problems. John Dewey, along with others of his day, criticized progressive schools for providing little in the way of organized subject matter for study and permitting no direction or guidance by adults.[16] Dewey could just as well have been talking about contemporary schools, the only difference being that today there are very few "traditional" public schools with which to compare them! Even psychoanalyst Erich Fromm pointed out that "progressive" schools are not nearly as liberating as their proponents thought. With respect to discipline, for example, by replacing the external authority of good and bad, "don't do that because it's wrong," with the internal authority of one's own feelings, "don't do it because you will feel bad if you do," the child may be confused by the lack of external authority and, according to Fromm, be even more oppressed than he was before: "The child is no longer aware of being bossed . . . and he cannot fight back and thus develop a sense of independence."[17] The lack of authority considered so essential to progressive schooling and the self-esteem movement, may, if Fromm is right, be even more damaging to a child than the more familiar constraints of the traditional school.

Low Expectations and High Self-Esteem: Psychology in the Public School

One of the early pioneers and one of the most influential researchers in educational psychology was Jean Piaget, who was active during the period when progressive education was gaining popularity. According to Piaget, every individual passes through distinct stages of development: sensorimotor, preoperational, concrete operational, and formal operational. The details of these stages need not concern us here, but the impact of his ideas may well have provided the intellectual foundation for the self-esteem movement. According to Piaget, each child goes through these stages at highly individualized rates, so it is virtually impossible to predict when a child will enter one stage or complete another. In addition, Piaget and his followers cautioned against trying to hurry children's development, arguing that it could be damaging to them.

Imagine the effect of this idea on a teacher. Most teachers-in-training are given the outlines of Piaget's theories, and therefore believe before they ever get into a classroom that trying to encourage a child to learn a little faster than he wishes can damage him. It is no wonder, therefore, that teachers are so anxious to let Johnny develop at his own pace, since that clearly seems preferable to possibly hurting his cognitive and emotional growth. The problem with this interpretation of Piaget's theories is that teachers accept the lowest level of their students' performance as the optimum they can achieve. If students are not encouraged to try the really difficult math equation or make sense of a complicated piece of literature, how do we know that they cannot do it? By erring on the side of caution, well-meaning teachers ensure that they have "developmentally appropriate" (i.e., low) expectations of their pupils, and as a result these kids may never know what their true abilities really are.

Lev Semanovich Vygotsky was a contemporary of Piaget who was also greatly influential. Vygotsky believed that children develop in stages but that learning takes place when children are working in what he called their "zone of proximal development"—the zone in which learning can take place—but only with the assistance of a student's peers or an adult. One of the principal applications of Vygotsky's theories, then, is the use of cooperative learning groups, in which students of varying abilities work together and help one another complete a task. Although cooperative learning can be a useful pedagogical and sociological tool, it is considered by many education professors and teachers as the *only* way to learn. Competition is out, cooperation is in. Once again, as in most issues relating to the self-esteem movement, there is no sensible middle ground.

The movement probably received its greatest boost during the 1960s, when humanistic theories of education and child development proliferated. Erik Erikson, like Piaget and Vygotsky, developed a theory of developmental stages, but he focused more on psychosocial than strictly cognitive development. He was interested in how individuals relate to each other and to the world at different stages of their lives. Erikson believed that between the ages of six and twelve it is essential that children experience success in school in order to preserve a positive self-image. If students do well, they feel good about themselves; if they fail, according to Erikson, they may experience feelings of inferiority about themselves that may hinder future learning. If school is a place where they feel bad about themselves, they may feel alienated from it and may become unwilling to try to learn new things, in case they fail again. The implications of this theory for education are significant. It means that teachers must ensure that students always experience success in school to protect their fragile self-esteem, and of course the only way to ensure success is to never ask them to learn things that cannot be picked up without effort or application.

Erikson is unequivocal: The preservation of self-esteem in the early years is critical to children's psychosocial development, and what they learn in school must not interfere with that. This creates a false and very dangerous distinction between achievement and self-esteem. Many educational psychologists do not believe that high self-esteem is promoted by effort and achievement but by a noncompetitive environment in which both teacher and student have low expectations. What is disturbing is the influence that Erikson's ideas wield, given that he never earned a degree.[18] Erikson, one of Freud's last students, trained as a lay therapist and began to publish papers and books that earned him international recognition by the 1960s and 1970s. His lack of formal qualifications did not hurt him, however, for he ended up a professor of psychiatry at Harvard University.[19] Erikson is a clear example of our readiness to accept ideas that sound intriguing, irrespective of their potential impact on us or of the qualifications of the person promoting them.

Robert Slavin, the author of a standard text in educational psychology, describes the downward spiral that he believes a graded, competitive environment creates. If, for example, students are put in reading groups according to ability early in elementary school, those in the low groups will feel bad about themselves and will lose interest in learning; subsequent negative teacher evaluations will confirm their fears and the situation will deteriorate: "By the third or fourth grade, or even earlier, students know who the winners and losers are. As they approach adolescence, the 'losers' are likely to turn to activities outside of school to salvage their self-concept—perhaps sports or social activities, but all too often delinquency, drugs, and other antisocial pursuits."[20] Again, imagine the impact of these statements on future teachers. Given the choice between (1) grading students and having high expectations for them and thereby effectively condemning them to a life of crime or (2) giving them an A for effort, having them like you, and ensuring their personal happiness, who would ever choose the first option?

However, as I discuss in Part 2, the real result of low expectations is not authentic self-esteem but a false sense of self, the social consequences of which are narcissism and the academic consequence—illiteracy. Ironically, narcissism was one of Erikson's interests, and it is his notion of it that Christopher Lasch developed in *A Culture of Narcissism*.[21] Erikson believed that narcissism is a common neurosis characteristic of modern life. People feel lost and confused and as a result they have a poor sense of identity, lack moral purpose, and eventually develop low self-esteem.[22] What Erikson doubtless did not foresee was the way in which his ideas would be introduced into education and how the current efforts in schools to promote self-esteem fail to create meaning, which is the source of self-esteem, and promote instead the very narcissism he warned about.

Slavin summarizes the influence of these psychologists on education: "Teachers must help students through the industry versus inferiority crisis. The behavior of teachers toward students, their evaluations, and the way they structure their classrooms can have important effects on students' self-concepts."[23] Teachers are taught that everything they do or say in the classroom affects a child's fragile self-esteem, which, according to the theorists, is a prerequisite for learning and must never be tampered with. The illogicality of the argument, of course, is that it is apparently only by students' *not* learning that their self-esteem can be perfectly preserved, since learning, if it requires anything, requires risk: leaping, running, or maybe just crawling into the unknown. And when we enter the unknown, we risk fear, pain, and failure. But without them, neither true learning nor true self-knowledge is possible.

A Time of Change: The Postwar Years

The progressive movement flourished in the 1930s and 1940s, but by the 1950s, schools were characterized more by a "back to basics" ethos. The United States had emerged from the war stronger than when it went in and was recognized as the leader of a new international economic and political order. The Marshall Plan, implemented in 1947, symbolized the new role of the United States in the world, and Americans were feeling optimistic. But when the Soviet Union beat the United States into space in 1957 with *Sputnik*, the first space satellite, the nation received a shock, and nowhere was it felt more profoundly than in the schools.

Schools were in something of a crisis in the 1950s owing to problems that had been brewing since the 1940s, including increasing enrollments boosted by the "war babies," the early baby boomers, who began to enter the elementary grades in 1946; budget problems exacerbated by the war effort, a need for more schools, and a flood of teachers leaving the profession.[24] This, compounded by the perceived need to compete with the Soviet Union and secure its place in the new world economic order, meant that America began to look closely at its schools and found them wanting.

In what is now a very familiar scene to us, countless pamphlets, essays, articles, and books were written criticizing schools for failing to properly educate the citizenry, and a war of words developed between critics of progressive schools—primarily academics outside the field of education—and their defenders: professional educators. Even as early as the 1950s, educators were unwilling to recognize the problems with their school reforms, and it was up to others to point out the error of their ways. But one thing was becoming clear. As Lawrence Cremin explains in *The Transformation of the School* as the 1950s progressed, there was increasing public appetite for education of a nonprogressive flavor.[25] *Sputnik*, combined with the endemic problems of public schools, shook the country and its education system to its foundation. America's technological, scientific, and intellectual authority had been challenged, and it was now up to schools to take up the cause.

Schools always reflect the political climate of the day, and so it is no surprise that they began to reflect the more conservative values of the 1950s, which, with its themes of scientific and economic advance, emphasis on the family, and a collective sense of patriotism, was considerably at odds with the somewhat self-indulgent anti-intellectualism of progressivism. The central focus of schooling in the 1950s was to redefine the purpose of public education and "to delineate those things that the school needed to do because if the school did not do them they would not get done."[26] In retrospect, while the renewed focus on the academic purposes of public schooling was certainly a positive change, the idea that schools could solve much of the nation's economic, social, and moral problems was hopelessly unrealistic and set up a standard that they could not possibly uphold.

In 1958, as a direct response to the *Sputnik* launch, as well as the growing public concern with education, Congress passed the National Defense Education Act, designed to give direction to education for the next several years. The NDEA directly tied education to economic and technical development and called for a heavy focus on education in science, mathematics, and foreign languages in order to bolster America's status nationally as well as internationally.[27] By the 1960s, however, while the Cold War continued to rage, schools and universities began to defy the old values and revisit the themes of progressive education. Psychology was set to make a triumphant return.

Psychoanalysis and Education: A Marriage Made in Hell

While politicians and the public were calling for a new kind of education, academics and educators were turning their attention to new developments in the field of psychology. Freudian psychoanalysis gained popularity in America after the war, when returning armed forces personnel were given psychiatric and mental health services. It also gained legitimacy in the medical profession, since, as one observer notes, "if therapy was good enough for American heroes overseas, or recovering in hospitals back home, it was good enough for middle-class Americans."[28]

But there are other reasons for the popularity of Freudian psychoanalysis. Norman Cantor, author of *The American Century*, suggests that the weak social, religious, familial, and economic infrastructures of the period between 1910 and 1940 drove people into themselves, and they needed a theory and a method of behavior that allowed them to function in spite of these eroding institutions.[29] Another reason could be that Americans have always been an isolationist people and tend to look inward for answers. Indeed, the burden of being, as many Americans believe, "the leader of the free world" is enormous and no doubt weighs heavily on the individual, as well as the collective, psyche. Perhaps it is too great a burden to carry alone. But if Americans are isolationist, they are also adventurous and entrepreneurial, often capitalizing on new ideas before they become popular in the rest of the world. Thus the lure of psychology and psychoanalysis, both highly lucrative, might have just been too enticing for Americans not to give it a try.

Whatever the reasons, psychological theories and clinics grew in popularity in the 1960s and the movement continues to grow to this day. Two of the most influential educational psychologists of this era were Carl Rogers and Abraham Maslow. Although both were identified primarily as humanistic psychologists and both influenced humanistic education, the precursor to the self-esteem movement, they saw themselves as philosophers and wanted to revolutionize the way we think about individuals, families, and schools. And they did.

In *Toward a Psychology of Being* Maslow discusses the role of psychology and psychotherapy in creating what he calls the "self-actualized" person— a phrase that has virtually become the slogan of the self-help and self-esteem movements. He believes it is difficult or perhaps impossible to achieve that idealized state but contends that we must continually work toward it. The self-actualized person, according to Maslow, is one who is fully in touch with his inner self. Becoming self-actualized is becoming fully human, which cannot happen unless one has dealt with one's demons, so to speak—the angers, frustrations, fears, and other traumas that exist in the unconscious and which, if unrecognized, can cause a variety of physical and mental illnesses.

The key to this process, Maslow argues, is accepting the core of oneself and others—the good, the bad, and the ugly—for without that acceptance, no such actualization can be possible. And the will to become self-actualized, which is something that we all have, is what makes for successful psychotherapy and is also a precondition for education.[30] While he recognizes that children may need some behavioral controls in education, he believes that "in our culture and at this point in history, it is necessary to redress the balance in favor of spontaneity, the ability to be expressive . . . unwilled, trusting in processes other than will and control, unpremeditated, creative, etc."[31] In his view, schools and society tend to inhibit any opportunity for authentic self-actualization because they encourage us to repress our inner desires.

Carl Rogers adopted Maslow's idea of self-actualization and took it a step further, arguing that schools must be completely transformed into places in which self-actualization takes place. In *Freedom to Learn* (1969) he provides specific plans for reinventing all levels of schools, from elementary school through graduate education. Subtitled "A View of What Education Might Become" Rogers wrote in the prologue that his book is for teachers, professors, educators, and others, to tell them about what he thinks learning should be: something that comes from the inside of the student and "has a quality of personal involvement" in which the "whole person" invests both his feeling and cognitive aspects in learning, which is self-initiated.[32]

He explicitly criticizes the "traditional and conventional"[33] approach to learning, saying that "when we put together . . . such elements as a prescribed curriculum, similar assignments for all students, lecturing as almost the only mode of instruction, standard tests by which all students are externally evaluated, and instructor-chosen grades as the measure of learning, then we can almost guarantee that meaningful learning will be at an absolute minimum."[34] Despite these damning statements, Rogers is charitable about educators, saying that he does not believe that they forced the traditional kind of education on kids because of "any inner depravity" (too kind!) but because they were not aware of any viable alternative, which he of course was quite ready to provide.[35]

Rogers believed that experiential, self-initiated learning makes for self-reliant learners. He describes a class environment in which a teacher, experimenting with these ideas, let the students do whatever they wanted for the day. Challenged by others who asked her how the students would learn new concepts, the teacher responded that the students would teach each other and teach themselves (apparently making teachers redundant). As well as refusing to teach the students academic material, the teacher (can we still call her that?) also allowed students to develop their own rules of behavior and classroom organization. While she found that there were still behavior problems, students nonetheless generally respected the rules that they made up and were relatively well-behaved. She continued to give out grades, as required by the school district, but she felt that the grades did not accurately reflect the real growth of the students, which was a growth in self-knowledge and self-concept.

According to both the teacher, who carried out her own informal evaluation of the experiment, and Rogers, who studied it, this new kind of classroom has a number of distinct advantages. Slow learners magically become fast learners and experience a positive change in self-concept. Students communicate better with others and are more in touch with their own feelings. They are more adventurous and more creative, and many of the students in the experiment tried things that they had not been willing to try in the traditional class environment.

Other teachers tried the experiment and failed because, according to the teacher, they did not have the appropriate commitment and conviction. Like any religion, self-actualized learning is only successful if one truly believes in it. In fact, Rogers noted that this new learning philosophy is so profound that it *cannot* be conveyed on an intellectual level from one teacher to another. Teachers themselves must experience self-direction and freedom in order to be able to communicate them to their students.[36] In addition, teachers must have a positive self-concept in order to be able to relinquish their customary role in the classroom and give over authority to the students.[37]

It is abundantly clear that, for Rogers, the acquisition of knowledge and the development of skills are vastly overrated products of the educational system. He claims, in fact, that "so quickly does change overtake us that answers, 'knowledge,' methods, skills, become obsolete almost at the moment of their achievement."[38] Self-actualization is what education should be about, and the development of "encounter" groups, or what is now known as cooperative learning, is the key. Through encounter groups students learn to relate to each other in a climate of openness, develop more constructive attitudes and behaviors, and thus deal with the world more effectively. Rogers's plan is in fact all about feelings and nothing else. He was interested only in the psychosocial self and how the self acts and reacts in the world; he virtually ignored learning discrete facts or developing intellectual capacities. It is a view of public schooling that goes far beyond the progressive ideals of the early part of the century; it is the total reorientation of the school from developing the intellect to a narcissistic focus on the emotions.

Perhaps the most important part of Rogers's idea for schooling is his view of education as therapy. He made no bones about it and said that the kinds of goals that the therapist has for his client in psychotherapy are equally applicable to education or to the family. By conflating therapy, schooling, and the family, Rogers was explicitly telling us that these institutions are identical in purpose, which is "the constructive development of persons."[39] The notion that each has a distinct, but complementary, function has been lost.

One of the most important consequences of therapy or schooling as therapy, is, according to Rogers, to become free and creative. This is done by loosening ourselves from our rationality. In contrast to most political and social theory, Rogers believed that man is an inherently rational animal—too rational. Depending on rationality rather than emotions is damaging. Rogers's ideal person would be so in touch with himself that he would be able to rely on his emotional and organic senses to tell him which behaviors are appropriate at which times and thus would always be in harmony with himself and with the world. Rationality is therefore the enemy of emotionality, the underlying ideology of the self-esteem movement.

It does not take much imagination to find the roots of the self-esteem movement in the works of Maslow, Rogers, and the like. The idea of radically child-centered learning, the notion of teacher authority as oppressive, the importance of creativity and freedom of individual expression, the limits on external behavioral controls, the introduction of self-evaluation rather than external (teacher) evaluation, and the emphasis on cooperative learning are all characteristics of contemporary schools, which have wholeheartedly adopted these ideas and now promote them as a new religion. And that new religion is therapy.

The reforms that the progressives suggested, along with the ideas of Maslow and Rogers, seem, at first glance, to have a lot to recommend them. Progressive and humanistic education have taught us to see children as active learners and not empty vessels in which we deposit knowledge. Dewey helped us see the child in his social context and helped us understand that effective education is an education that in some way addresses the needs of the whole community. We now know that standardized tests need not be the only method of evaluation and that effective evaluation involves a variety of methods. And there is certainly no virtue in making students memorize facts separate from any real-world context, nor in refusing to allow them to collaborate on work with others. Education as force-feeding, or overly strict behavioral controls, does not do much for anyone except, maybe, giving the teacher a sense of power.

But neither is there virtue in the notion that education is only about self-discovery and emotional rather than intellectual development. The main problem with the self-esteem movement is that it has not satisfied itself simply with integrating some of the more humanistic and progressive notions in educational psychology but has used them to turn all our traditional notions of education on their head. As a result, we have schools in which children's perceived interests override all other considerations in school, and the development of rationality and intellect are seen as dispensable or even dangerous. As has always been the case in public education, we seem unable to adopt anything in moderation. Everything that comes along must be the new magical cure. Sadly, since only common sense and tried and true remedies will fix what ails public education, what seems to be the latest prophet inevitably turns out to be just the latest fad. Rita Kramer, in *Ed School Follies*, puts it very well: "Lacking any tradition, with no sustaining belief in the value of a liberal education, the 'ed psych' learning theorists have no authority to appeal to except 'research,' most of which is trivial when it isn't obvious, and much of which is in the service of political aims rather than objective knowledge."[40]

The self-esteem movement says to the nation: "We are no longer going to fit students into any particular idea of what schooling should be." But not only is there no longer any preconceived mold (a good idea as far as it goes), but the mold itself has been thrown away. In many ways this is the ideal of democratic education in practice: schooling of, by, and for the children. But as I frequently have to remind my future teachers, while the policies and purposes of public education must be democratic, classroom practice rarely is.

Why Classrooms Aren't Democracies

Democracy does not require agreement among citizens, but it does require participation. But in order to create a workable, stable democracy, individuals must have the emotional and intellectual maturity to understand the responsibilities that democracy entails. They also need the knowledge and skills that will permit them to make rational, moral choices that are in the best interests of society as a whole and not just in their own interests. That is the connectedness that combats narcissism and separatism. Many Americans believe that democracy is all about fundamental rights—the inalienable right to speech, thought, and association, for example. But rights are only half the equation. An educated population understands that rights necessitate responsibilities and that it is precisely because those rights are inalienable that they must be exercised judiciously and not at will.

While schooling writ large must be democratic because it must serve the public interest, educating young people cannot be done in a truly democratic environment because true participation and shared decisionmaking will prevent teachers from fulfilling their proper role. Schools must be places where people participate, but they cannot be places where everyone participates equally. In fact, perhaps the most important educative function that schools provide is precisely to teach students about democracy. We need to understand the rights and responsibilities of democratic citizenship before putting them into practice. Democracy must be earned, and it is by becoming educated persons that we earn it.

Although the rights of speech and association may be inalienable, the right to democracy has not been, as much of American history tells us. If the desegregation and civil rights struggles taught us anything, it is that democracy is hard fought and sometimes impossible to win. African Americans and women should not have had to fight to earn their place in the democracy, but their struggles did something very important for the nation: They woke up the rest of America to the fact that by excluding them, this country was not yet a complete democracy. And the continued political and economic disenfranchisement of certain groups is evidence that we still have not learned the lessons of history and democracy's true meaning. America may have its stars, but it is still earning its stripes.

The Death of Teacher Authority— and a New Beginning

There is a reason that schools have always had teachers—it is because they have a distinct role to play. We need them! Their role is—or should be—to help lead and guide the students in the learning process, give them necessary foundational knowledge and skills, and teach them appropriate behavior, morals, and values. Parents, are, of course, the first and most important teachers and moral role models. In the last section of this book I provide suggestions for improving education for parents and others who have an investment in public schooling, but I do not address them directly in much of this book for the simple reason that we do not, as a society, have very much input or control over what parents do in terms of child rearing. Some have suggested that everyone who wishes to have a child should go through parenting classes (and there is little doubt that many of us could benefit from them), but this idea is not likely to ever catch on, since people view the bearing and raising of children as a highly personal decision. Although we can suggest to interested parents that they might help their children's education by reading to them and spending more time talking with them, parents do not like being told they're doing a bad job. And if we did, those who were guilty as charged wouldn't be listening anyway.

Thus for better or for worse, parents rear and educate their children in relative obscurity and often, sadly, with relative impunity, even when the children are abused. But teachers are another story. Teachers are answerable to society for the job they do. While there is little doubt that society today expects far more of teachers than is reasonable, there is just as little doubt that there are some things for which they must be held responsible. Even the most motivated teacher cannot make a child think if the child has absolutely no motivation herself; nonetheless, the teacher is responsible for doing everything reasonable to get the child to think and to learn. This does not mean teachers should cater to the child's every wish, as is current school practice, but use the tools that they already possess to create an environment in which learning is an exciting, challenging, and never ending experience.

Teachers' tools include the knowledge they have accumulated as a result of their academic studies, the pedagogical and teaching skills they have acquired in their teacher education programs, and the practical experience they gain in the classroom. This is all part of the science of teaching. They are what gives the teacher authority, and it is that authority that allows the teacher to be effective. "Authority" is a word that is frequently misunderstood, particularly when it comes to the teaching environment, in which one adult has control over thirty-five children and young people at any given moment. People are concerned about that environment because the authority of the teacher can easily be abused. But a teacher who abuses her power is authoritarian, and that is something completely different.

An authoritarian teacher is one who takes advantage of her position of authority in the classroom to be overly controlling. But a teacher exercising authority need not be authoritarian. A teacher who exercises her authority takes responsibility for her class and is always prepared. If she's a good teacher, she uses all the tools at her disposal to help her students learn. It is not just her right to exercise her authority in the classroom, it is her responsibility, for she is the person whom *society* has authorized to do so. It is only when she abuses her authority that she becomes authoritarian. This is a very important point, for in our efforts to make public schooling more "democratic" and child-centered we have seriously undermined the authority of the teacher and thus lowered her even more in her students' eyes, in the eyes of the public, and also in her own. How ironic. By trying to foster student self-esteem, we've undermined the self-esteem of our teachers!

It is inevitable that, when the classroom becomes entirely child-centered, the authority of the teacher must change. If all learning comes from the students and they have nothing to learn from the teacher, that part of the teacher's authority becomes obsolete. If the class is rarely together as a whole but students are always grouped together and teach each other, then the pedagogical skills of the teacher remain unexercised. And if students are to make up the organizational and behavioral rules of the class, there isn't any need for a teacher to make them, so the third leg of teacher authority is knocked out as well.

This is exactly what Carl Rogers proposed, and his wish for education to conform to his views has been fulfilled probably more than he ever imagined. The teacher is no longer respected for the unique skills and talents she brings to the classroom and becomes nothing more than a caretaker, babysitter, or counselor for kids who spend their time learning about their feelings and experiencing encounter groups. There are some schools in which common sense prevails over self-esteem ideology, but the ideas of child-centered education are very powerful in the education establishment and are considered sacrosanct by many teachers and professors.

Indeed, the idea of education as therapy pervades not only K–12 education but higher education as well. A book I discovered in a college bookstore in Canada gives an insight into how professors of education, not content with indoctrinating teachers, are promoting the self-esteem movement in higher education as well. This was a required text in the teacher education program, *Teaching Tips,* aimed at university teachers. It contains a plethora of information on grading, group work, preparing for class, and other relevant concerns. The fascinating part is not so much the content, which, if one relies only on the table of contents, is unremarkable, but the ideology underlying it, which is verbatim self-esteem.

Written by American university psychologists and experts on "teaching effectiveness," it gives the reader a very clear understanding of just how far the self-esteem movement has entered our consciousness. For example, under the section entitled "Motivating Students for Your Course and for Lifelong Learning" the authors explain how students need to feel competence in order to get motivated. Teachers must provide situations in which success can be guaranteed so that students can feel good about themselves.[41] The problem is, as I noted earlier, that the only way to ensure success is to never challenge the student. They do point out that the brighter students need challenge, but the irony is that the slower students probably need it even more, if they are ever to improve.

Under the same section they also criticize competition, arguing that "when there are few winners and many losers, it may be easier to protect one's sense of self-worth by not trying, than to try and still not succeed."[42] I always find it interesting that psychologists view failure and low self-esteem as a necessary result of competition, when competition can simply mean trying to do one's best. Indeed, the most meaningful kind of competition is arguably competition against oneself; setting one's own goals and trying to meet them.

In the chapter on "problem students" the authors discuss what to do about students who are chronically unprepared for class. Rather than suggest that some students just can't be bothered, the authors claim that the professor has not been sufficiently clear about what he or she expects from students regarding readings, tests, or other requirements. This is of course a possibility: I once had to take over a class from a professor who had never even given out a syllabus. But some students simply decide that they do not feel like doing the work, no matter how clearly it is written down, explained, re-explained, or discussed.

I remember one student who just couldn't seem to do his research paper, even though, like everyone else in the class, he had written instructions on how to do it. To encourage him I had discussed his topic with him personally and given him two chances to redo it. After a lot of excuses and arguments he finally came out with it: He didn't think he should be made to do a research paper. His believed he was *entitled* to do just as he pleased and refused to recognize my authority, as the instructor, to determine what the assignments in the class should be. It was as simple as that.

In another section on how to teach effectively in large classes, the authors of *Teaching Tips* give suggestions for professors for getting to know their students. There is no question that it can be very alienating for both the student and the teacher not to know each other a little, but it is an unfortunate reality in most universities, primarily because of budget limitations. (Smaller classes mean more instructors and instructors cost money, which some university administrators apparently consider better spent in jacking up their own, or the athletic coach's, salary.) As lamentable as it may be, university students are adults and need to accept the fact that they probably will not become the professor's best friend.

At any rate, in order to become acquainted with students, the authors propose that professors pass out invitations to a few students to join them for coffee and get to know them after class, asking some to make evaluative comments on the course or scheduling an extra class session in order to discuss issues of concern in a smaller group.[43] The last suggestion is a good one (if the professor has the energy), but the first two suggestions smack of favoritism and are virtually guaranteed to provoke student complaints that the professor is getting "cozy" with some students and not others. Absolutely nothing is more important than treating students fairly.

It comes as no surprise that the authors of *Teaching Tips* are strongly in favor of cooperative and collaborative learning, and indeed there is something to be said for integrating these methods of teaching and learning into schools and universities. The authors state that the best method of teaching must depend on the context—the students, the level, the professor, and so on—but that overall, the best method of teaching is students teaching other students.[44] Once again, it's cooperative learning to the exclusion of everything else. And once again, Carl Rogers and his team triumph. According to these "experts" the professor is just as expendable as the teacher, and both are reduced to referee or, if they're lucky, "facilitator."

Of course a teaching guide in a college course is not necessarily evidence that the self-esteem movement has completely infiltrated higher education. But there are indications that it is gaining a foothold. Of the many conversations I have had with colleagues on everything from remedial education to admissions policies, the emphasis is virtually always on student feelings and almost never on excellence, achievement, or standards. And it is broader than schools of education. There is a movement afoot to make emotional education the center of university life as well as public school life.

An example of this is the recent book by Jane Tompkins, formerly an English professor but now transformed into a professor of education. Her memoir, *A Life in School: What the Teacher Learned,* describes her travails as a scholar and an educator, and how she became convinced that the world of higher education should be about feelings and not academics. According to Tompkins, her education, which led to a Ph.D. from Yale University and a full professorship at Duke, "stunted and misshaped" her for life.[45] (One wonders how many people who didn't have her opportunities would have jumped at the chance to experience such oppression.)

Tompkins then turned to "experimental" teaching, which has all the hallmarks of the self-esteem movement, and now calls for education of "the whole human being" and gives workshops with titles like "The Inner Life of Teachers and Students."[46] Apparently disillusioned with the academic rat race, she decided to change her teaching philosophy and "surrendered control in the classroom," allowing students to plan the syllabus, lead discussion, and figure out their grades.[47] Tompkins writes of her revelation of this new approach to teaching: "I could never fool myself into believing that what *I* had to say was ultimately more important to the students than what they thought and felt" and that "I wanted them to discover themselves."[48]

She describes how as a result of this revelation her whole approach to teaching changed: "I began to teach courses where there was no syllabus— just some readings I'd put together in order to set the stage for the students to take over."[49] From then on "students supplied the course material" and Tompkins says, "and all I did to prepare for class was make cookies or buy Danish, make coffee, bring fruit."[50] She did experience some doubts: "I simultaneously thought of myself as a fraud—someone passing for a teacher who didn't in fact have anything to teach" but was apparently able to dismiss these intrusive feelings of guilt by telling herself that "one thing I've learned from doing experimental teaching is that you never know, really, what you've accomplished. You never know what the students have learned, or if they've learned anything, anything solid."[51] Despite the doubts, and despite this admission, the experimental approach won out and is even officially sanctioned: Tompkins recently gave a talk at the annual meeting of the Association of American Colleges and Universities, which honored her memoir.[52]

The response from fellow academics has been mixed. A recent article in the *Chronicle of Higher Education* on Tompkins and her book quoted one admirer as saying that Tompkins was "doing God's work."[53] Self-esteem as religion again. And in the weeks following the publication of the article, letters to the *Chronicle* varied from fervent admiration: "Bravo for Jane Tompkins . . . If you doubt the effectiveness of Tompkins's ideas, try five or 10 minutes of guided imagery before delving into (work)"[54] to admonition: "To Jane and others like her I say: Go for it! It's not too late to get out of academe and do something else. Help people. Become a therapist. But don't spoil a wonderful field for those of us with real commitment."[55]

Indeed, the rest of us end up having to clean up after the mess made by people who believe in letting the class "discover" themselves. When I took over the class from the chap with no syllabus, I met a group of people who were completely bewildered as to what they were supposed to be doing and justifiably angry that they had spent good money to be taught nothing. Rather than resent my intrusion (which I feared they might) they actually thanked me for taking over and universally welcomed the structure I brought to the class with a written syllabus, clear assignments, deadlines, and all the other symbols of so-called academic oppression that self-esteem advocates so revile.

At Least the Public Isn't Crazy

Children can learn a lot just by reading or by working with their classmates, but they cannot learn everything on their own. It seems crazy to be obliged to defend the necessity of teachers and teacher authority, but the self-esteem movement has pushed us this far. Defining school as therapy is another way to undermine teachers. Apart from the idiocy of the idea itself, teachers are not trained therapists and therefore have little authority in that area to begin with. Fortunately for all of us, hope for our nation's schools ultimately lies with parents and the public at large, who understand that schools and universities need teachers; not teachers who are content to be just "team facilitators" but teachers who want to assume their responsibility as the educators of a nation.

If we really want to improve public education, we must strengthen teacher education programs and support teachers. We cannot castrate them, making them pedagogical eunuchs, and still expect them to educate our children. If we can recognize the damage that the self-esteem movement has done our teachers as well as our children, then we can begin to turn the tables and create an education system that respects and supports both child and teacher.

Maria Montessori, like many educators, may have been well-intentioned, but we all know where good intentions lead. In fact, Ms. Montessori had it wrong. There should be neither master nor slave; only a leader and her students, working toward a better future for all.

PART TWO

Therapy Nation

Culture and Schooling in Contemporary America

The Rake's Progress

Self-Esteem Takes Over

The schools ain't what they used to be and never was.
—Will Rogers[1]

IT IS VERY EASY TO LOOK at the problems of schools today—violence, low teacher morale, poor-quality learning materials, unsafe facilities, and a lack of parental participation, to name a few—and look back nostalgically to the good old days when schools were safe, happy places, and teachers were not afraid to go into their classrooms. We watch reruns of *Happy Days* and fondly remember the two-parent household: Dad earning an honest living and Mom baking pies at home, the nice clean-cut look of the boys, and the fresh prettiness of the girls. Families were recognizable in those days, and schools were places where you respected your teacher and felt proud to be an American. Even the music made us feel good. Those were the days, we sigh and then ask ruefully, "How did we get here?"

There is little doubt that Americans had reason to be optimistic in the 1950s, as the country and the economy began the process of rebuilding after the war. While Europe struggled to overcome the hardships of the 1940s the United States emerged from the war as a nascent superpower in a new world order. In this new order, the Cold War era, rearmament was a priority and a policy that not only garnered public support in the prevailing political climate but was also highly profitable. Preparing a war machine to counteract the "evil empire" that Ronald Reagan identified three decades later was, and continues to be, big business. In addition, the Marshall Plan of postwar reconstruction for both former allies and former en-

emies gave the United States unprecedented economic and political influence throughout the developed world. These two aspects of American
postwar reconstruction—rearmament and the Marshall Plan—were
closely connected, since building up the military capabilities of Western
European allies was a principal part of the plan.

Thus the Cold War gave the United States permission abroad, and support at home, to put vast resources into creating a huge military-indus-
trial complex. And, ironically, the very existence of a recognizable enemy,
particularly an ideological one—communism—gave a peculiar stability to
the era. The opposition could be clearly seen. The bad guys were as identifiable as the cowboy with the black hat in any Western. It was a war of
rhetoric in which a show of might on both sides gave their respective
viewers someone to cheer and someone to boo. Americans are always at
their best when waging a war of ideology because they have a real need for
heroes. And if one thing differentiates Americans from other peoples, it is
their unwavering belief in the rightness of American institutions and their
particular interpretation of democracy. Not for them the masochistic self-
analysis of Canadians, the bitter ideological and class wars of the British
or the cynicism of the French. Americans' unflinching patriotism has
elicited criticism from other democracies, but it almost invariably ensures
public support for any measures aimed at promoting American values
abroad.

Thus America's greatest strength in the 1950s, as today, was the strength
of Americans' belief in their ideological, economic, and moral superiority.
Although that belief has been variously interpreted as ignorance, arrogance, or both, Americans' almost unassailable optimism has allowed
America to prosper—sometimes in spite of itself. When we look back to
what are usually referred to as "simpler times," we tend to view things
much more rosily than the reality warranted. Will Rogers was right:
Schools are not now and have never been what they ought to be. And in
the 1950s and 1960s, while the Cold War raged, there was also a storm
brewing at home that would turn education, and society, on its head.

Race: The Great Divide

Historian Eric Hobsbawm calls his history of the twentieth century the
Age of Extremes, and perhaps nowhere have the contradictions and con-
flicts been so painful to a nation as the racial divide in the United States.
As a people that prides itself on practicing democracy, liberty, equality,
and tolerance, the ethnic and race wars continue to scar the soul of Amer-

ica; a classic example of the contradictions between ideals and practice that Gunnar Myrdal explored in *An American Dilemma*. In this particularly American drama, the public school has played the role of both hero and villain. Horace Mann's common school was not, in fact, common at all, but was discriminatory, as African Americans, if they were educated at all, were educated in separate facilities from white Americans. In the early 1800s, state laws in the South prohibited slaves' being taught to read and write[2] because if blacks could be kept illiterate, they could also be kept subjugated. Although slavery had been abolished in the northern states by 1825, blacks were still discriminated against in schooling.[3] State and local laws in the South segregated the races in schools, hospitals, transportation, hotels, theaters, and in most other public and private facilities[4] well into the twentieth century, and even today the health, political, and economic infrastructure in black neighborhoods is often far inferior to that in white neighborhoods.

Nonetheless, black Americans were becoming educated. Even if the schools they were attending were inferior, they provided access to the ideals of equity, justice, liberty, and freedom—American ideals, they were told—and the seeds of their discontent grew roots. Equity and excellence are the twin pillars that support the public school and as much as they are in conflict, they are also necessary: another dilemma. Equity means providing the same quality of and access to education for all individuals, while excellence means ensuring high standards of expectation and achievement. During the 1950s and 1960s, it was the blatant absence of equity in education for African Americans that fueled the ideological fires.

A fight for social justice on the basis of inequity was exactly what racial separatists had been hoping to prevent with their segregationist measures. The 1896 court decision *Plessy v. Ferguson* was a classic example of this. Homer Plessy, who was seven-eighths white and one-eighth black, had been arrested in Louisiana for refusing to ride in the "colored" section of a train. The Supreme Court, examining the case, ruled that segregation did not necessarily imply inferior conditions for black Americans as long as the facilities they used were equivalent to those of whites. Thus the so-called separate but equal doctrine was born, which segregationists hoped would enshrine the perpetual separation of blacks and whites. The problem, of course, was that facilities and opportunities for African Americans had never been equal to those of whites; "separate but equal" just provided a convenient legal excuse to continue discrimination.

The NAACP had been fighting for equal rights for blacks since it was founded. Progress was slow and piecemeal until 1954, with the landmark Supreme Court decision in *Brown v. Board of Education* of Topeka,

Kansas. This decision overturned *Plessy*, ruling that state-imposed racial segregation in public schools was unconstitutional. "Separate but equal" had taken a fall from which it would never recover. The decision is historic not only in exposing the hypocrisy of the separate but equal doctrine but also in thereby affirming the ideals of equality and social justice. These ideals are not reserved for whites only, the Court was implicitly telling the nation; they are for all men and women, for all colors.

Education, then as now, was seen as the tool that Americans could use to begin to practice the egalitarian ideals upon which the United States was founded. But it was an enormous undertaking. At the time of *Brown*, approximately 40 percent of the nation's public school students attended segregated schools.[5] Although a Supreme Court ruling has significant juridical as well as symbolic value, it cannot be implemented without the cooperation of legislators and communities across the country who are charged with overseeing the actual implementation of desegregation. In 1955 the Court issued a ruling called *Brown II*, which left implementation of desegregation to local school authorities answerable only to federal district judges.[6]

Unfortunately, both *Brown II* and the language of the first *Brown* decision ensured that the process of desegregating schools would drag on for years. *Brown I* called on school boards to desegregate with "all deliberate speed," a phrase whose vagueness permitted any unwilling district to move at a snail's pace, all the while giving reasons for not going any faster. And *Brown II*, in allowing district judges to oversee desegregation efforts, meant that judges who were resistant to desegregation policies could be depended upon to permit slow application of the law.

As a result of these problems, we are still trying to ensure desegregation today. Students continue to be bused from one area to another to ensure desegregation, and we have created other ways to desegregate, such as magnet schools, that attract a mixed population by offering specialized and high-quality academic programs for a diverse population. Sadly, as Jonathan Kozol describes in *Savage Inequalities* (1991), minority children in cities across the country are still, at the end of the 1990s, often taught in schools lacking basic materials and sometimes lacking walls or a roof. As the title of his book suggests, these children are the victims of unequal funding, unequal expectations, and unequal—or no—respect.

Nonetheless, the *Brown* decision provided an important catalyst for the civil rights movement of the 1960s. In 1964 Congress voted in the Civil Rights Act, which extended federal regulation in the areas of voting rights, public accommodations, education, and employment.[7] Title IV and Title VI of the legislation provided federal authority for implementing the

Brown decision and ending school segregation. Ironically, school desegregation moved more slowly in the North than in the South, where de jure segregation had been the rule. De facto segregation existed in the North as well, however, and in the late 1960s, courts were ruling that the *Brown* decision applied to all schools, whether segregated by law or by intentional practice.[8]

The issue of race continues to divide America and underlies all education policy and practice from kindergarten to the college level. Up to the 1960s, efforts by the NAACP and other groups in support of equal rights had focused on making society color-blind (instead of classifying people on the basis of race). Since then the focus has gradually turned into something quite different. It was perhaps inevitable that fighting discrimination on the basis of race would result not in a color-blind society but in a society that is hyperaware of race and how it informs culture, language, family life, politics, and economics. Once the racial consciousness of blacks was raised, not even Martin Luther King Jr.'s stirring calls for an integrated society would put race in the background. Many African Americans feel, not unreasonably, that after centuries of slavery and discrimination on the basis of their race, only a strong affirmation of it will help to balance the scales. This is quite a change. During the hearings on the Civil Rights Bill the NAACP argued that a quota system was unfair, whether used for or against African Americans.[9] Today we argue over the relative merits of affirmative action, supported by many minorities as a way to access government jobs and higher education that they might otherwise have little chance to get because of institutional discrimination in schools and in the public service. "Separate but equal" has been resurrected, ironically, *in support of* African-American identity, but it has helped foster increased mistrust among individuals and the resegregation of various ethnic groups.

It is important to understand this legacy because it underlies most of what we call multicultural education, which is an important tool that the self-esteem movement uses to promote its message. Briefly put, multicultural education is a total school reform of curriculum, pedagogy, and learning environment that places the learner's ethnic and linguistic identity at the center of the learning process. Everything from teacher materials to the class seating arrangement must reflect the diversity that now characterizes many of the nation's classrooms. The purpose of multicultural education is to help all students feel pride in their identity and have high self-esteem. Since identification with and focus on race is considered by most academics and most teachers as one of the main keys to high self-esteem, these programs, first instituted in the late 1960s, now enjoy huge popularity, both in the United States and in Canada.

The 1960s: "Discovery" Learning and the "Open Curriculum"

If the 1960s was the era of the civil rights and race movements, it was also the era of self-discovery, "free love," Woodstock, and women's rights. It would be surprising if the school system were not somehow affected by the social and political movements of the time and of course it was. Following the launch of *Sputnik* and the ensuing hysteria over raising achievement in math, science, and foreign languages, schools adopted a kind of "back to basics" approach, but the methods used to teach those basics were new. As a result of the legacy of the Progressive movement in education as well as the liberal politics of the 1960s, curriculum reformers in this era rejected the traditional concept of teacher-led classrooms, replacing it with ideas of open classrooms and learning by discovery.

Discovery learning was invented by Harvard psychologist Jerome Bruner. He contended that students would learn better if they discovered ideas and concepts for themselves, rather than have them drilled into them by teachers. Like the progressives of the 1930s and 1940s, Bruner believed that learning should be an active, not a passive, process and that the goal of education should not be restricted to delivering information and knowledge to students but should have them claiming it for themselves. This would teach them to think.

Open education was a similar idea and its influence is seen in the self-esteem schools of today. In open education, classrooms are informal places where students are free to express their imagination and creativity. Adult direction is limited and teachers follow student direction as much as possible, rather than the other way around. If this sounds very much like the ideas of the Progressive movement, it was. Progressives and promoters of open education both believed in the idea of teacher as facilitator, in tailoring education to the needs of individual students and in allowing the curriculum to be determined by student interests.

The reformers of the 1960s had an advantage over the progressives in that they were not battling politicians and the public. Academic theories of education were beginning to receive much more attention in the media and therefore the public eye than they had before, and thus teachers were able, if necessary, to refer to the new learning theories if required to defend their methods. For example, one of the important ideas of the 1960s was the idea that children are intrinsically, rather than extrinsically motivated, and only need to be given the opportunity to express that motivation in order to learn and succeed in school. This idea supported open education, of course, because the implication is that teacher-led instruction—extrinsic motivation—is unhelpful, or even antithetical, to an authentic learning process.

Open education and discovery learning affected not only pedagogy but curriculum as well. Up until the progressive movement took hold, curricular materials had been largely in textbook form; teachers would use a standard text for a particular course, and all classwork and evaluation would be based on it. But students who are expected to discover knowledge for themselves are not likely to do so if their work consists solely of memorizing the textbook. So in the 1960s and 1970s texts in most courses began to be supplemented with laboratory manuals, primary sources, films, extra readings, and hands-on activities, among other things. These new learning materials not only gave students more opportunity to be active and imaginative learners but also gave teachers more leeway with course requirements and allowed them and their students to exercise their creativity.

Besides being organized differently, curricular materials began to be conceptualized differently, too. In the past the emphasis had always been on covering the prescribed amount of material in a certain time frame, which meant that quality and depth of understanding were often sacrificed for breadth. The new curricula, by contrast, were organized around fundamental concepts or principles that students were expected to master. The idea was that learning core ideas would be more beneficial in helping the student develop critical thinking skills and was thus more useful academically than simply learning a collection of unrelated facts.

Trying to balance depth with breadth is always difficult. While observers like E. D. Hirsch, author of *Cultural Literacy*, argue that there are certain ideas and pieces of knowledge that all students should know, others contend that developing problem-solving and critical-thinking skills is just as important. The battle between these two positions continues today in another example of the kind of all-or-nothing debate that characterizes arguments over public education. In reality, of course, both are needed. There is no question that a graduating high school senior needs to be literate, to know a fair amount of U.S. history and geography, to have a foreign language and computer skills, and to meet other basic requirements. It is very difficult to quantify exactly what she should know, but she should have had sufficient exposure to a variety of subjects, learning styles, and learning environments to support continued learning throughout her life. But she also needs to have critical-thinking and problem-solving skills. She should have studied enough literature to be able to identify a protagonist from an antagonist and to understand imagery, metaphor, simile, and the underlying themes that define a good piece of fiction or poetry. And perhaps most important, she needs to be able to make connections across disciplines and begin to understand her place in the world and how her actions affect others in the community. These are the critical thinking skills that will serve a student not only in his or her academic endeavors but in all areas of life.

The 1970s and 1980s: Back to Basics (Sort Of)

Just as the pendulum had swung back to the basics in the 1950s and then toward more progressive education in the 1960s, in the late 1970s and into the 1980s, it swung back again. Proponents of open education had hoped that relaxing academic standards, encouraging a more casual relationship between students and teachers and teaching a curriculum "relevant" to pressing social and political concerns would invite student interest and also prevent discipline problems.[10] What researchers found, however, was that open classrooms were too often characterized by a lack of teacher authority, disorganization, and serious discipline problems. All of this undermined national confidence in the public schools. This dissatisfaction in the 1970s, along with a more conservative political climate in the 1980s, meant that schools began to return to a more traditional orientation, both in curriculum and pedagogy.

The most visible sign that public education was undergoing another transformation came in 1983, when the Department of Education published its indictment on the state of public education, *A Nation at Risk*. This document was the product of the National Commission on Excellence in Education, established in 1981 to assess the quality of public education at all levels. The commission assessed the quality of learning in both public and private schools and colleges, compared U.S. schools with those of other countries, studied the relationship between achievement in high school and performance in college, and other indices of the state of American education. Their findings were damning.

The commission essentially concluded that American schools are not doing a very good job of educating American youth. Specifically, the report cites insufficient time spent in school, low expectations and low standards, dumbed-down and homogenized curricula, and poor teacher preparation, among other problems. The report's authors recommended raising standards, requiring every student to take a certain number of basic liberal arts and science courses (math, science, English, a foreign language, etc.), lengthening the school day or the school year, assigning more homework, and restructuring teacher education programs. They also identified the necessity of public commitment to improving education, including addressing student apathy and encouraging parental and community involvement.

A Nation at Risk was a seminal report in the history of American education for a couple of reasons. First, as with every major policy paper on education, it is of course a political document. Written under a conservative administration, it reflects a particular view of education—one that many liberals have criticized. The report focuses almost entirely on excellence and standards and gives little or no attention to the issue of equity. Liberals find this very problematic, since the report recommends raising standards but does not tell us how those students—often poor and minority students—who are not reaching present standards are going to reach the new standards, or what the consequences will be if they don't. Indeed, in the absence of any information, one can only conclude that those who don't reach the new standards will simply be left behind. Standards can be a good thing, but they are of little use if a large percentage of the student population cannot ever hope to reach them.

Second, the report gave the most comprehensive overview of decades of schooling in the United States and therefore its conclusions, however displeasing they may be, cannot be ignored. Although it does not identify particular learning theories or paradigms as the cause of school problems, it does criticize the low standards, poor attendance policies, lax disciplinary codes, and the general attitude of low expectations and permissiveness that characterized schools during the 1960s and much of the 1970s. Most significant in terms of the progress and evolution of American education is the statement that for the first time in American history the present generation of students will not outperform its predecessors. In fact, the report notes that while the average citizen today is better educated than the average citizen of a generation ago, the average high school and college graduate is not as well-educated as her peer of twenty-five or thirty-five years ago.[11] In other words, more people are being educated but the standards are lower. Of course, the economic and ethnic diversity of contemporary schools is not the same as it was twenty-five years ago, and therefore straight comparisons can be misleading. Nonetheless, the absence of positive progress over that time in terms of basic literacy and numeracy and general level of education cannot but be troubling.

Not surprisingly, *A Nation at Risk* has been both praised and reviled. Liberals call it misleading and argue that it was intended to divert the nation from real issues of poverty and inequality while conservatives claim it provides irrefutable evidence of the decline of the public school. In this sense *A Nation at Risk* achieved much the same notoriety as Allan Bloom, who announced the end of intellectual and moral life in this country with his book *The Closing of the American Mind*, published a few years later. So much has been written about each, both pro and con, that the average citizen or parent could be forgiven for wondering just exactly what things are like in schools and what we can do about it.

I will not here attempt to arbitrate between liberals and conservatives on this, but point out two things that seem to me rather important. First, whatever its shortcomings (and they are many), *A Nation at Risk* did what no other report and no other theory or learning fad could do: put education at the forefront of the national political agenda. Education today is as topical an issue as the economy, foreign policy, or race problems, and, indeed, it is tightly interwoven with each of them. For the first time the public, and not just academics or policymakers, became aware, whether they liked it or not, that everyone has an investment in education and that therefore we all have a responsibility to be involved in it. Although sadly some parents still believe that it is the school's job to raise as well as educate their children, the growth in parental and community involvement in education over the last fifteen years has been almost exponential. The constant media coverage of education (although sometimes unduly negative) is evidence of the public concern with schooling and ensures that it will never again be something that is relegated to school boards alone (or the back pages of the local newspaper). And, perhaps most important, no politician can hope to be elected at the local, state, or national level without a clear platform on education and all its attendant concerns: equity, standards, teacher quality, funding, community involvement, and so on.

The second point is that, like it or not, the report described what a lot of people had been thinking but couldn't prove: that whether or not America is truly "a nation at risk" because of its education system, there is little question that things are not at all the way they ought to be. Sadly (but predictably) it is primarily professors of education and to a lesser extent, teachers, who have disclaimed the report's findings. Entire academic journals have been dedicated to dissecting the report and explaining how it grossly misrepresents, or at least grossly exaggerates, the state of the nation's public schools. The reason professors reject the report is easy to understand in psychological, if not in ethical terms, because the report implicitly condemns the ideas that educators have embraced for decades: the progressive, child-centered, open learning, discovery model of schooling, which is the essence of what we today call the self-esteem movement. It is not much fun to be the inventor of the latest "creative" way to teach mathematics and then be told that actually the old way was much better. Without question, the report's lack of attention to the needs of at-risk students is a very significant problem. But that should not nullify the majority of the findings.

Teachers who have eighth-grade students who cannot read know that something is wrong; parents who never see their children do any homework know it; business leaders know it when they have to train their employees to write a letter or teach them proper grammar. That knowledge is what inspired—or maybe the word is "provoked"—me to write this book because *I* knew it too. When the vast majority of my students (remember, they all have degrees and are all future teachers) have no idea how to write a research paper and make serious spelling and grammatical errors, I know something is wrong. When they have little knowledge of geography, only a smattering of U.S. history, and no world history, and they evince little interest in knowing more, it is clear there is a problem.

By the 1980s the public and most policymakers were focusing their efforts on improving education along the lines suggested in *A Nation at Risk*. In the years immediately following the publication of the report, states and local school districts across the country implemented a whole host of reforms, from overhauling curricula to improving teacher preparation and standards to greater business involvement in schools and higher standards across the board. Change was amazingly rapid. By 1984, one year after the report's release, 275 state-level task forces had been created to study the report and implement its findings, forty-eight states were considering new high school requirements, twenty-one had initiated textbook reform, and eight had approved lengthening the school day, doubtless the most controversial change of all, because of traditional opposition from teachers, students, and parents.[12]

The trend away from progressive kinds of schooling and toward a more standards-based, goal-oriented model, at least in terms of public policy, continued during the 1980s. In 1989 President George Bush met with the nation's governors for a national summit on education, and with the leadership of Bush and Bill Clinton, then governor of Arkansas, a blueprint for American education, called America 2000, was created. Its name has been changed to Goals 2000 under the Clinton administration, but the objectives remain the same. They call for U.S. students attaining first place in the world in math and science by the year 2000; raising the high school graduation rate to 90 percent or higher; ensuring that each child is ready to learn when he or she enters school; ensuring student competency in basic subject areas; improving teacher education and academic performance in key subject areas; keeping schools safe and free from drugs and alcohol; promoting parental participation in their children's learning; and helping to make education a lifelong commitment of all Americans.

It is worth noting that although Democrats and Republicans often disagree on the details, such as how to define standards or what level of standard should be required, since its inception Goals 2000 has received
considerable bipartisan support. This general measure of agreement over
the aims doubtless explains the slow but steady progress achieved in the
1990s toward some of the goals. For example, mathematics achievement
in grades four, eight, and twelve improved between 1990 and 1996 by an
average of about 7 percent, and children's readiness to learn, measured by
childhood health indices, immunization rates, and the amount of reading
done in the home, has also improved. However, more kids reported using
drugs in 1997 than in 1991 and more public school teachers reported incidents of classroom disruptions in 1994 than in 1991.[13]

Although *A Nation at Risk* can conceivably be dismissed as a conservative document, the same cannot be said of Goals 2000, and I believe that it
is a sign that common sense may yet prevail in the education wars. Although we do not seem destined to meet the goals by the year 2000, the fact
that there is consensus on them is reason for considerable optimism. The
common sense does not appear to extend to professors of education, however, some of whom still contend that the whole notion of standards—national or otherwise—is actually detrimental to the learning process.

We have a disjuncture in perspective between the public, particularly
parents, who see the problems in schools, and the education profession,
which by and large commits itself to denying the problems. A recent study
of teachers' views on education provides evidence of this. Teachers share
the public's opinion that higher academic standards are necessary, but
they do not rank standards as highly as does the public. Sixty percent of
the general public believes that there is insufficient emphasis on the basics, compared to only 34 percent of teachers overall. And 86 percent of
teachers said that the public schools in their communities are doing a
good or excellent job, whereas only 55 percent of the public share their
optimism.[14] Even teenagers yearn for higher standards. According to a
study conducted by the public opinion research organization Public
Agenda, nearly 80 percent of students said that they would learn more if
schools made sure that students were on time and completed their homework. More than 70 percent of respondents said that schools should require after-school classes for students earning D's and F's, and 75 percent
of those surveyed said that students shouldn't be allowed to graduate unless they had mastered English.[15] Out of the mouths of babes . . .

With all this evidence facing them, one would think that professors and
researchers would be spending their time focusing on how to improve
things, but sadly the opposite is true: they seem to spend an inordinate

amount of time and effort trying to explain how things are not as bad as they seem. Books are even written on the subject of how the news media and the conservatives (interesting bedfellows) are attempting to create a distorted picture of public education merely to further their own subversive interests. The recent book *The Manufactured Crisis,* by David Berliner and Bruce Biddle, is one of the more prominent of these. In it the authors disclaim what they perceive to be the many myths about American education, including myths about aptitude and achievement, selective schools, and other important issues. Although their observations on the issue of IQ testing (very biased, unreliable, and not very useful) are right on the money, their belief that the prevailing negative perspective of American education grew from "organized malevolence" gives their discussion a somewhat defensive and paranoid flavor that significantly undermines the force of their arguments.[16]

Berliner and Biddle use a variety of statistics to explain that test scores are not falling and that *A Nation at Risk* was misleading. There has indeed been a sharp increase in SAT scores since 1995, but that is more likely due to the College Board's decision to "recenter" the mean score rather than any real increase in student aptitude.[17] Berliner and Biddle's overall judgment is that the problems in education are largely manufactured by "powerful people who—despite their protestations—were pursuing a political agenda designed to weaken the nation's public schools, redistribute support for those schools so that privileged students are favored over needy students, or even abolish those schools altogether."[18] It seems a little unfair to put everyone who is seriously concerned with the nation's schools in the same political basket; not everyone subscribes to the Allan Bloom philosophy of education. Unfortunately, in their desire to expose these so-called myths, Berliner and Biddle, like the conservative policymakers they criticize, use statistics to make a political point rather than simply inform. One set of statistics can be manipulated to defend any number of competing views, as all researchers know, and it might be more to the point to address what we can all agree are problems rather than continue to wage endless ideological wars.

More Ammunition for the Self-Esteem Movement

Educational researchers are helped in their defense of the public schools generally, and the self-esteem movement in particular, by the continuing publication of research that directly or indirectly provides fuel for the movement. Howard Gardner's theory of multiple intelligences, one of the

most influential educational ideas of the 1980s, is one of these, as is Daniel
Goleman's work on emotional intelligence, which captured not only academic but public interest in the 1990s. Their ideas are complementary in a
number of ways, and Gardner and Goleman have recently collaborated
with another colleague on a video called *Optimizing Intelligences: Thinking, Emotion, and Creativity.* Each has had growing influence in the other's
arena: Gardner's work is beginning to reach the nonacademic audience
while Goleman is being increasingly examined in academia. This cross-
fertilization illustrates both the reliance of the self-esteem movement on
external (non-academic) validation and its increasing influence on that
external environment and on popular culture generally.

According to Gardner, each of us has one or more different kinds of intelligences (not just one, as has been traditionally assumed), and he believes that schools should be reoriented to developing them. Goleman's
thesis is that emotional intelligence is just as important for success in life
as IQ and that we should therefore be focusing more time and attention
on child rearing, schooling, and society in general. The popularity of these
theories has two causes. First, both Gardner's and Goleman's ideas are relatively easy to understand and, second, both can be used to support the
ideology and practice of the self-esteem movement. I am not contending
that either author deliberately fashioned his theory with that in mind but
that their ideas lend themselves to educational policies that promote the
ideals of self-esteem.

Gardner's thesis is based on the notion that intelligence testing (indeed,
the whole idea of IQ) is severely limited and that intelligence is not one set
of talents but is multidimensional. He promotes a "pluralistic view of
mind, recognizing many different and discrete facts of cognition, acknowledging that people have different cognitive strengths and contrast-
ing cognitive styles."[19] Referring to research in cognitive science and
neuroscience, Gardner tries to answer the age-old question of just what is
intelligence.

Since Alfred Binet developed the IQ test in France in 1900, Western culture has typically regarded intelligence as easily measurable and unidimensional. But Gardner believes that individuals may express one or
more of at least seven different intelligences. He defines these intelligences
as follows: linguistic, logical-mathematical, spatial, musical, bodily-kinesthetic, interpersonal, and intrapersonal. The first two are the intelligences
that have traditionally been valued and are what IQ tests, as well as other
standardized tests, are typically designed to measure. Spatial intelligence is
the ability to form a mental model of the world and use it to function in
some way. Sailors, engineers, and painters are examples of people who

typically exhibit spatial intelligence.[20] Musical intelligence is easily identifiable: anyone with a clear musical ability would fit into this category while bodily-kinesthetic intelligence is expressed by athletes and dancers, among others. Interpersonal intelligence is the ability to understand others and work cooperatively with them. Lastly, intrapersonal intelligence is the ability to look inward, create an accurate model of oneself, and use that model to function effectively in life.

Gardner is very explicit about the educational implications of his theory. He believes that schools should be places in which these intelligences are developed and where "people reach vocational and avocational goals that are appropriate to their particular spectrum of intelligences."[21] Schools must, perforce, be individual centered—geared to the optimal development of each student's particular assortment of intelligences.[22] Gardner believes that education must be organized around two assumptions, first, that each of us has a different set of intelligences and therefore learns in a different way and, second that no one is capable of learning everything there is to learn.[23]

A central purpose of schooling, and of teaching, would be to determine just what each child's intelligences are so that he or she can be directed to make educational choices commensurate with those aptitudes. Teachers would become "assessment specialists"[24] and, after identifying a child's gifts, would direct students toward the "student-curriculum broker" who would match students' intelligence profiles and interests to curricula.[25] There would also be a "school-community broker" who would help match those interests to opportunities in the larger community, thus ensuring a smooth transition between school and work.[26]

Gardner's ideas have begun to be put into practice at several school sites across the country. One project, Arts PROPEL, a collaborative program with the Educational Testing Service and the Pittsburgh school system, seeks to assess learning in areas like music, creative writing, and visual arts.[27] A school in Indianapolis is organized entirely according to the principles of multiple intelligence (MI) theory and offers special classes in "bodily-kinesthetic" activities, a "flow" center, and "pods."[28] And Project Spectrum of Tufts University has developed curriculum activities "suited to the 'child-centered' structure of many preschools and kindergartens."[29] Gardner writes that "the final story on Multiple Intelligences may turn out to be more complex than we envisioned" but that even if these specific intelligences turn out to be related to a global intelligence level (the traditional view) "the goal of detecting distinctive human strengths, and using them as a basis for engagement and learning, may prove to be worthwhile, irrespective of the scientific fate of the theory."[30]

It goes (almost) without saying that Gardner categorically opposes standardized testing. He believes that testing allows individuals to express only some of their intelligences and that it is therefore a very limited and inaccurate measure of a person's true aptitudes and abilities. The problem, then, is how would we know which people have which intelligences (if that is in fact what they are) if we *don't* measure them? Goleman clearly states that we need to identify the intelligences, but it is not clear exactly how we would go about doing that. Schools and colleges still rely on IQ tests, subject matter tests, and aptitude tests for college, such as the SAT and the GRE for undergraduate and graduate admission, and the MCAT, LSAT, and GMAT for admission to medicine, law, and management, respectively. If the intelligences are to be used as the organizational basis of each student's education, they *must* be in some way measurable.

There are a couple of likely outcomes of Gardner's proposal, neither of which is desirable. Let us assume that (1) these intelligences do exist and (2) we are able to accurately identify them in each child (both statements as yet unproven). If we then tailor education directly around these intelligences—making schools more "child-centered" than ever before—children will either choose to study something they are interested in, to the neglect of other important areas, or they will be forced to choose what an evaluator (the teacher) has decided is their forte. Either option would result in very narrowly *trained,* not *educated,* individuals and could result in academic and vocational tracking, in which students are corralled into a field that they may neither enjoy nor be suited for. Gardner denies that his approach demands "early overdetermination"[31] and contends that by identifying strengths and weaknesses early on we can find ways of addressing both. But he does not explain precisely how to avoid these very real pitfalls.

Gardner's theory also has implications for teaching and teacher preparation. Today the idea of multiple intelligences is usually taught in a teacher education program. Although it is one of the favorite topics of professors, teachers do not come out of their classes with anything like the kind of in-depth understanding or skills required to appropriately assess students according to Gardner's rubric. And this is where the real damage is done. It means that teachers are likely to stop expecting all students to do well on standardized tests, having been told that they do not accurately reflect intelligence (and anyway, they're told, standardized tests are inherently biased against women, the poor, and minorities). With the best of intentions, they start to look wherever they can for evidence of little Bobby's kind of intelligence. If he can't read, no matter. No good at math? Don't worry. We'll find *something* Bobby can do. Maybe he's good at music. No luck? What about drawing? That's spatial, isn't it? Yes, that's it. And if the drawing doesn't look much like anything, that's okay too because we're not here to judge, we're here to encourage (and isn't art totally subjective anyway?).

The picture is clear—and it's not a pretty one. Since, according to the educational psychologists, we all learn in different ways and at different speeds, and we all have different intelligences, from a practical point of view, it is all but impossible for a teacher to accurately gauge either a student's progress or her achievement. Add to this the messages teachers already receive about how grading, competition, standards, and testing are bad for children's self-esteem, and there is virtually no possibility of either accurate assessment or uniform standards. Teachers might be content with identifying just one intelligence, which would mean of course that others would never get developed.

Daniel Goleman's theory of "emotional intelligence," although slightly different in emphasis, has the same implications as Gardner's for education. Goleman uses recent developments in neuroscience to argue that our success in academia, and in life generally, is far less determined by IQ than by our ability to harness our emotions to make sensible, rational life choices. According to Goleman, "academic intelligence offers virtually no preparation for the turmoil—or opportunity—life's vicissitudes bring" while "emotional life is a domain that, as surely as math or reading, can be handled with greater or lesser skill, and requires its unique set of competencies. And how adept a person is at those is crucial to understanding why one person thrives in life while another, of equal intellect, dead-ends: emotional aptitude is a *meta-ability*, determining how well we can use whatever other skills we have, including raw intellect."[32]

Goleman believes that emotional intelligence governs how we function in all areas, including intellectually, and he seeks to find an "intelligent balance" between reason and emotion.[33] The relationship between reason and emotion has, of course, been a central concern of philosophers for centuries, but until now that relationship has been described in terms of a dichotomy or perhaps a hierarchy with reason on top. Since the Enlightenment man has attempted to use his reason to curb his emotion, but what Goleman and others are suggesting is that we have perhaps overemphasized rationality and underestimated the importance of emotion in our daily lives. He explicitly acknowledges Gardner's influence on his work, calling him a "visionary" who was instrumental in revealing the limitations of our traditional conceptions of intelligence, including our dependence on the IQ test.[34] Two of Gardner's intelligence categories—interpersonal and intrapersonal—are of particular interest to Goleman, since they come closest to his emphasis on emotions.

To help explain his theory, Goleman gives us examples of a "pure" high-IQ man and woman, and their pure emotionally intelligent counterparts.[35] Of course these are only hypotheticals; most of us have a mixture of emotional as well as intellectual abilities, but they serve to explain his theory. The high-IQ male is typically ambitious, productive, critical, condescending, and emotionally cold. His female counterpart is also intellectually confident, has a wide range of intellectual and aesthetic interests, but has a tendency to be anxious, self-involved, and reluctant to express anger openly. On the other hand, the man with a high emotional quotient is socially poised, outgoing, sympathetic with others, and generally feels comfortable with himself and others. High-EQ women are very similar: they express their feelings well, are outgoing, and have considerable social poise. They too feel comfortable in a variety of social situations.

Although much academic research on education has focused on academic illiteracy, Goleman contends that the real danger to our children is emotional illiteracy, which he believes has been steadily growing for the last couple of decades.[36] In order to help prevent or address some of these problems, emotional skills, such as self-awareness, impulse control, listening to others' perspectives and so on, are needed.[37] Mere information—intellectualizing problems, as it were—is not enough.

Goleman believes that schools should be redirected toward developing the emotions as well as the intellect and notes that classes in emotional literacy are becoming increasingly popular in schools. Courses in "social development," "life skills," or "social and emotional learning" are examples of this trend, which has its roots in the affective-education movements of the 1960s (remember open education and discovery learning?).[38] The difference, however, is that instead of using the emotions to educate, emotional literacy educates the emotions themselves. Goleman describes a model of emotional intelligence that has been used for almost twenty years: the Self-Science Curriculum at the Nueva School in San Francisco. In this class teachers use kids' everyday experiences to examine how they feel in situations of conflict and disagreement in order to provide them the tools to deal with situations in a peaceful, just, and cooperative manner.

The content list of Self-Science includes Goleman's main ingredients for emotional intelligence: recognizing feelings and building a vocabulary to deal with them; handling stress; developing self-acceptance; developing empathy; seeing the links between feelings, thoughts, and reactions; knowing if feelings or thoughts are ruling a decision and examining consequences of various choices. No grade is given in Self-Science; "life itself is the final exam."[39] Wouldn't it be interesting, though, to bring the class back together years later to see what effect, if any, this course had on them and whether it did indeed give them tools to become more emotionally mature and stable? Goleman notes that there have been a "handful" of objective evaluations, some of which have assessed behavior before and after such programs, but his book is astonishingly thin on evidence that they actually work. He lists six programs that have been evaluated and that seem to indicate success, but the results are distressingly vague. Six programs hardly seems sufficient evidence to promote a notion that Goleman himself admits would demand a fundamental transformation in the purpose and mission of the public school.

We should be concerned about the conspicuous lack of evidence regarding the efficacy and utility of promoting emotional intelligence in schools. Do we really want to transform schools into places that focus more on emotional and less on intellectual development? Goleman himself admits that the emotional mind is "childlike": categorical, in which everything is seen as black or white, and personalized, in which all events are perceived as centering on oneself.[40] He also explains that the rational mind is tentative, examining new evidence and avoiding judgments or decisions until all relevant information has been processed. The emotional mind, however, "takes its beliefs to be absolutely true, and so discounts any evidence to the contrary. That is why it is so hard to reason with someone who is emotionally upset: no matter the soundness of your argument from a logical point of view, it carries no weight if it is out of keeping with the emotional conviction of the moment. Feelings are self-justifying, with a set of perceptions and "proofs" all their own."[41]

Precisely. It is because emotion recognizes only itself and, he says, its own proofs, that reason is essential. This also shows us that emotion is the basis of narcissism, since it is by definition consumed only with the self, with the here and now: "The working of the emotional mind is to a large degree *state-specific*, dictated by the particular feeling ascendant at a given moment."[42] How he expects to avoid the consequent narcissism were schools to focus on the emotions even more than they already do is not clear.

The problems with Goleman's and Gardner's theories is that in practice just about anything could qualify as a kind of intelligence. While it is surely a good thing to recognize musical and artistic, as well as linguistic or mathematical aptitudes, since we do not know how to accurately evaluate them, we are forced to let go of any ideals of standards or excellence. This sort of democratization of intelligence, while intellectually appealing, actually lends itself to a dumbing down of school in general, since according to Gardner all intelligences are equivalent and thus cannot be ordered into any value hierarchy. If we include Goleman's ideas of emotional intelligence in here along with Gardner's, where do we end up? Should all intelligences really be considered of equal value? Do we really want to say that having good social skills is just as important for a second-grader as being able to read at grade level? Does working cooperatively help one learn algebra? Or perhaps we should put it another way. Even if these are important skills, are they not ones that should be developed in the home? Isn't school primarily for developing the intellect?

Unfortunately, these are questions that have not, as yet, been seriously examined. Both Gardner and Goleman have interesting hypotheses, but educators treat them as prophets in education rather than examine them critically to determine what use, if any, they might have for public schooling. And of course their ideas fit perfectly (whether they wanted them to or not) into the ideology of the self-esteem movement by lending support to the call for lowered standards, radically child-centered education, and an overall move to emotional training instead of academic education. If we continue to move in this direction, the ideal of a liberal education, and the original purposes of the common school, will forever be lost. Then schools will *really* be "what they never was."

Nothing More than Feelings

The Naked Truth About Self-Esteem

Men become civilized, not in proportion to their willingness to believe,
but in proportion to their readiness to doubt.
—H. L. Mencken[1]

WE HAVE SEEN HOW, OVER SEVERAL DECADES, the self-esteem movement has slowly infiltrated education to the point that today most educators believe developing self-esteem to be one of the primary purposes of public education. As a result, schools are providing more courses in "life skills" and less attention to academics, which is the core of a liberal education. The very essence of public schooling is thus being transformed. We are in danger of producing individuals who are expert at knowing how they feel rather than educated individuals who know how to think. This is a radical transformation in the role of schooling. The questions that arise are the following: Should self-esteem be a central focus of public schooling? Are there research data that demonstrate the importance of promoting self-esteem in schools? What specific benefits does it provide?

Because self-esteem has been part of our educational discourse for so long and because the public tends to trust what academics and policy-makers say about education, the concept of self-esteem has seeped virtually unexamined into our consciousness. But it behooves all of us to determine whether or not it is the concept around which we should organize public policy and practice in education. Unfortunately, we cannot always rely on the educational community to tell us the truth, since many in it have a vested interest in promoting self-esteem. It is a concept upon which, after all, countless careers have been made. In an attempt to continue to justify their existence (and their influence in the public schools) educational researchers invent new learning theories every year and declare them the answer to all our problems, sometimes with little evidence to prove it. In so doing they have managed to turn the aphorism "necessity is the mother of invention" on its head: Invent something to prove your importance and try to convince the public to buy into it!

The self-esteem movement infiltrates virtually all aspects of schooling, from teaching methods to evaluation to curriculum planning. It is the most popular of all the fads, and the most dangerous. But as we will discover, it is not essential. In fact, it doesn't even make much sense.

Undressing the Emperor

I have remarked how nice it would be if educational researchers could put aside their political squabbles for a moment in order to address substantive issues. This is unlikely to happen, however, since education is a national concern as well as an individual one, and our views on it are embedded in our personal political perspectives. The issue of self-esteem, which grew out of progressive notions of education, is no different. It is a concept that we see and hear everywhere, and yet almost nowhere is it clearly defined. Likewise, we hear all the time that it promotes achievement and good behavior, and most teachers will tell you that it is absolutely essential to a child's overall academic success. In fact, high levels of self-esteem are believed to be necessary for not only academic achievement and good behavior but also a positive outlook on life, a happy marriage, good sex, and just about everything else that relates to having a successful life.[2]

After hearing all this, practically no one in her right mind would want to publicly argue the importance of self-esteem, since it would tend to make one appear rather like Dr. Seuss's Grinch at Christmas: mean, bad-tempered, unsociable, and loath to let anyone else have a good time. But are we really sure that self-esteem has these wonderful effects on children and that it should be a fundamental part of schooling? What is the research on self-esteem? Has it been proven in practice? Let's take a closer look at this emperor and see what, if anything, he's wearing under his robes.

The Evidence

A recent article in the *American Educational Research Journal,* one of the most respected journals published by the American Educational Research Association, surveys the research on self-esteem. The author, Joseph Kahne, reviewed a massive amount of literature on self-esteem and notes that self-esteem has been demonstrated to be only modestly correlated with good behavior and academic achievement and that, furthermore, the direction of causality is unclear.[3] In other words, we do not know whether self-esteem promotes achievement and good behavior, or the other way around. Although an enormous amount has been written about self-esteem, there is precious little in the way of evidence regarding its efficacy in these areas. On the contrary: The preponderance of the data illustrate that self-esteem is irrelevant in all areas of education.

A few examples from the literature available show how strenuously researchers have attempted to illustrate the importance of self-esteem and correlate it to behavior or achievement and how, despite their best efforts, they have failed. A recent article in the *Journal of Educational Research* examines perceptions of school administrators, counselors, and teachers about student self-esteem. The authors explains that it is important to understand how these individuals view students and student self-esteem, since students' academic progress and social behavior are affected by those perceptions. They come up with some interesting results. Thirty-five percent of administrators, compared to 60 percent of teachers and 69 percent of school counselors, believe that student self-esteem should be addressed by "providing more unconditional validation to students based on who they are rather than how they perform or behave."[4] Little surprise that counselors, who are trained as therapists, should support the idea of "unconditional validation" while administrators, who are trained in organizational management and not self-esteem, are less supportive of the idea.

But the authors express concern regarding these results, suggesting that students will suffer if not all school personnel share the same view of how self-esteem is to be developed. They argue that "in order for school personnel to make an enduring difference in students' self-esteem, they must construct a consistent and ongoing series of specific situations in which students can receive both positive and constructive feedback."[5] It is revealing of the research bias that the authors believe the counselors' view is the correct one and that administrators and to a lesser extent teachers, must be brought in line with the counselors.

They conclude that "one of the most significant findings of this study was the overall agreement of school personnel regarding the importance of being responsible and dependable as characteristic of students with high self-esteem" but acknowledge that "this notion has yet to be empirically supported."[6] They also point out that respondents indicated "clear linkages between family and school in helping students build self-esteem" but that, again, these results have not been "empirically substantiated."[7] This suggests the difficulty of correlating self-esteem with anything, even such positive characteristics as parental involvement. Common sense suggests that these should be instrumental in developing a positive self-concept, but there is in fact little evidence to prove it.

Another study examines whether enhancing self-concept improves educational achievement, one of the central claims of the self-esteem movement. The authors note that "the proposition that a person's self concept influences his behavior has long been a part of American individualistic social philosophy. A belief in the power of self concept is incorporated into diverse strands of psychological, sociological and educational theory, all of which have emphasized the influence of subjective inner experiences as sources of individual behavior."[8] The authors reviewed dozens of studies on self-concept and achievement and note that "empirical evidence validating the causal role of self concept has lagged behind its incorporation into theory and educational interventions."[9] In other words, we are using the notion of self-esteem in schools before determining whether or not it has any value. They conclude that "while several studies to be reviewed have found positive correlations between self concept and educational achievement, the causal direction, if any, of this relationship cannot be ascertained from such cross-sectional studies"[10] and that "little direct evidence exists in either psychological or sociological literature that self concept has an independent influence on behavior."[11]

The authors also examined evaluations of existing programs designed to promote self-esteem and found that "the overwhelmingly negative evidence reviewed here for a causal connection between self concept and academic achievement should create caution among both educators and theorists who have heretofore assumed that enhancing a person's feelings about himself would lead to academic achievement."[12] Another article from the *Review of Educational Research* arrived at similar results: "Although some researchers convey the impression that a moderate and positive association exists between self and measures of performance and achievement, an initial and cursory assessment of the literature suggests that this relationship is neither precise nor clear."[13]

Lacking evidence of causality, researchers often look for what they *can* prove (if anything) and come up with some pretty bizarre results. One study, which compared the self-esteem of college-ready students and academically underprepared students found that the latter demonstrated more test anxiety than their more prepared peers, completed fewer courses, but had roughly the same grade point averages (GPA), learning and studying strategies, and self-esteem. Amazingly, those who were unprepared but persisted, as well as those who were college ready, exhibited *lower* self-esteem overall than whose who did not persist.[14]

Behavior as well as achievement is supposed to be positively affected by having a high level of self-esteem. One study examined the extent to which subjects' self-esteem affected their behavior by giving participants false feedback from a personality test aimed at increasing their self-esteem, lowering it, or leaving it unchanged. The participants were then told to play a game of cards in which they were provided opportunities to cheat under circumstances that made it appear impossible to be detected. What they found was that significantly more of the people who had their self-esteem lowered cheated, compared to those whose self-esteem had been raised by the test feedback.[15] The trouble with this experiment, as even the researchers themselves note, is that there are a number of possible reasons why those with low self-esteem cheated more often. They could have been angry at the evaluators and decided to cheat as a way of punishing them. Or they may have felt that cheating on the card game would somehow compensate for having fared badly (so they thought) on the personality test. Thus in this particular experiment it does seem intuitively correct to assume that those with low self-esteem exhibit bad behavior (cheating). But it is difficult to determine it absolutely and, perhaps more important, equally difficult to explain why.

A question that this article brings to the fore is, How stable is self-esteem in our personality? Is it stable over time or can it be crushed by a simple personality test? The evidence indicates that self-esteem remains fairly stable and cannot be either instantly created or suddenly destroyed. Most of the psychological studies suggest that one's sense of self is developed quite early in childhood and stays more or less constant through adulthood. Jerome Kagan, professor of psychology at Harvard University, contends that "it is an error for educators to argue that they can raise children's self-esteem merely by praising them."[16] Although many adolescents experience challenges to their self-confidence during those often trying years, as adults they often regain the sense of self they held before adolescence.

Perhaps the only general aberration from this pattern is the sense of self-confidence that many of us experience as we go through our twenties and on into our thirties and forties. In early adulthood we are busy struggling to figure out what we want to do with our lives, getting through college, finding a job, and relating to a variety of people. By our thirties and forties most of us have settled into a career, have found a partner, and have generally decided who we are or who we want to be. In fact, researchers have found that most people generally get happier as they get older.[17] The hang-ups and self-doubts we had in our high school and college years slowly fade into the background as we begin to construct our own identities, have our own families, and enjoy success and satisfaction in our work. Even for those who had a difficult or abusive family life it is often a time of re-evaluation and renewal, coming to terms with life experiences, learning to move forward, and taking responsibility for their own destiny.

The point, of course, is that if self-esteem is relatively stable and does not significantly affect academic achievement or behavior, then all the programs intended to raise it may be quite useless. We would do much better to focus on academics and hope that feelings of self-confidence will result from achievement, which they almost invariably do. If self-esteem does develop early in life, we should be redirecting scarce resources now used to foster self-esteem into early childhood education programs, family support groups, reading groups, health programs, and other programs designed to help students take full advantage of their education.

Problems with self-assessment of self-esteem continually confound researchers' efforts to relate it to school behavior and achievement. For example, a recent study compared the extent to which black, white, and Hispanic students based their overall self-esteem on academic performance during high school. The researcher found that African Americans had the highest levels of self-esteem at all ages but that over time, African-American males detach their self-esteem from academics. They retain a high sense of self-esteem but do not relate it to success in school.[18] The peer group, sports, or other aspects of their lives become more important than academics in determining their self-worth.

What does this tell us? Well, it may be that self-esteem has, in the end, little to do with success in school, or even school at all, and the African-American males are simply reflecting that in their responses. Or it could mean that the self-esteem indicated by the boys was simply bravado; they do not feel all that good about themselves but did not want to admit it. This seems a likely possibility because adolescents often try to act tougher, smarter, or stronger than their peers in an effort to win praise and acceptance from them or from rival groups. It also tells us that we need to regard with caution studies that rely on self-reporting of self-esteem in their data. In addition, as Jerome Kagan points out, self-esteem is a complex thing, involving many aspects of our personality. He notes that "each person makes separate judgments for each of a variety of qualities, including academic skills, memory, courage, physical attractiveness, popularity, athletic talent, morality, wealth and social status. No one computes an average of the many different characteristics to arrive at a general self-concept."[19]

Not only does self-esteem not seem to correlate with good academics and good behavior, it may actually exert a negative effect on them. This is graphically illustrated in a recent study in *Psychological Review*. In it the authors examine the relationship between egotism and violence and aggression; what they called "the dark side of high self-esteem."[20] They studied a significant body of research on that relationship and found that it contradicted the accepted view that low self-esteem was a cause of violence. They found that "violence appears to be most commonly a result of threatened egotism—that is, highly favorable views of self that are disputed by some person or circumstance."[21] They illustrate, moreover, that most studies that purport to show a positive relation between low self-esteem and violence fail to do so, "and many provided clear and direct contradictory findings."[22] They note, however, that this does not mean that high self-esteem per se is a cause of violence, nor that all people who think highly of themselves are violent, but that "violence is perpetrated by a small subset of people with favorable views of themselves."[23] They sum up the issue rather well: "Viewed in this light, the societal pursuit of high self-esteem for everyone may literally end up doing considerable harm."[24]

If programs designed to foster self-esteem are either useless or harmful, why are we so intent on promoting them? Perhaps it is because we do not yet realize what the costs can be. There is another explanation, however, one that is more serious and even rather sinister. I am far from suggesting that the self-help movement is part of some kind of conspiracy, but there is little question that it has taken hold of the American psyche and is hanging on for dear life. I have explained how it got into our collective consciousness and in our schools. One of the reasons it has stayed there is that so many people have so much invested in it that they are unwilling to give it up. But academics are not the only ones at fault here. How self-esteem has insinuated itself into our lives despite the evidence against it is at least partly the result of what can only be called either willful ignorance or a deception of truly massive proportions.

The Big Lie

Of all the studies of self-esteem and its role in public policy, the California Task Force on Self-Esteem probably produced the most comprehensive. This task force was created in 1986 by several members of the California legislature to study self-esteem and demonstrate the importance of it in virtually all aspects of society and education. The sum of $245,000 was appropriated by the task force for implementation of its provisions. The task force, in a state bill, defended the use of self-esteem as a concept central to public policy by arguing the following: Californian society is afflicted with a number of serious social problems that the government alone cannot fix; it is the government's duty nonetheless to address these problems in the most cost-efficient way possible; low self-esteem "may well have a wide-ranging, negative influence on individual human conduct" and that therefore "human costs and the costs to government (to solve these problems) could be reduced by raising the self-esteem level of our citizenry."[25]

The legislation also stated that "it is incumbent upon all Californians, in order to promote the exercise of responsible citizenship, to . . . explore . . . environments which are most conducive to the development of high self-esteem."[26] The bill listed the specific goals and functions of the task force: to establish the relationship between self-esteem and various social and education problems (note that there is already an assumption that *there is* a relationship); disseminate this information to the public, and recommend legislation and public and private initiatives that utilize this information to address those problems.

One of the task force organizers, then Assemblyman John Vasconcellos, called self-esteem part of a "social vaccine" designed to cure many of the major social ills of contemporary society.[27] The task force chairperson, Andrew Mecca, argued that the report "demonstrated that self-esteem may well be the unifying concept to reframe American problem-solving."[28] Indeed, it is clear that the task force took this issue very seriously and very personally. Vasconcellos states that his desire to create the task force grew partly out of his personal struggle to develop his own self-esteem, and he notes with apparent satisfaction that the task force "has already served to legitimate self-esteem as a crucial factor in our lives" and has "moved self-esteem from an object of Garry Trudeau's satire to a subject widely and deservedly respected."[29] In 1990 Trudeau wrote several strips on the California task force satirizing the group's promotion of self-esteem—despite all the evidence against it. In one series* the task force is shown describing its findings to an audience. One panel has the moderator asking for questions and an observer says, "I notice buried in your report a statement from the professor who reviewed all the reasearch. He says, 'the associations between self-esteem and its expected consequences are mixed, insignficant or absent.'" And the observer continues: "In light of that, isn't it possible that self-esteem isn't causal at all, but simply the happy side effect of a sturdy character, itself the product of unambiguous moral educa-

---

* Garry Trudeau, *Doonesbury*, Thursday February. 22, 1990.

tion?" The final panel has the moderator calling for security, mumbling that his interrogator must be from out of state. "Just asking," the man says.

Trudeau shows just how foolish the task force looked, trying to promote its findings, which turned out to be groundless. And the fact that Vasconcellos uses the term "legitimate" in his comments illustrates just how eager the task force was to convince the public of the meaning and importance of its work. The fact that he employed the term "legitimate" suggests that the agenda was already determined before the research was completed. This was not to be an objective study of the function and effects of self-esteem but an exercise in proving the importance of self-esteem.

Indeed, the resulting book that includes all the research is entitled *The Social Importance of Self-Esteem*. The only problem is that the title and the contents don't match. The book was written by several social scientists—all experts in their fields—to document the correlation between self-esteem and the following social problems: welfare dependency, teenage pregnancy, drug and alcohol abuse, poor scholastic performance, child abuse, and criminal activity. The task force depended on the researchers to find a causal connection between self-esteem and these problems, namely, that low self-esteem is responsible for them and therefore high self-esteem can resolve them. The results would then form the basis for new social policy initiatives. Unhappily for the task force, the researchers' findings were not exactly what they had expected.

The Truth

Overall, the researchers found that there was a "non-relationship" between low self-esteem and teenage pregnancy, child abuse, alcoholism, drug abuse, or chronic welfare dependency. Regarding alcohol and drug abuse, for example, one researcher writes that although "there is a logical relationship between one's level of self-esteem and membership in groups, cultures and families . . . there is a paucity of empirical evidence linking the two" and that this problem is exacerbated by the difficulty in accurately defining self-esteem.[30] He notes that from a sociodemographic point of view, self-esteem can only be indirectly related to drug or alcohol problems[31] and that sociocultural theories in general illustrate "little direct linkage with self-esteem."[32] His overall conclusion is that "there is a paucity of good research, especially studies that could link the abuse of alcohol and drugs with self-esteem."[33]

With respect to welfare dependency, the researchers note that "the widely held assumption that low self-esteem has predictable behavioral consequences that are necessarily associated with low motivation or lack of initiative or social responsibility is not supported by the empirical literature"[34] and that "evidence suggests some individuals with low and moderate levels of self-esteem may be more driven, competitive, and motivated than individuals with high self-esteem."[35] The chapter on crime and violence showed similar results: "The vast body of quantitative studies does not establish level of self-esteem as a cause of crime and violence."[36] In fact, the chapter's authors go out of their way to make their point (italics in original): "*Even reviewers who are completely sympathetic to the intentions of the quantitative studies acknowledge that these studies have produced no results*"[37] and they ask: "How many inconclusive studies will be conducted before basic premises are examined?"[38] These statements are as forceful as any I have seen in academic research on any issue.

In the chapter called "Self-Esteem and Failure in School" author Martin Covington, who has written extensively on self-esteem, found himself forced to admit that it has little apparent relevance or use in education. Covington writes that although some relationship may exist between self-esteem and academic achievement, the findings are "of little more than circumstantial value in making a case for causation or for the direction of any causal relationship"[39] and they generally indicate a "low magnitude of association . . . between self-esteem and achievement."[40] Similarly, the research that has been used to demonstrate that intentional (manipulated) changes in self-concept lead to improved performance "is somewhat contradictory and the effects of the manipulation are typically short-lived."[41] Covington's meta-analysis of studies of achievement and self-esteem in school is, in fact, quite unambiguous. He notes that self-esteem is typically poorly defined, difficult to measure, and therefore of little use in understanding the causes of academic success and failure.

Covington also points out that there are many puzzles in the literature on self-esteem that have no apparent solutions. If, for example, high self-esteem promotes achievement, "and if noteworthy accomplishments increase esteem even more, then why should there be so little relationship between a sense of personal satisfaction in school and grade point average?"[42] Why does failure seem to actually motivate some students, when self-esteem theory tells us otherwise? Covington poses these and other questions that are part of the conundrum of self-esteem. He asks the questions that the evidence begs: "If feelings of self-esteem are so important to achievement, then why is the demonstrated relationship between self-esteem and academic performance so uniformly low? On the face of this evidence alone, would we be better advised to concentrate our limited educational resources on potentially more effective and more immediate ways to offset educational failure, such as teaching improved study habits or increasing the amount of time students spend on a task?"[43] The answer must be a resounding yes!

These results must have shocked and disappointed the members of the task force, who were counting on the studies to prove "the social importance" of self-esteem. Nonetheless, one would assume that, in publishing the results, they would be obliged to acknowledge that lack of self-esteem or low self-esteem is not the underlying cause of all these social problems, but a tangential issue at best. But the task force was clearly made of stern stuff and was not going to allow a group of researchers to stand in the way of their plan to use self-esteem as the basis of public policy in California.

The task force, in its final report, makes a couple of rather interesting comments. They reassure the reader that "we who served on the Task Force were determined that our findings and recommendations would be grounded in the most current and valid research available, including lay experience and anecdotal wisdom."[44] But then they add that "many of us on the Task Force are convinced that a sizable number of practitioners in functioning programs are well ahead of academic researchers in their appreciation of self-esteem's central role in the social problems that plague our society."[45] The problem is that these statements are contradictory. Did the task force rely on the best research or on anecdotal (unproven) evidence? The task force effectively undermined the whole research enterprise, suggesting that practitioners (teachers and others) really know more about self-esteem than any researchers.

The reason for this contradiction becomes clear in the final report. The task force admits that Neil Smelser, editor of *The Social Importance of Self-Esteem*, "contends that the variable of self-esteem remains elusive because it is so difficult to pinpoint scientifically."[46] And the writers admit that no consistently accepted definition of self-esteem exists, making it difficult to compare different studies, and that "as a result, our researchers felt unable to establish *causal* relationships."[47] They go on to say, however, that research indicates "correlations" between self-esteem and the various social problems and that "just because the causality chain is incomplete with regard to self-esteem, it does not mean that it is implausible."[48] Unfortunately, the longer the task force goes on like this, the more absurd their pronouncements begin to sound, and the reader can clearly see what is happening. The researchers did not produce the results the task force was looking for, and so they undermine their own researchers' efforts by saying that practitioners know better than researchers.

If this were all there was to it—some politicians trying to save face by undermining research they commissioned—it would be unfortunate and embarrassing but little more. But their bad faith apparently infected some of the researchers, too. Neil Smelser in his introduction to *The Social Importance of Self-Esteem* joins the chorus, insisting that we all intuitively know how important self-esteem is and that "it is really not necessary to create a special California task force on the subject to convince us."[49] Despite his own findings, Smelser goes along with the task force and claims that "low self-esteem is the causally prior factor in individuals seeking out kinds of behavior that become social problems."[50]

To support this contention, Smelser suggests that all the research in the book *he* edited might have been flawed and therefore correlations between self-esteem and social problems and education would not be found. For example, he notes that because measuring self-esteem is difficult, some of the research results could be questioned. Smelser offers a number of reasons why the research might be flawed, but we should take his criticisms with a grain of salt because, first, the researchers convened to study the issue (*including* Neil Smelser) were all respected experts in their field. Second, their conclusions were drawn not just from their own work but from an analysis of years of work by others. Can *all* those studies be flawed? Are *all* the researchers wrong? I leave the reader to decide this for herself.

At this point the Alice in Wonderland effect sets in: the world appears normal at first, but the more one delves into things, the stranger they look. Everyone talks as if self-esteem means something, yet where's the evidence? Where is the substance? Where is the meaning? People deny things they themselves write, and then say it wasn't necessary to write it in the first place! And to make matters worse, the task force members, despite all the evidence against their pet idea, seem to have exerted great influence over the public and academics, as well as other policymakers.

Future teachers certainly seem to have absorbed the message. A question on the survey I gave to several classes of future teachers asked whether they believe that high self-esteem helps reduce social problems like juvenile crime, teenage pregnancy, and drug abuse—the same question that the task force researchers were investigating. Seventy-four percent said they did, and most wrote that feeling good about oneself would help one resist peer pressure and make responsible decisions. However, a minority seemed to have seen through the myths of self-esteem. One respondent wrote that "lately, there appears to be a 'culture' of self-aggrandizement . . . unrelated to accomplishment or social concern" and another noted with considerable acuity that "it depends on one's self-identification. A person can feel like the greatest thief . . . or the greatest Drugee [*sic*] ever."

Overall, the task force succeeded in accomplishing what it set out to do. Vasconcellos notes in his preface to the book that their work "seems to have provided permission for many individual Californians to initiate their own endeavors to promote self-esteem" and has "served to legitimate the notion of self-esteem as a respectable focus of concern and analysis."[51] Apparently that was the goal from the beginning, and nothing, not science, not logic—and certainly not the truth—was going to stand in their way.

The influence of this task force and its proclamations on self-esteem have been incalculable, although one can get an idea of the impact by perusing the appendixes to the final report. The appendixes list individuals, agencies, resources, and programs in California dedicated to the promotion, preservation, and practice of self-esteem in a variety of contexts, and it includes everything from counseling groups for Latino girls to twelve-step programs for adult children of alcoholics—and everything in between. A few examples of these programs give an idea of the various guises of self-esteem.

The section on available programs includes "Creative-Mind Life Control Training" or "Women Who Love Unwisely" and, for educators, "Astra's Magic Math" and "Self-Science: The Subject Is Me"—one of Daniel Goleman's favored projects. A very comprehensive list of self-help books includes such titles as "What You Think of Me Is None of My Business"; "Vulture, a Modern Allegory on the Art of Putting Oneself Down"; "Transforming Education: The New Three R's" (I'm afraid to ask), and "Unicorns Are Real; A Right-Brained Approach to Learning." The individuals listed as resources (experts on self-esteem) sound just as intriguing and include a "human potential specialist" (also listed as a poet, presumably in case one has low literary, as well as low personal, self-esteem), a motivational speaker (no surprise there), a "stress consultant," and sundry educators, psychologists, and psychotherapists. Finally, the section on books and other resources includes an audiotape, made by none other than John Vasconcellos, called "Politics for Growing Humans," which "addresses the need for a more humanistic, integrated approach to politics. Assemblyman Vasconcellos speaks to leadership, economic perspectives, and the need for all Californians to acknowledge their responsibility as co-creators of a healthier state."[52]

All this would be quite amusing if it weren't so depressing and if the consequences weren't so serious. It is no laughing matter that Vasconcellos et al. used this report to try to legislate self-esteem into the lives of Californians. It took me some time to realize that the title of the final report, *Toward a State of Esteem*, with the drawing of the state on the cover is doubtless meant to be taken literally. The task force clearly intended California to actually become a state in which self-esteem is the concept around which public policy revolves, and all the available evidence indicates that they are well on their way to succeeding. Their influence has spread far beyond the Golden State, however, to the rest of the nation and beyond. Their pronouncements are cited everywhere in popular magazines, books, and academic articles on self-esteem. Despite the inevitable cracks about how this is just the kind of thing that flourishes in California—and it is—a browse through the Internet or a glance in any bookstore shows that the self-esteem and self-help movements are alive and well all over the country.

What is most disturbing about all this is the hypocrisy involved. The final report issued by the task force gives the impression that self-esteem is everything they hoped it would be and more. There is little reference to the researchers' conclusions in *The Social Importance of Self-Esteem* that in fact self-esteem has little or no educational, social, or public policy value whatsoever. And since few members of the education profession or the public are likely to wade through this weighty document, all most people know about self-esteem is what they read in the final report or, more likely, what they get from second- and third-hand versions of the report in the media or from friends. In our willingness to believe, we have been truly led down the garden path—with some devastating results.

"Why Isn't 'Phonetic' Spelled the Way It Sounds?"

If the self-esteem movement had only marginal influence in education, it would not be something we would need to worry about. But today it influences virtually all aspects of public schooling, from teaching methods to curriculum and evaluation. And it seems that the more important the aspect of education, the more it is corrupted by the ideology of self-esteem. Nowhere is this more visible, and more tragic, than in the area of language and literacy, the very foundation of a liberal education.

When I was in elementary school in Canada in the 1960s, teachers began implementing a program called Initial Teaching Alphabet (ITA), designed to help kids learn to read. Instead of teaching kindergartners the alphabet as it actually is, ITA had its own alphabet, which combined sounds to create a phonetically based language. English, of course, is not very phonetic; the pronunciation and the spelling of a word are often very different, unlike Spanish, for example. It reminds me of an *I Love Lucy* episode in which the difference between English and Spanish became evident to Ricky when he tried to read a children's book to Little Ricky. The book contained a number of words that look the same but are pronounced differently: rough, bough, cough, through, and so on, and Ricky's attempts to pronounce them are some of the most memorable and hilarious moments of that show. In the end he gave it up, deciding the whole thing was too difficult. I don't know whether the inventors of ITA had seen the same show, but they had evidently absorbed the same message: English is just too darn hard, so let's change it! Let's make it easy.

The subheading at the beginning of this section is something I recently saw on a billboard advertising Mexican beer. What it has to do with beer escapes me, but the question it poses is one of those imponderables. The answer, of course, to why "phonetic"—or any other word for that matter—is spelled differently than it sounds, is that (without examining the etymology of every word) there is no answer. It is just the way English is. But rather than teach the language as it really is, some educators, in their wisdom, decided to change the spelling to make it easier. The rationale, of course, is that if children are forced to learn real English, which is indeed quite difficult, they might start to feel bad about themselves. Kids taking ITA thus learned to read (if you can call it that) by spelling words incorrectly, but in a way that could be easily sounded out. As a child, I had already mastered the fundamentals of reading using a phonics book at home (more on phonics in a minute), but just to be sure I wasn't going to be confused by ITA, my parents enrolled me for kindergarten in a school where ITA was not taught. When I returned the following year to my local school, my English was strong enough so that I was not overly influenced by it.

For some of my friends who stayed in the class, however, the following years were nothing less than a nightmare. They had to gradually unlearn this false alphabet and begin to learn English for the first time. Consequently they mastered English much later than those of us who had not been made to learn ITA. An even more serious consequence is that many are still, to this day, poor spellers, even though most are educated professional people who hold responsible jobs. But their early indoctrination into ITA was so profound that they were never able to completely rid themselves of it. Now if one were to read about this in a newspaper, one would think it was a type of indoctrination imposed by a dictator on his people, for as we all know, the best way to control people is to keep them illiterate. But like everything relating to the self-esteem movement, it was done "with the children's best interests" in mind.

Although ITA may sound like an isolated example of a kind of temporary madness that overcame educators, it is neither the only nor the most damaging effect of the self-esteem movement on language acquisition. That honor is reserved for "whole language learning." This is the idea that reading is best taught by, in effect, not teaching at all. The underlying assumption is that children learn to read in the same way they learn to speak: by being in a literate environment. Children learn to speak by being spoken to and by hearing language all around them on a daily basis. The rationale regarding reading, then, is that if they are surrounded by books and other written materials, they will learn to read in much the same way. Rather than teach children the basics of language by breaking it down into phonemes, or manageable pieces they can sound out, children are given "literature" while teachers sit back and wait for them to figure out how to read all by themselves. Yet the overwhelming evidence indicates that learning how to read is *not* the same process as learning to speak. Reading requires instruction.

Like many ideas born of the self-esteem movement, whole language learning started out with a germ of good sense and then went out of control. It was invented as an alternative to the often very dull and dry way reading had been taught for decades, phonics. The phonics method teaches children to sound out words, beginning with the alphabet and then gradually putting words together: a, at, cat, sat, and so on. The books that were used to teach this were often excruciatingly boring stories of a boy, a girl, and their dog (usually imaginatively named "Fido" or "Spot"). Not only were these primers boring, but they were frequently sexist and racist as well. Girls were often portrayed as foolish and subservient, and people of color were not portrayed at all (or only as "savages" of some kind). Educators thus decided that there had to be a better way to get children interested in reading, primarily through giving them real books to read, rather than unreal stories of plastic people.

Whole language was right to throw out the boring primers. Why should kids be forced to read them when there is a wealth of fine literature available? But the reading reformers didn't stop there and decided to throw out the method (phonics) too. The reason? Making children learn language in a logical, sequential way was considered oppressive because, again, if children have to struggle a little, their self-esteem might suffer. Instead they should be "experiencing" language, enjoying it, even making up their own language ("invented spelling," the contemporary version of ITA, is a key part of all this) until they somehow manage to pick up English.[53]

The extent to which whole language learning was embraced by the academic community and thence by teachers in the 1980s and early 1990s cannot be overemphasized. Until very recently anyone who ventured to suggest that phonics is still the best foundation for teaching reading was regarded as ill informed or worse—*uncaring*. For whole language learning is the icon of what self-esteem is about: making education a therapeutic and caring experience rather than a deliberately demanding intellectual one. But the tide is now turning because whole language has been demonstrated to be an utter failure. Children are not learning to read unassisted but are still struggling with the basics in the fifth and sixth grades and even later. At Fern Bacon Basic Middle School, for example, in Sacramento, California, where 80 percent of students read at fourth-grade level or below, teachers are using flashcards to teach thirteen- and fourteen-year-olds basic English.[54] But those who are not fortunate enough to have teachers who care that they don't read may never become truly literate. Although the home environment, poverty, poor libraries, and overcrowded classrooms can all seriously affect a child's reading skills, whole language drives the last nail into the coffin. Instead of helping children to read *despite* such hurdles, we have thrown another hurdle in their way—one that can be insurmountable.

The crisis in reading has become so severe that it has captured national attention and legislatures, school districts, and parents across the country have initiated efforts to remedy the problem, which has now reached epidemic proportions. The most recent national assessment of reading found that 20 percent of fourth-graders read too poorly to keep up in school.[55] California, which helped lead the charge into whole language learning, is seriously failing its children. More than 100,000 third-graders in southern California failed to achieve grade-level reading in the spring of 1998, and about two-thirds of those could not read at all—they were completely illiterate.[56]

California provides an interesting case study of the rise and fall of the whole language movement and its effects on our children.[57] In 1987 the state officially adopted whole language as the favored method of teaching reading and in 1989 California reading test scores for third- and sixth-graders fell after years of steady improvement. The state's response? The testing program was killed. In 1993 California failed reading on the National Assessment of Educational Progress (NAEP); only Guam, the District of Columbia, and Mississippi scored below California, the richest state in the nation. In 1995 a task force was established to examine the reading issue and the state, finally assuming its responsibility, demanded that textbook publishers include more attention to phonics. In September of that year the task force declared that there was indeed a reading crisis, and in September 1996 Governor Pete Wilson signed legislation authorizing more money for reading texts that emphasized phonics and for teacher retraining. In addition, funds were provided to reduce class size in the early grades to no more than twenty students. In December 1996 the State Board of Education selected new reading textbooks, rejecting some hitherto popular whole language books.

Other states and school districts across the country are also reinventing or reintroducing phonics. In Houston, for example, a uniform teaching strategy has been imposed on all 280 schools in the district, focusing on a basic-skills approach to reading.[58] Changes in teaching reading necessitate reforms in teacher education, and the Maryland State Board of Education recently passed new reading course requirements for elementary and secondary instructors.[59] And the changes are beginning to show results. Reading scores were up in several states in the latest NAEP; in both Maryland and Texas the percentage of fourth-grade students who scored at or above proficiency level rose from 24 percent in 1992 to 29 percent in 1998.[60] California has shown slight improvement from 1994 but still has a long way to go.

Changes are taking place in other countries too as a response to the failure of whole language learning. A researcher in Canada, alarmed at the worsening results of reading tests and the increasing numbers of children being labeled "reading disabled," studied the effects of a British method of teaching reading called "Jolly Phonics" and found it to be very successful. It has now been adopted by three education authorities in the Toronto area. The researcher, Professor Dale Willows of the Ontario Institute for Studies in Education, notes that "for the past 20 years in Canada, teachers have accepted the fallacy that reading is a natural process just like learning to talk. . . . Twenty years of research have now shown us that this appealing idea is wrong. We need to teach reading and writing."[61] And Jolly Phonics isn't the only game in town. Phonics has become big business for reading entrepreneurs, who are jumping on the bandwagon and selling phonics books and games at record rates.[62]

In England, as in the United States and Canada, concern over low test scores has made literacy a new priority. A "crusade" to promote reading, the National Literacy Framework, has been launched, which requires that students first be taught phonics.[63] And New Zealand, which led the worldwide promotion of whole language instruction, has been forced to admit its abject failure and return to phonics. In 1970 New Zealand's children scored first in the world on an international test of reading. But whole language learning caught on shortly thereafter. Marie M. Clay, an Auckland child psychologist, toured the United States promoting her views on how children just "emerge" as readers and a New Zealand publisher made a fortune selling 85 million books around the world based on this idea.[64]

By the 1990s teachers across the United States were hooked on whole language, rather than phonics, and were paying New Zealand consultants $3,000 a day for the privilege of unlearning everything they knew about reading.[65] Sadly, New Zealanders, like Americans, began to feel the fallout from the whole language revolution. In 1996 the New Zealand government's Educational Review Office warned that eight out of ten high school students in one area of Auckland were illiterate. University researchers found that 90 percent of working-class children in other areas were up to three grade levels behind.[66] And in the worst embarrassment of all, New Zealand's ten-year-olds fell from first to sixth place in the most recent international rankings of reading skills.[67]

Despite the incontrovertible evidence of the failure of whole language teaching, however, some professors and teachers are loath to part with it. Many still defend it, arguing that its apparent failure is due not to the philosophy behind it but the ways in which it has been implemented. A few reluctantly admit that some phonics may be necessary while continuing to defend whole language, "invented spelling," and other bright ideas. But the most absurd example of the extremes to which some people will go to avoid the strain of teaching English can be found in an article in the journal *English Leadership Quarterly* that urges teachers to make intentional errors in English as "the only way to end its oppression of linguistic minorities and learning writers." Think that's bad? The article (written in oppressively good English, notes one observer) won an award from the journal, a publication of the National Council of Teachers of English.[68]

The long and the short of all this is as follows. First, there is absolutely no evidence that teaching phonics (or any other necessary skills, for that matter) is damaging to children's self-esteem. On the contrary, if given the tools to read as early as possible, children will experience success in reading and in all academic areas—the surest foundation for building self-confidence. Second, there is no reason to use uninteresting materials to teach phonics. We are fortunate today in having a wealth of instructional materials and literature that can make learning to read fun and exciting. And third, the consequences if we don't teach children phonics are simply too great. If you wonder whether little Johnny's self-esteem might suffer a blow if he is challenged by phonics, imagine how damaged his self-image will be when he finds himself in high school illiterate. There is simply no excuse for *not* teaching children to read.

Now for Something *Really* Oppressive: Ebonics

Whole-language learning is dangerous, but at least it does not discriminate: It is as damaging to white kids as it is to black kids. But leave it to educational researchers to dream up—again, in the name of equality and self-esteem—an even more outrageous notion of teaching reading that discriminates against the very individuals it claims to help: African-American children. It is Ebonics, a word created from "ebony" and "phonics," and it refers to the notion of allowing black children to learn Standard English through their own vernacular, or what is known in some quarters as Black English. It is a debate that raged throughout 1996 and 1997 and then died down somewhat, but its implications for the nation's literacy, particularly the literacy of minority students, is profound.

The firestorm over Ebonics was ignited by a resolution passed in December 1996, by the Oakland, California school board, recognizing Ebonics as a valid language system. Part of the goal of the resolution was to have more teachers participate in California's Standard English Proficiency program (SEP), which trains teachers to understand the structure of Black English and how it differs from Standard English. The SEP program began in Oakland in 1981 but until 1996 had been strictly voluntary. The impetus for the move to broaden the program was the very low achievement levels of African-American students in the Oakland school system. Although they constitute 53 percent of the students enrolled in the only predominantly black school district in California, African-American children account for 80 percent of the school system's suspensions. Seventy-one percent of these students were classified as having special needs. Their average grade was a D+.[69]

The resolution called for the implementation of educational programs in which teachers would focus on the nature and history of Black English, or Ebonics. Teachers would themselves be educated in the principles of African language systems and instruct children both in their "native language" and in English. The idea was that through their understanding of the "first language," so to speak, they could help black students improve their reading and writing skills.[70] The resolution is very explicit, describing Ebonics as a "genetically based" language system with origins in West and Niger-Congo African languages, and not as an English dialect.[71] The resolution also notes that other states have recognized the "unique language structure of African-American pupils" and that the interests of equal opportunity would be served by recognition of Ebonics, just as we acknowledge the needs of other students "whose primary languages are other than English" by offering them bilingual education.[72]

The resolution instantly became front page news, and the fight was on between those who felt that teaching Ebonics was a way to give struggling African-American students help in making the transition to Standard English and thereby improving their school achievement, and those who argued that there is no such thing as Black English; that it is at best a dialect of Standard English and at worst a corruption of it. Pretty much everyone who was anyone on the left and right put in their two cents' worth, but the lineup on each side was not exactly what one might have expected. The Reverend Jesse Jackson of the Rainbow Coalition, NAACP chief Kweisi Mfume, and poet Maya Angelou joined with such conservative luminaries as William Bennett, George Will, and even Rush Limbaugh to criticize the Oakland decision.[73]

One observer contends that this strange alliance can be at least partly attributed to the media's tendency to polarize the issue, misrepresenting the position of the Oakland school board and equating Black English with slang.[74] Not only the media: Jesse Jackson was quoted as saying that "while we are fighting in California trying to extend affirmative action . . . in Oakland some madness has erupted over making slang talk a second language."[75] The National Head Start Association also weighed in on the issue in an unexpected way, running an ad in the *New York Times* with a figure of a man meant to represent Martin Luther King, symbolically turning his back on Ebonics with the words "I Has a Dream" superimposed on him.[76] (The association was unhappy with the ad after it came out, however, and claimed that its own board never approved it.)[77]

The debate continued for a year after the Oakland decision, and in early 1997 the school board amended the resolution. It maintained that Ebonics is not simply a dialect of English but stopped short of suggesting that Ebonics is genetically based. In addition, the resolution no longer insisted that students be taught in their "primary language," Ebonics, but called for the district to implement programs that move children from the language patterns they acquire at home toward English proficiency at school.[78] And although in California a school board member introduced a bill to expand language programs for African-American students in Los Angeles, lawmakers in Massachusetts and Virginia have introduced bills to prohibit public schools from teaching Ebonics.[79]

Although the initial furor over Ebonics has subsided, the fires of debate are likely to be reignited at any time, essentially because it touches on some of the most controversial issues in education: language differences, bilingualism, race, equality, and achievement. I am not going to weigh in on the question of whether or not Ebonics is a language. The interesting point here is the underlying rationale for it: that black students need to be addressed in the speech that they use outside the school in order to feel good about themselves. This is really self-esteem at its worst, for whether or not Black English qualifies as a language, young African Americans need to learn Standard English in order to succeed in this country. Encouraging them to speak and write a nonstandard form will help them neither in school nor in the workforce.

To compound matters, many of these students come from some of the most impoverished communities in America and therefore need and deserve the best education we can offer them. Standard English is the cornerstone of that education. As one observer writes, "(Ebonics) directs us

away from the problem—the poor academic performance of black children—by emphasizing self-esteem and weak racial identity as the root
causes of the problem" and concludes that "now we no longer have students with academic deficits; we have racial victims, identity victims."[80] Instead of creating victims we should be helping young people develop real
self-esteem by helping them raise their expectations and their achievement. And it is certain that teaching a nonstandard language like Ebonics
does not help us do that. In this respect it is no different from invented
spelling or ITA: Both encourage the acquisition of, if not a false language,
a language that is not in general currency.

As is often the case when it comes to doing the right thing by our kids, it
is the kids themselves who steer us in the right direction. Shortly after the
Oakland resolution was passed, TV reporters interviewed the potential
subjects of Ebonics: Oakland's black students. And although a couple of
TV interviews cannot be considered a representative sampling of opinions, the responses were unanimous. "We need to learn Standard English,"
they said repeatedly. "If we want to go to college or get a job, we need to
learn how to write properly." The kids know what they need. Why don't
the educators? The answer is sadly obvious. These children have not (yet)
been completely indoctrinated into the self-esteem movement. They still
know what's what. And in their readiness to doubt the wisdom of Ebonics,
they show us what real wisdom, and real education, is all about.

6

Practicing Self-Esteem

Magic, Myths, and Masquerades

Headmasters have powers at their disposal with
which Prime Ministers have never yet been invested.
—Winston Churchill[1]

IN REVOLUTION FROM WITHIN: A BOOK OF SELF-ESTEEM Gloria Steinem traces the history of self-esteem, noting that the phrase "selfe-esteem" can be found in the 1600s in English literature[2] and that similar concepts have been popular in a variety of societies perhaps as far back as 2500 B.C.[3] For most of its history, however, self-esteem has been a peripheral concept in societies and not the "organizing principle" of public life that the California task force recently hailed it. Even in this century it was balanced, until recently, with a sense of shared community and responsibility.

In its early days, then, self-esteem posed little threat to the integrity of the public school system. The schools' increasing emphasis on self-awareness, self-esteem, and self-gratification was still balanced by an expectation that these other values would be upheld. Today, however, the self-esteem movement has so insinuated itself into the policies and practices of schools that their very purpose has been completely transformed. The very notion of a *public* school, that is, a school to serve the needs of the public, the community, and the nation, has been subverted by the apparently innocuous notion of helping kids feel good.

"Now You See It, Now You Don't"

One of the reasons that self-esteem is such a powerful concept is that although it permeates virtually all areas of schooling, few people are currently aware of its influence. It is embedded in a variety of school policies and practices that further the ideology of the self-esteem movement but make no obvious mention of it. Today almost all aspects of public schooling, including evaluation, standards, expectations, curriculum, and class environment reflect the goals of the self-esteem movement. This is no accident but the ultimate goal of self-esteem advocates. As one of them writes, "Whatever else schools do, effective learning cannot take place until all areas of the curriculum—instructional methods, student evaluation, subject-matter selection, scheduling, room topography, learning climate, everything—make self esteem consistently possible. Without such conditions, education in America and around the world will remain a human wasteland."[4]

Self-esteem policies promote the worst in political correctness. Evaluation is no longer intended to provide feedback on progress but to make the kids feel good, even if that means deceiving them about their true ability and achievement. Curriculum must be organized around student interests; whether or not they are actually learning what they need to learn no longer matters. And the class environment must emphasize cooperation, never competition, so that all believe themselves to be winners.

This is the remarkable sleight of hand that the self-esteem movement has been able to pull off. It has transformed the very mission of the public school to serve the individual at the cost of quality, standards, and the public interest without anyone getting wise to it. The public school is being transformed from a vehicle for public education to a vehicle for mass indoctrination into a very damaging set of ideas. Educators have a term for this sort of thing: the "hidden curriculum." We usually think of curriculum as what is expressly taught in schools and defined in state standards. Formal course requirements, standard texts, and examinations are all examples of the "manifest" curriculum: what kids are *officially* learning in school. Learning is determined by other things as well, however, including teacher attitudes and expectations, the relationship between teachers and administrators, the physical environment of the class (are the walls falling down? is there heat and air conditioning? is students' work displayed?), how girls and minorities are represented in class materials, and so on. This is what is known as the hidden curriculum.

There is no question that the ideology of the self-esteem movement is part of the hidden curriculum. The fact that, as far as I know, it has never been identified as such up to now is undoubtedly because it is so interwoven with our expectations and beliefs regarding public schools that it is *really* hidden—kind of the secret basement of the hidden curriculum. Even those of us who claim to "get" what schools are all about are deceived by it, just like everybody else.

"Positive" Discipline, "Constructivist" Teaching, and Other Marvels, I–IV

Where there is a fad there is money to be made, and bookstore shelves are bursting not only with the usual adult self-help books but countless teacher manuals on how to promote self-esteem in schools. Some of these books can be easily identified by their titles, which usually include the words "self-esteem" or "self-concept." Much of the time, however, one needs to either be a good sleuth or be already familiar with the jargon of self-esteem to ferret them out. Words like "positive discipline," "constructivist teaching," and "authentic assessment" signal that the work is self-esteem based or oriented.

Publications for elementary and middle school teachers often include a variety of games and activities, whereas those intended for secondary school instructors include more sophisticated exercises along with discussion and explanation of the role of self-esteem in the learning process. On the face of it they appear relatively harmless, and some contain sensible suggestions on building cooperation or stress the importance of service to others. But for the most part the activities only serve to emphasize a narcissistic, emotivist, and separatist view of the world.

One of these manuals, *Self-Esteem and Conflict-Solving Activities for Grades 4–8*, by Beth Teolis, is a good example. She identifies the components of self-esteem as security, positive identity, friendship building, goal setting, and competence, based on another program of esteem building.[5] Another author identifies the goals of self-esteem a little differently for grades 7–12, but the same elements are there. In *Self-Awareness Growth Experiences (SAGE)* author V. Alex Kehayan tells the reader that the purpose of his book is to "facilitate the personal and social development" of students in grades 7–12 and he identifies eight primary goals or skills to be developed: self-awareness, self-esteem, social interaction, problem-solving and decision making, coping ability, ethical standards, independent functioning, and creativity.[6] Both authors clearly see self-esteem as a concept that encompasses a variety of skills and attitudes. Teolis also concurs with the California Task Force on Self-Esteem, contending that enhanced self-esteem combats anorexia, drug and alcohol abuse, school

truancy, gang affiliation, gender inequity, and any number of other problems.[7]

Teolis lists a variety of activities designed to promote the components
of self-esteem listed above. Under "positive identity" students are encouraged to look at how they think of themselves, list positive and negative
thoughts, and then try to erase the negative. An example she gives is a student who says, "I am a poor catcher in baseball."[8] According to the author,
it is very bad for the student to say such a thing about himself, even if it is
true, so he must be taught never to say it or even think it. Here we see the
self-deception that is endemic in the self-esteem movement: denying reality through "positive talk." But avoiding the truth about oneself or the
world is never a good idea and is a very bad idea for kids in school, since it
is only by recognizing our limitations and failures that we can experience—and appreciate—real success.

To be fair, however, Teolis suggests more worthwhile pursuits in other
sections of the book. The section on competence includes an activity designed to help children withstand peer pressure and the temptations that
go along with it, like drug use, gang involvement, and sexual activity, in a
discussion reminiscent of the California Task Force on Self-Esteem.[9] It
also includes a critical-thinking exercise that encourages students to weigh
both sides of an argument in a controversial issue before making up their
mind about it.[10] What it does not include, however, is a suggestion that
one answer may be better than another, and how to get there. That would
be imposing a value judgment on an issue, which is something self-esteem
advocates avoid like the plague. Self-esteem devotees consider everyone—
and everyone's opinion—just as good as anyone else's, and thus the very
notion of analyzing an idea for its veracity, morality, or logic is out of the
question. This is one of the most serious problems with the self-esteem
movement because it threatens to undermine our collective allegiance to
certain basic values, without which the very essence of a civilized society is
at risk.

I: How to Succeed in School Without Ever Trying

Another book, *Esteem Builders: A K–8 Self-Esteem Curriculum for Improving Student Achievement, Behavior, and School Climate* by Michele Borba
includes activities similar to those found in Teolis and cites the same resources and "experts": Jack Canfield, Robert Reasoner, and Nathaniel
Branden, along with a few others. It is interesting to note that for all its influence, the world of self-esteem is a small one. All the literature support-

ing self-esteem includes the same ideas, but, as the research reviewed in Chapter 5 illustrated, there is little or no evidence to support them. In her book Borba includes a section designed to get children to focus on themselves: how they look, what they like, what they're good at, and so on. She suggests that children write a commercial about themselves in which they say positive things about their looks, personality, skills, and friendliness. [11] The notion that it is just as rewarding, and a better learning experience, to learn about *other* people is apparently of no interest.

In another section of the book, Borba suggests activities designed to help students identify goals.[12] This is certainly a worthwhile activity, but she emphasizes that they must be "achievable" goals. Self-esteem proponents believe that if the child doesn't reach her goal she will feel bad about herself. Yet as a matter of fact we never know whether our goals are achievable or not, although it is important to be realistic about our abilities. All of us know people with physical or mental disabilities who have gone on to achieve things that one might never have expected. Paraplegic cyclists who participate in marathons are an example.

And one person who comes to my mind is Terry Fox, a young man with cancer who, despite having only one leg, started a run across Canada to raise money for cancer research. Tragically, he made it only part way when he became ill again with cancer and ultimately died. But his incredible bravery, will, and strength of character affected the entire nation. He did not finish his run as he would have liked. But the money and awareness he raised for cancer research and the impression he left upon the nation made a profound impact, and he achieved far more than he probably ever dreamed. Indeed, our ability to achieve our goals is limited only by our imagination.

Setting the bar as low as possible and aiming only for the lowest common denominator may inhibit failure, but it also prevents success. And what it produces in schools is lowered standards, subjective grading, and inaccurate evaluation. Standards and evaluation are complex but very necessary aspects of schooling, without which there is no way to gauge student progress and achievement. But by introducing gradeless report cards, or report cards with numbers instead of letters (that's what they had when I was in school), or dispensing with them altogether, we have no way to determine whether Johnny has learned what he was supposed to. Educators have invented portfolios as a way around this problem, but although they can be useful, they do not, by themselves, provide a complete picture of progress or achievement. Portfolios are a collection of a student's best work in a term or a year and thus are a good measure of progress over time. They provide no information however, on how one student compares to her peers or whether or not she has reached a desired standard, so they have limited value.

To make matters worse, rather than use old-fashioned words like "excellent," "good," "fair," or "poor" (or, heaven forbid, A, B, C, or D) portfolios are typically judged using words like "distinctive," "appropriate," and various other euphemisms that make it virtually impossible to understand just whether Johnny can write or not.[13] Because the words are so vague, each of us will likely interpret them differently. Consequently, it is virtually impossible to obtain either a consensus or a clear understanding on just what Johnny's capabilities and achievements are. The assessors of Vermont's portfolio programs, for example, recently found the scoring reliability "so low that most planned uses of the data had to be abandoned."[14]

Vermont isn't the only state with portfolio problems. A report commissioned by the Kentucky legislature criticized that state's portfolio-based system as being "seriously flawed" and concluded "the public is being misinformed" about statewide results.[15] None of this should come as a surprise. Portfolios were part of an enterprising and well-orchestrated attempt by educators and self-esteem advocates to avoid anything like accurate, objective assessment (things like tests, actual grading, comparing students to a clear standard), and they have succeeded beyond anyone's wildest dreams.

Grading on the curve is another example of distorting grades in the interests of self-esteem. The bell curve represents the idea that, statistically speaking, in any given class, one can expect a few A's, many B's and C+'s, and a few D's or fails. Grading on the curve means that, irrespective of the real scores in the class, the teacher will manipulate the mean so that the grade distribution will look the way it statistically "should." The defense of this practice is usually that if too many students in the class fail or do badly, it won't look good for the school and the students will feel bad about themselves. What it really does, however, is distort everyone's grade, so no one knows how he or she is really doing. The kids who are failing end up being promoted to the next grade, even though they didn't really pass, and if there were "too many" kids who earned an A, some of them will be given a B, just to make the curve look the way the statisticians think it should. This is a terrible idea. The high achievers are cheated out of their rightfully earned grades and the slower students are cheated of knowing what they must work on, and thereby learning what they need. But again, it is all done with the intention of preserving self-esteem.

Once again, self-esteem advocates are doing a great disservice to students in an attempt to shield them from the illusory ill effects of an objective evaluation. Students should not have to be afraid of being evaluated.

Nor should they be afraid of taking risks or being challenged in school. As Margaret M. Clifford, a professor of educational psychology at the University of Iowa writes, the maxim "nothing succeeds like success" has driven educational practice for decades and as a result, success has become the means and the end of education and become a higher priority than learning.[16] To ensure success educators keep standards and expectations low, mistakenly believing that it is more important for kids to experience success than to actually learn something; sadly, it apparently matters little whether or not that success is a fiction.

Research over the last twenty years, however, indicates that children's self-worth relates to their achievement in areas of their life they consider personally important.[17] And we need to remember that real success involves risk. Clifford argues that students need to be able to experience risk in learning because "from every risk-taking endeavor—whether it ends in failure or success—risk takers learn something about their skill and choice of strategy, and what they learn usually prompts them to seek another risk-taking opportunity."[18] She recommends that teachers create an environment in which making errors is considered an acceptable part of learning and suggests that every activity should include 10–20 percent of content that provides a challenge to even the best students.[19] It is one of the great ironies of the self-esteem movement that in trying to protect students from challenge and failure, educators have managed to turn risk taking and the possibility of failure into something shameful.

Some self-esteem proponents go to literally any lengths to ensure "success," even if it means teaching something that is patently false. One observer writes that "ADDING 2 + 2 AND GETTING 5 IS NOT 'WRONG.' If two plus two gets you an answer of five, you've not been 'wrong.' Instead, your behavior, getting an answer of five, *didn't work* in the system of mathematics accepted by society. Whether done in the classroom or making a purchase in a store, adding two plus two and getting five *won't work effectively* for you"(all emphases original).[20] Thus even when an answer contravenes basic mathematical principles, even when it is by any and all measures wrong, it must not be called wrong. Since it would be difficult, if not impossible, to invent a new kind of mathematics, as ITA or invented spelling is substituted for English, the teacher is encouraged to refute basic mathematical truths because someone believes that kids cannot handle being told that if they believe that two plus two is five, they are wrong. What a very low opinion we must have of our young people! The reality is, of course, that the truth, whether about mathematics or about oneself, is never oppressive, however difficult it may be to accept. Truth is liberation from real oppression: ignorance.

Michele Borba in *Esteem Builders* notes quite rightly that it is important for students to feel that they achieve something. Now one would think that in order to develop competence we would simply teach it by ensuring that students master required course material and evaluating them regularly to gauge their progress. Borba argues, however, that for some students a report card is just another reminder of their failure, and she advises that "a student with low competence *must be shown progress in highly concrete terms*"(italics in original).[21] That means breaking down skills into small components so that the slower students can see where they make progress. This is a sensible suggestion that may help motivate some students to continue more challenging tasks. Borba concludes, however, with a warning that these students must only compare themselves to themselves, never to anyone else, since "cross comparisons defeat the purpose of the esteem builder's work."[22]

Antipathy to competition is rife in the self-esteem literature; cooperation is the law of the land. V. Alex Kehayan, for example, refers to competition as something that must be merely "tolerated."[23] The use of the word "tolerate" tells us that he is not exactly thrilled about competition. Self-esteem advocates actively discourage comparison and competition, since they promote an environment in which there is a general recognition that some kids are better than others at certain things. The fact that competition can be a wonderful motivator for students to strive toward something is forgotten.

Take the Olympic Games, for example. They represent the ultimate in competition: the world's best athletes competing for the privilege of being called the best, the fastest, the gold medal winner. Anyone who has participated seriously in competitive sports knows that the possibility of going to the Olympics, indeed, the very existence of the competition, is the best motivator. Competitors know that only a few win, but they also know that they are winners for getting that far, for trying despite the odds and not giving up. And the best ones—Jackie Joyner-Kersee comes to mind—are connected to those who have not won, as well as those who are less fortunate, and are symbols of hope for their communities. Being competitive has not undermined their relationship to their families, their communities, or their countries; on the contrary, it has only deepened it.

Few people suggest there's anything unhealthy about the Olympics; on the contrary, despite the inevitable politicization (and the recent charges that potential host cities tried to bribe Olympic officials) the games are still hailed as an example both of the ideal of excellence in athleticism as well as a healthy outlet for the expression of national pride. Competition is what fuels the economy and, for better or worse, is one of the driving forces of capitalism, of which the United States is the worldwide symbol.

In our working lives, we are compared to others in one way or another on an almost daily basis. Cooperation is a fine thing, but it is competition that drives the nation.

II: Twenty-One and Still in School: The Promise of Social Promotion

The logic (if we can call it that), behind these efforts to dull standards and competition is that effort suggests the possibility of failure as well as success, and failure means low self-esteem, so therefore it is better not to try. (Promoters of self-esteem are presumably unimpressed with the athlete's maxim, "no pain, no gain.") Consequently we have scores of kids who do not have the skills required to complete their grade level and go on to the next. What should be done with them? The sensible answer, of course, would be ensure that all children, starting in kindergarten, possess the necessary skills and knowledge before progressing on to the next grade. If children are held accountable for their learning from the very beginning there is far less chance that they will find themselves hopelessly behind in middle school or high school and then give up on their education altogether.

And if they do need additional help early on, split classes (with two grades in one) can be helpful for the slower students. Another idea is "transition grades" in which students take extra classes during the year and over the summer to help them stay up to grade level so they can progress with their peers, at the same time ensuring that they will have mastered the necessary material.[24] Holding kids back is never an easy decision, but it may sometimes be necessary for the child's educational future. This idea is anathema to self-esteem devotees, however, who contend that holding kids back does irreparable harm to their self-image. Critics of accountability also point out that more minority kids are held back than white kids and that therefore retention is discriminatory. Holding kids back because of race or ethnicity is clearly quite wrong. But that is a reason for *improving* the education of minority kids, giving them the education they deserve, *not* an argument for irresponsibly promoting them to the next grade and letting them slip through the cracks because of some misplaced sense of guilt. Educational psychologists contend that one of a person's basic needs is to fit in with a group. But are their social requirements really always more important than their intellectual ones?

Some apparently believe they are. The authors of a book called *Encouraging Children to Learn: The Encouragement Process* claim that "belonging is the basic need" and that "the significance of belonging deserves more emphasis than it usually receives."[25] They go on to describe the close ties between the formation of self-concept and the need to belong: "Much of the anxiety which influences our personal adjustment is produced because we do not feel we belong; to the extent that we feel inferior, we lack a sense of belonging."[26] One finds versions of this view in much of the literature in educational psychology. The child's emotional state is considered paramount and fragile, and thus academic concerns come second.

This is exactly what the self-esteem movement has done with its relentless defense of social promotion, the practice of passing children on to the next grade for social rather than academic reasons. As a result of it, young people are graduating from high school in record numbers without the skills they need to succeed outside school, but they do not realize this until they are in college or until they can't get a job. Consequently, colleges and universities across the country are forced to provide remedial education in math, English, and other basic courses for students who are not prepared to enter freshman-level classes. It is an epidemic of mediocrity for which the self-esteem movement is largely responsible. (So much for John Vasconcellos's "social vaccine.")

In 1995, almost 100 percent of public two-year institutions and 81 percent of public four-year institutions offered remedial courses. Twenty-nine percent of incoming students that year took at least one remedial course in reading, writing, or mathematics.[27] That is up considerably from the 1992–1993 school year, during which, according to a recent study by the American Council on Education, 13 percent of undergraduates in public and private institutions needed some kind of remedial class.[28] In 1995, at my institution, part of the California State System, a full 47 percent of freshmen were enrolled in remedial English, and 54 percent in remedial math.[29] Those numbers are up from 1990, when about 22 percent of regularly admitted freshmen in the California State System needed remedial math and about 38 percent needed help in English.[30]

Similarly, in 1997, about 50 percent of incoming students in colleges of the City University of New York system required some remediation.[31] Needless to say, both the students and the institutions affected by this are fed up. For the institutions, it is a question of money, space, and reputation, and some are taking steps to end their role as the dumping ground for products of a poor K–12 education. In February 1997 the Board of Trustees of the California State System issued an executive order issuing new requirements for remedial students, which also noted that "campuses are encouraged to establish and enforce limits on remedial/developmental activity."[32] And in the fall of 1998 California lawmakers passed legislation aimed at clamping down on social promotion. The legislation also provided $115 million for remedial programs such as summer school and tutoring for students who are falling behind.[33] In May 1998 the trustees of the City University of New York took similar action and voted to phase out most remedial education beginning in September 1999, changing forever CUNY's historical commitment to a policy of open admissions.[34]

CUNY and the California State System have clearly chosen to try to maintain standards while in some way addressing the needs of unprepared students. The only other option is to abandon standards altogether, which apparently some teachers would prefer. In a recent article on the subject, one teacher is quoted as saying that high schools have done all the adjusting to the "new" (read: unprepared) students but colleges have not and that if a college does not adjust to the realities of the students it gets, it's going to be disappointed, for "there's definitely a difference between what it wants and what it gets."[35] What a brilliant idea: lowering standards so schools don't have to do their job and students can (temporarily, anyway) feel good about themselves. One trembles to think what the next great idea might be.

III: Let's Be Friends: The New Teacher–Student Relation

The classic self-esteem handbook for teachers must be *100 Ways to Enhance Self-Concept in the Classroom: A Handbook for Teachers and Parents* (1976) by Jack Canfield and Harold C. Wells. Jack Canfield has been writing on self-esteem and self-help issues for many years now and is probably best known these days as coauthor of the *Chicken Soup for the Soul* self-help series. Part of the foreword to *100 Ways* was written by John Vasconcellos, late of the California Task Force on Self-Esteem. In it Vasconcellos notes that in 1976, a study of school and community goals revealed that every school and community in California had declared self-esteem one of its primary goals for children,[36] giving us an idea of how strong the movement was even then.

Vasconcellos also writes that we are in the middle of a cultural revolution "from self-denial to self-actualization"[37] and says that this new understanding, and Canfield's book, breaks us "out of our old cultural traps of founding self esteem in having or doing. Those lead to the materialistic and performance mores that are at best substitutional, at worst downright unhealthy for the human."[38] Vasconcellos spells out here (albeit unwittingly) the fundamental principle of self-esteem: *feeling good for no good reason.* The notion that one's worth as a person should be somehow related to character or achievement is rejected outright. According to self-esteem believers, the only meaning is the meaning that comes from within.

I agree with Vasconcellos that material concerns should not affect our estimation of our own self-worth, but the idea that it is not necessary to do anything, be anything, or serve anyone but ourselves to feel good about ourselves is quite shocking. The self-esteem movement is not a revolution. It is more like a terrorist coup that has succeeded in hijacking and destroying all our notions of intellect, character, and community. And as a result, as I discuss in the last chapter, it threatens the very essence of science, progress, and education.

But back to Canfield. He begins the book with some basic principles underlying the idea of self-esteem, along with some general suggestions for teachers. Among these are "accepting pupil contributions without judgment" and "being, in all ways, a friend."[39] These are two of the most popular ideas of the self-esteem movement, and one is as dangerous as the other. Students should never be ridiculed for their class contributions, but neither should they be totally accepted. Students should be challenged to go further in their thinking when they are right and gently directed to a better answer when they are wrong. Total acceptance means stasis; if there is no room for improvement, there is no opportunity to learn.

The idea of teacher as friend, one of the more enduring myths of the self-esteem movement, is just as dangerous. Many parents have unfortunately adopted this idea for themselves, and the idea of parent as friend is also hugely popular. In both cases, the danger is the same. By becoming a child's friend, teachers and parents lose their authority and thereby their ability to direct the child in any pursuit, academic or behavioral. Parents and teachers should be the first leaders in children's lives. Children need our guidance.

And if some parents and teachers don't know this anymore, at least their children do. In a recent survey of Seattle schools, for example, students—*students*—complained that teachers were not doing anything about kids smoking and taking drugs at school. Eighty-eight percent of high school students and 86 percent of eighth-graders said they had tried drugs, and 40 percent said that they or a friend or family member had been shot at. But the really telling part of this story is that underlying the statistics are unheeded cries for help. One student wrote, "If you actually cared, you wouldn't sit there and give us condoms and wipe our tears when our friend gets shot and killed, you would tell us what is right and wrong and that there are consequences to our actions. DO SOME-THING!!!"[40] If nothing else wakes up America to the crime of the self-esteem movement, that must.

As I have stressed throughout the book, however, teachers are more influenced by the self-esteem movement than their students. Beth Teolis, in her book *Self-Esteem and Conflict-Solving Activities for Grades 4–8* begins with a section on teacher empowerment, providing a number of suggestions for teachers to raise their self-esteem so they can help their students do the same, among which are "rescripting your self-talk" (replacing the bad thoughts with the good) and listening to empowering tapes on the way to work.[41] But the influence of the movement goes far beyond empowering tapes. It also greatly influences instructional theory.

The latest and most popular of these is "constructivist teaching." I discuss constructivism in more detail in Chapter 9, but briefly, it is the view that the world only exists through our construction of it. There is no such thing as an objective world or an objective perspective, for that matter. What that means, of course, is that my version of the world could radically differ from yours, and there's no way to tell whose version is the right one (because there *is* no right version, from this point of view).

Constructivist teaching involves getting students (and teachers) to become clear about their own perspectives by putting their feelings and experiences at the center of the learning process. One book describes three goals of constructivist teaching: (1) to help students actively understand subject matter with reference to their past experiences and personal purposes; (2) to help students actively understand themselves; and (3) to help students actively understand participatory democracy.[42] The ideology of the self-esteem movement is clear here: School must be made relevant to students' personal lives; the primary goal of education is to get students to understand themselves; and, finally, schooling must be a democratic process in which everyone's opinion is given equal weight. As I pointed out in Chapter 3, however, schools were never intended to be places where democracy is fully practiced but rather places where it is fully learned.

IV: The New Behavior Therapy

The self-esteem movement profoundly affects not only curriculum, instructional methods, and evaluation, but also behavior. Self-esteem advocates have a particular take on how to deal with behavior problems. Most of us are relieved that the days of corporal punishment (and its liberal use of the principal's strap) are long gone in favor of more humane methods of behavior management. But we need to look at what has replaced them. Just as in the phonics–whole language debate, the baby has been thrown out with the bathwater. Having recognized that brutal punishment is immoral and largely ineffective, some educational researchers have thence concluded that any kind of punishment—consequences for actions—is necessarily a bad thing. Instead of punishment we now have "behavior modification," "mediation," and "positive reinforcement."

These are all "therapeutic" ways of addressing inappropriate behavior, and the idea behind each is the same. Since children do not respond to coercive methods of behavior control, let's try to get them to change the way they behave by having them talk about how they feel when they're upset, by role playing, and by reinforcing their good behavior. In fact, some observers believe that even behavior modification is too harsh. One writes that behavior modification "is less severe in its punishing characteristics (than traditional punishment) but more than makes up for this with subtle ABSENCE OF REWARD AS A PUNISHMENT. It eats away, like an unseen cancer, at the self esteem of students, leaving them resentful, anxious and eventually IMPAIRED AS LEARNERS."[43](Presumably the caps are necessary in case the reader didn't quite get the point.) And one researcher claims to have identified whole new categories of mental illness caused by the embarrassment and humiliation supposedly produced by traditional methods of punishment.[44]

Although there is nothing wrong per se with talking about feelings or doing role playing, these strategies are useless without something very important: an overarching sense of right and wrong. Educators are so afraid of saying or doing something politically incorrect that they refuse to acknowledge their role as the moral, as well as intellectual, leaders in their classrooms. More than one teacher trainee has told me, "It's not my job to teach them right and wrong; that's what their parents are for." Unfortunately, some parents have abrogated that particular responsibility, and so it falls to the teachers to take on that role as well. But since students spend so much time in schools, being a moral leader is, irrespective of what the parents do, necessarily part of a teacher's job. And all the behavior modification in the world will not make Johnny a decent individual unless he is taught moral principles because before he can change his behavior he needs to understand *why* he should change his behavior. Principles must precede practice.

The whole concept of discipline is one that self-esteem advocates treat with distaste and clearly consider a regrettable aspect of public schooling. From their point of view discipline must not intrude in any way on an individual's free will, self-expression, or self-esteem. These are paramount. For example, one of Canfield and Wells's proposals for raising student self-esteem is to have them group together and boast about themselves to one another. They rationalize this ridiculous suggestion by saying that "if a person is to become fully self-actualizing, it is important for him to learn to express his positive as well as his negative feelings."[45] They note that kids don't get a lot of opportunity to do this in public since society frowns upon it. In the subsequent section on bragging in pairs (variation on the theme) the authors note that "most people feel uncomfortable bragging" often because of "an imagined fear of rejection for being too self-centered."[46]

There are a couple of things to be said here. First of all, there's a very good reason why society frowns on braggarts: Bragging or boasting is one way of putting oneself above others and makes others feel bad. It is not nice and, moreover, is just not considered good manners. In fact braggarts are not only bad mannered but usually feel that they have to talk about themselves in order to hide, ironically, an unusually low self-esteem. With respect to the "imagined" fear of rejection for being self-centered, I would say that kids *should* be reprimanded for bragging and showing off. However, typically, the perceived need to protect children's fragile egos far outweighs any concerns about individual decency or concern for the feelings of others.

Self-esteem promoters advocate "logical consequences" for behavior rather than punishment, which sounds quite reasonable on the face of it. But what exactly is meant by logical consequences? According to the authors of *Positive Discipline in the Classroom*, logical consequences means focusing on what they call solutions, rather than consequences: "Some people get fixated on consequences and forget the ultimate goal of helping. The most effective strategy is to look for solutions. It is a mistake to think there must be a logical consequence for every behavior or to solve every problem."[47] They recommend focusing on preventing future problems instead of teaching consequences for past misbehavior: "Rather than focusing on making students "pay" for what they've done, look for solutions that will help them learn for the future."[48] Their example of how to do this was a scenario in which one student was unhappy that a classmate had scribbled on his test while correcting it. The appropriate response, according to the authors, is not to convey to the scribbler that that was inappropriate behavior but provide him a piece of paper on which to scribble when correcting in the future.[49] Apparently logical consequences are no consequences at all.

Self-esteem advocates believe that anything that is at all evaluative in nature is by definition punitive and, as a result, discipline and academics become inextricably intermingled. Grading is the best example of this. A small section in Canfield and Wells is reprinted from the *Association for Humanistic Psychology Newsletter*. The author writes that an instructor must never, under any circumstances, use red pencils to make corrections on student papers, because "red symbolizes violence, blood, STOP, (immoral, godless) communism—a whole host of authoritarian, painful, paranoiac associations"[50] and notes that even editors, with their reputation for being merciless, use blue pencils.[51] And to think I thought red was great because it shows up on papers a lot better than, say, blue or black. It makes one wonder how many lives one has ruined or how many psychoses one might have created because of an overly liberal use of red pencils. . . .

Grading is considered central to "positive reinforcement," and Canfield and Wells describe some of the author's creative suggestions for avoiding the unpleasantness of assigning meaningful grades—grades for work done, for example. "The best way to affirm student performance via grading is to give grades only for that which can be affirmed."[52] If that is not quite clear, as it wasn't to me at first, read on. The author describes approvingly the grading system that a number of junior colleges have adopted, whereby no grading record is established until the student has passed the course in question.[53] Although a student might fail a course and thereby lose time and money, he will not have to actually see the fail on his grade card and thereby face his reality. He will never get less than a pass. Grades are not considered a reflection or expression of the student's actual achievement (or lack of) but a punishment.

One of the more absurd examples of this kind of mentality is the new practice of introducing tests that allow the test taker to manipulate the difficulty level, thereby presumably reducing test anxiety. The idea is if the test taker feels too stressed-out to deal with the standard test level, he or she has the opportunity to individualize the test by making it easier. This is called "self-adaptive" testing, and it is likely to cause great excitement among those in the academic community who consider the almost universal phenomenon of exam jitters a sickness rather than a natural biological reaction to perceived stress.

Self-adaptive testing is not a fringe notion, however nutty it sounds, but has the support of a number of researchers, including Howard T. Everson, a senior research scientist for the College Board.[54] Everson admits that an obvious practical problem with the test is the possibility of abuse: someone faking exam stress to take an easier test and score better.[55] In fact, who *wouldn't* be tempted to fake it, since doing so would virtually assure a higher grade? The absurdity of this notion is almost too great to comprehend. Following the reasoning behind it to its logical conclusion would mean recommending that all test levels be set as low as possible from the outset to avoid stressing the most fragile of students. Or, better yet, why don't we just get rid of tests altogether?

The fact is, all students at one time or another experience various levels of fear or anxiety before a test, but the adrenaline produced by stress is often what gets us through those trying moments. I recall very clearly my worst experience with exam jitters. I was starting university and had to take an English placement test. I had taken two years off to work and travel after high school before going to college, and going into this placement test I was absolutely petrified, fearing that in the intervening period I had forgotten how to write. This didn't make much sense, especially since English was my best subject, but then fears are often irrational, if not groundless. I got through about two-thirds of the exam, sweating and fidgeting, until I looked up and realized I couldn't see anything. I had blacked out but was still conscious. Somehow I made my way down the auditorium stairs to the proctor, gave him the unfinished exam, and was taken somewhere to lie down.

The episode only lasted a couple of hours, but it was terrifying and did negatively affect my performance, since I ended up in a middle-level English class rather than the advanced class that I had frankly expected. I was embarrassed and angry at myself for getting hysterical over a simple placement test. But in the long run it didn't do my academic career any harm or undermine my self-confidence. In fact it had the opposite effect. Since then I have told myself before every exam that it is, after all, only an exam, and if I am prepared, that is all I can do. And if I'm not prepared, well, it's a little late to worry about it! I used the experience to learn something about dealing with a stressful situation. If I had been protected from the experience by choosing an easier test (or no test at all) I probably would not have learned that lesson or perhaps not until it was more critical, such as during a job interview. If one is going to have an anxiety attack from stress it would be far preferable to do it in school and learn to deal with it than to make a real fool of oneself by fainting from fright in front of a potential employer!

The notion of learning from experience is not one that thrills self-esteem advocates, however. In fact, they consider almost any kind of real experience involving learning, risk taking, accepting challenges, or identifying goals very bad. Grades are not something one earns but a punishment or reward given to the student by the teacher. This would explain my students' continual demands to receive an A in the course. I have always responded that I hope they get their A but that it is entirely in their hands, since they know what the requirements are and how grading is determined. They seem to think that this is some kind of mean professor trick on my part and continue to repeat their demands until they realize that they are not having the desired effect. As far as I am concerned, grades are simply the

formalization of students' actual achievement in class. But many firmly believe that they should be given grades they haven't earned.

This view that teachers and not the students themselves are responsible
for student learning produces the mentality that students have to be protected from challenges and are potential victims of an overdemanding educational system that punishes them through tests and grading. Canfield
and Wells's suggestions regarding self-expression are typical of this view.
When a student has a statement to make, the class is to listen and not respond, and the teacher is not to challenge, grade, or correct the student.[56]
This suggests that students are much more fragile and much less creative
and resilient than they really are. Although speaking in front of a class is a
stressful experience for many kids (and adults), getting the class involved
can make it much less so. It also gives the student a chance to defend her
ideas in more depth or to reevaluate them with the help of her peers. And
if the teacher is respectful and supportive, speaking can be an exciting
learning experience for everyone.

In fact, debate, which Canfield and Wells expressly say must *not* develop
from this exercise, is one of the lost arts of the American public school.
Kids are not taught how to defend a point or make an argument, skills
that are absolutely essential in the development of critical thinking and
logical reasoning. Creating opportunity for debate is one of the most interesting and creative ways to hone those skills. If given a chance and a little help, most kids can excel at it. This is one of the great ironies of the
self-esteem movement: It leads teachers to underestimate our kids. Since
they are not challenged, their skills and talents lie dormant.

The self-esteem movement's approach to behavior also undercuts the
notion of civility, perhaps the biggest behavioral casualty of the movement. Canfield and Wells provide an excellent example of how civility is
undermined. In a section in their book called "Making Your Wants
Known" they suggest that teachers encourage students to express their desires in a straightforward manner, saying "I want to be heard on this matter" or something similar. They acknowledge that "some teachers will
cringe at the thought of encouraging students to state their demands," but
they justify it by saying that it "helps pupils realize that they do have a
right to make demands on people."[57] They advise that students begin by
issuing general demands to get used to the experience of being assertive
and then move on to making specific demands on the teacher and on their
classmates, such as "I want the members of this class to listen to me when
I am talking."[58]

The purpose of this exercise, according to the authors, is twofold: to
help students become more comfortable asking for what they want and to

facilitate more direct communication between individuals. Although both ideas are good in theory, as is so often the case, the theory is incomplete and therefore the practice leaves something to be desired. Assertiveness is fine but must be tempered with the idea that it is not always appropriate to demand what one wants and often one should not or cannot get it. In addition, one's demands may well be in conflict with others, which requires the recognition of oneself as part of a community of individuals, something that is conspicuously absent in much, if not all, of self-esteem ideology. And finally, whatever happened to politeness? Most of us were taught that one does not ever say "I want" such-and-such but that one should express oneself in a more polite manner, saying "I would like" or "could I have, please" rather than making outright demands.

Ruben Navarrette Jr., author of *A Darker Shade of Crimson: Odyssey of a Harvard Chicano* and a frequent commentator on public education, discusses the consequences of years of a lax approach toward discipline: "Many children and adolescents have little fondness for rules or those who enforce them. So accustomed are many of them to talking their own way, acting their own way, dressing their own way and generally having their own way in schools that, when confronted with rules and discipline, they rebel."[59] As a substitute teacher in a California junior high school Navarrette quickly acquired a reputation for zero tolerance, which his students initially greeted with anger and resentment, but gradually their anger gave way to a respect for his authority in the classroom *because he demanded it*. As Navarrette notes, "Once upon a time, there was no mistaking who was the parent and who the child. No longer."[60]

Unfortunately, as others have observed, very little of any sense is written in teacher texts regarding how to apply effective punishment. In *Reclaiming Our Schools: Teaching Character, Academics, and Discipline* Edward A. Wynne and Kevin Ryan explain: "Teachers are cautioned about the ill effects of even mild sarcasm toward students, raising their voices in anger, and simply pointing at a misbehaving student. They are admonished that publicly embarrassing students is not to be tolerated under any circumstances."[61] A handbook I received at work entitled *Toward Enhancing Communication with Students and Helping the Emotionally Distressed Student* clearly spells out this kind of attitude. Under the section on "the verbally aggressive student" faculty are reminded to not "become hostile or punitive yourself, e.g. 'You can't talk to me that way!'" nor to ask for explanations or reasons for their behavior.[62] Instead, they are advised to "acknowledge their anger and frustration, e.g. 'I hear how angry you are.'"[63] It is *verboten* to demand that someone speak to you in a respectful manner, but *you* must legitimize their aggression.

Perhaps the most important message to give children is how fortunate they are to have access to education. It is a responsibility and a privilege, one that millions of children around the world will never know. According to the United Nations Children's Fund (UNICEF) more than 130 million primary school–aged children in developing countries are without access to basic education.[64] Remedying negative attitudes and behaviors is not very difficult. It requires only common sense and a little backbone: establishing rules, ensuring compliance, and identifying consequences if the rules are violated. Punishments must be appropriate and applied swiftly with authority and empathy in order to be effective. Perhaps we need to remind teachers and professors that they are also privileged to be in their profession and that public education must be treated with respect—something many of them seem to have forgotten.

In sum, the self-esteem movement has woven a whole tapestry of myths masquerading as truths that seem to promise magical things for schools but are, in fact, misleading, mistaken, and frankly moronic. Here, then, I review the ten major myths of the self-esteem movement, the reality they conceal, and the solutions we need to remedy them.

Myth 1: High Expectations for Students Are Damaging to Their Self-Esteem

This is what we might call the all-encompassing myth because it relates to virtually everything that goes on in a classroom. It is based on the ideas that kids are much less capable than we think they are and that failure is shameful and permanently damaging. Of all the ideas of the self-esteem movement, this one does the most to prevent students from exploring and finding their potential.

The Consequences: The first consequence is the most serious. Teachers lower their expectations of students, which research shows is one of the most damaging things we can do, since students will fulfill our expectations, high or low. Lowered expectations lead to a poor-quality, low-level curriculum, since that is all students are assumed to be able to handle. Thus course materials may suffer. The overall result is that students will achieve less, will be less motivated (because little is expected of them), and will therefore fail to take advantage of their education.

The Truth: There is no evidence to demonstrate that high expectations are damaging. Research tells us about the self-fulfilling prophecy—that students usually live up (or down) to the expectations we have of them. High expectations, and the achievement that usually results, develops self-esteem in children because they feel confident as a result of their successes. In addition, students usually adopt others' expectations of them, and thus if we expect much of them, they will expect much of themselves. This is the source of intrinsic motivation, an essential ingredient of successful learning.

The Solution: Parents and teachers must always have high expectations for all students. Students have varying ability levels, but all students can and should be challenged. And because we never truly know what students' abilities are, we should always encourage them to do more, not less, than they believe they can. Finally, we need to teach them that not reaching our greatest expectations is not shameful. The only shame is in not trying.

Myth 2: Evaluation (Grading, Testing, Report Cards) Is Punitive, Stressful, and Damaging to Self-Esteem

Like Myth 1, this is a far-reaching myth, since schooling involves some kind of evaluation every day. The belief is that informing students of their progress and achievement will (almost) always disappoint them and they will therefore experience a drop in self-esteem. Therefore, every attempt is made to avoid frequent, objective evaluation of students.

The Consequences: Students will be examined very infrequently, which is likely to damage their schooling. Frequent evaluation provides necessary feedback to student, parent, and teacher, and without it there is no way to gauge a student's progress. Evaluation is becoming significantly less objective overall, since writing descriptive evaluations has largely replaced the standard letter-grade format. Consequently students develop fear of tests, report cards, and anything else do with assessment.

The Truth: Evaluation is a necessary part of any educational process. It need not be punitive. On the contrary, if done correctly, it provides feedback to the student and the teacher as to student progress, and it provides an opportunity for early intervention should there be a problem. It is also a good preparation for students' working lives, when their job performance will be evaluated regularly.

The Solution: The more frequent and the more varied the evaluations, the more accurate our assessment of the student will be. Evaluation should include both information on progress over time as well as student performance gauged against a fixed standard. Evaluation should include both individual and group work, should gauge their writing skills, and should test all the different ways children learn: kinesthetically (physical or motor learning), visually, orally, and aurally. Expectations for assignments must be made clear, and the purpose and process of every evaluation explained.

All students must be evaluated, and, except for exceptional or learning disabled students, evaluated the same way. Fairness is of the utmost importance. Students must be made to realize that they will be individually evaluated throughout their lives on a number of levels and that the key to dealing with it is to be prepared and to look at it as a learning experience.

Myth 3: Teaching and Learning Must Always Be "Relevant" and Student-Centered

Relevance is one of the central concepts of the self-esteem movement. Everything must be made to fit students' needs and desires, whether or not it is educationally warranted. Self-esteem advocates believe that students should be able to decide what courses they take and what they do and do not learn. Teachers and schools must bow down to the whims of each of their students, no matter how nonsensical or self-defeating.

The Consequences: Students may not get the education they need because they are not always wise enough to know what courses they should take. Therefore, schools that are entirely student centered actually do their students a great disservice. Since "relevance" is construed as something that directly relates to students' immediate lives, students are not encouraged to study subjects that they know nothing about and they may therefore learn very little. For example, music students interested in jazz piano or guitar frequently want to skip the boring scales and harmonics and go directly to the improvisational (fun) part, not realizing that creativity and improvisational ability depend on *both* (1) natural ability and (2) extensive training in musical theory and practice, with (2) being even more important than (1). Improvisation without knowledge and experience is merely dilettantism.

The Truth: "Relevance" is of course important, but it should not be the central principle of public education. In fact, students only progress if they are challenged to learn something that they initially believe has no relevance to them. That is what learning is about: acquiring new knowledge. If we only learned what we were sure was relevant, we'd never learn anything. Although learning should take into account students' wishes, they should be exposed to a breadth and depth of learning that takes them out of themselves for a change. Education should be about discovering the world, not just discovering oneself.

The Solution: When appropriate, curricula should be related to material that students have already mastered or experiences they have had but not at the expense of learning. Relevance should be used as a stepping-stone for going from what is familiar to something that is unfamiliar. Relevance is less important than ensuring that kids acquire necessary information and skills that can be taught only in schools. But perhaps the most important thing to understand about relevance is that real knowledge is always relevant. But most of us do not know enough to know that!

Myth 4: Effort Is More Important than Achievement

This is one of the more enduring myths of the self-esteem movement; I remember hearing this when I was in elementary school. The notion is that, since all students have different ability levels, it is unfair to hold them to a fixed standard or even to any standard at all. What we should do instead is look at how much effort they have expended.

The Consequences: This idea destroys the notion of working toward a goal and thereby undermines the very idea of excellence. It says to kids that there is no point in trying to achieve a high standard because we are not interested in that standard anymore. To the slower students, it says that because you aren't as bright as the other students, you don't need to even bother trying to compete with them.

Since there is no way to accurately measure effort, students can claim they did the best they can, and we will never know if it is true or not. And of course suggesting that they didn't is a hazardous policy, since if it turns out that they really did do their best, both teacher and student end up feeling pretty bad. Finally, students figure out pretty quickly just how they can manipulate the system for their own ends.

The Truth: In American society, effort does not get you very far. It is results that count. All the effort and good intentions in the world do not matter one whit if there is no product to show for it. The economy could not function that way, and neither can schools. The only way to ensure that we really are teaching children what they should be learning is by examining them on it.

The Solution: Students do not all have the same abilities and therefore cannot be expected to achieve at the same level. We should nonetheless hold all students to a high standard while explaining that there is no shame in not reaching it. Effort, therefore, *is* important, but since it cannot be accurately measured, we measure what we can: results. Effort should be recognized and praised, but students must be made to understand that they have to produce something tangible so that their effort *and* their achievement can be appropriately acknowledged.

Myth 5: Competition Leads to Low Self-Esteem and Should Be Replaced by Cooperation

The idea here is that if students compete with one another in either academic or athletic pursuits, some will do better than others—some will win and others won't. Those who don't do well will suffer a blow to their self-esteem. Competition is one of the most dangerous ideas in contemporary society and should be replaced by friendly, cooperative games and activities that are designed to help us work together.

The Consequences: Without competition, many students will have little motivation to work toward a goal. Although some students have sufficient internal motivation to succeed simply for the feelings of self-confidence that it produces, many kids need the external stimulation of competition with others in order to become motivated. Without this stimulus, many kids will not see any point in trying to improve on anything they do. If we, the parents and teachers, don't care if our kids do well, neither will they.

The Truth: Competition is an integral part of human biology and sociology. Darwin's theory of the survival of the fittest is in essence the explanation of how competition between animals (or people) with different strengths and abilities creates an environment in which the best competitor wins. That competition is what ensures the survival of the species. It is also the underlying principle of capitalist economies and is therefore what makes America tick.

In fact, the economic consequences of a lack of competition provide a very instructive lesson for schools. As a result of being protected from competition, industries in former communist states often experienced very low productivity and worker disengagement—alienation that was perhaps worse than the alienation that Marx foresaw for capitalist economies—and as a result depended on government subsidies for their survival.

There is little reason to think that the consequences would be any different for kids in schools. Without competition, kids have little reason to produce any work. They become alienated from school because they have no reason to be there and no goal to work toward. They become dependent on kind, but ill-advised teachers who "subsidize" their learning by giving them grades they didn't earn—what is known as grade inflation. When they finish school, because they have been given grades they didn't earn, they may then be dependent on government subsidies because they are not qualified to get any kind of job. No competition, no success, no independence, no future.

The Solution: Keep competition in the schools but make it healthy competition. Teach kids that competing is good but that winning does not make you a better person than anyone else. Winning for the sake of winning should not be the point of competition. It should be about measuring one's skills and knowledge against others in order to test oneself and in order to learn from the successes of others, as well as one's own successes—and failures.

Competition and cooperation can work hand in hand; team sports are an excellent example of that. By competing in teams, whether in sports or in spelling, kids learn how to work together and celebrate the virtue of teamwork while keeping their eye on a collective goal of excellence. Students should be evaluated primarily on their own work but should also be evaluated as part of a team, whether on the court or in the class. When it comes to competition and cooperation, balance is the key.

Finally, anyone who believes that competition is damaging to students who are somehow "less able" need only look at the Special Olympics. For at least a brief time, these kids learn just how special they are, not by being protected from competition but by competing with their peers and experiencing the exhilaration and true self-confidence that come from the challenge of doing their best.

Myth 6: Students Should Be Promoted from One Grade to the Next, Irrespective of Achievement (Social Promotion) in Order to Preserve Their Self-Esteem

Self-esteem advocates believe that a child's social development is far more important than his intellectual, moral, or physical development. Thus anything that threatens his sense of belonging or changes his peer-group status is considered dangerous. They therefore believe it is better to pass a child who fails academically on to the next grade for social reasons.

The Consequences: Social promotion is a very serious practice because it has a snowball effect. If a student who experiences academic difficulties early in elementary school is passed on from grade to grade without those problems being addressed, she will fall farther and farther behind as the years go on. Not only will her problems remain unsolved, they will multiply. This is because learning is not only cumulative, with new knowledge based on what the student already knows, but is also horizontally connected. The more we learn in one area, the more connections we are able to make to other areas.

Thus the student who does not have an adequate foundation is limited both from vertical (cumulative) learning as well as horizontal learning. To make matters worse, parents and teachers naturally assume that a student is in a particular grade because she deserves to be, and thus her learning deficits may remain hidden—to them and to herself.

The Truth: There is little evidence that the practice of social promotion does what it sets out to—protect the child's self-esteem by ensuring that she progress through school with her age-group. Although some students experience discomfort or embarrassment by being held back a grade while their friends go on to the next, there is no reason to believe that this discomfort will cause irreparable damage to their self-esteem.

Social considerations are important but should not outweigh academic considerations in schools. Children may prefer to move ahead at the same rate as their classmates even when it may not be in their best interests: what serves them well academically. But their social needs should be taken care of primarily in the home and in the community.

The Solution: Happily, there is a very simple answer for the problem of social promotion: Don't do it! We can help prevent the problem of students not being at grade level by holding them back, if necessary, in the early grades. The first few years are, hands down, the most critical period of education because it is during those years that children acquire the fundamentals upon which the rest of their learning will be built. If children who are not ready for first or second grade are kept back in kindergarten or grade one, we can be sure that they have not missed these essentials. By retaining them as soon as a serious problem is identified, we prevent the snowball effect from occurring and help ensure that they are prepared to succeed in the next grade. No child should be held back if not absolutely necessary, but when it is necessary, we must have the courage to do so to protect the child's educational future.

Myth 7: Discipline Is Bad for Self-Esteem and Should Therefore Be Dispensed With

Anything that suggests a restriction on individual liberty or control of a student's impulses is considered a threat to self-esteem, since the core of self-esteem is freedom of emotional expression. Thus mediation is used as a way to help direct students to appropriate behavior while avoiding the idea of punishment or consequences for bad behavior.

The Consequences: When students are not held responsible for their actions, do not have to make any restitution for serious infractions or are not punished for bad behavior, they lose all sense of respect for the teacher as an authority and for school as a place in which certain norms and values are enforced. If they are not taught consequences for actions, they have no opportunity to learn from their mistakes. Thus there is no opportunity for growth.

The Truth: Unfortunately for teachers, establishing and enforcing disciplinary rules is a necessary part of schooling. Since children spend the better part of their formative years in schools, teachers have as much responsibility as parents for identifying appropriate rules of conduct and sticking to them. There is no evidence that effective, compassionate, and relevant disciplinary measures adversely affect student self-esteem. The opposite, in fact, appears to be true: Children who are allowed to run wild end up not only hurting others by their behavior but hurting themselves. Most parents know that kids often act out as a way to get some attention, structure, and discipline in their lives because without it they are lost. Having high disciplinary, as well as academic, expectations for kids is one of the most caring things we can do for them.

The Solution: Teachers should let their students know at the very beginning of the year just what their expectations are in terms of behavior and general comportment—etiquette, in other words, to use a term that has become sadly out of date. If the class can be encouraged to participate in the creation of these rules, they will be that much more effective, since children are more likely to adhere to rules in which they have a personal investment. However, the rules should reflect primarily the teacher's and school's position on behavior.

Teachers must also ensure that the consequences for violating these rules are clearly stated and restated throughout the year and that consequences are enforced with absolute consistency and fairness. They must take care to explain to students that there are consequences to all actions and that we all must be responsible to rectify our mistakes whenever possible. Kids need to know that there is no shame in making mistakes, as long as they learn from them and try not to repeat them. But we need to teach kids that when they make mistakes, they need to own up to them and that when they see others do wrong, they have a responsibility to report them. We need to change the rules of the playground, the code of silence that says that no one "tattles" on anyone else, no matter what they've done.

What may have begun as a notion of respecting someone's privacy has turned into the very dangerous idea that exposing a bad or illegal act done by someone you know is wrong. That *view* is wrong. We need to teach our kids that telling about someone beating someone else up or using racist language is the morally courageous thing to do; it makes you a good person, not an outcast. If we taught our children this, some of the shooting tragedies at our schools may have been prevented and the children responsible for them may have been given the help they needed *before* anyone was killed.

But a word of caution. Teachers must also try to treat all children with caring and respect and avoid treating some kids as troublemakers—even if that seems to be what they are! They will only learn from their mistakes if they are treated as equals with their peers. Once they are labeled "bad" or something worse, they are likely to live up (or down) to that ideal.

Myth 8: Teachers Should Be Therapists

Since self-esteem advocates believe that the role of the school is to develop the emotional health of the child, they believe that it is the teacher's job to act as a therapist. Teachers are to help students express their emotions and "get in touch" with their feelings, the two things that are considered essential to building high self-esteem.

The Consequences: This myth has effectively transformed the role of the teacher from intellectual leader to counselor, day care worker, parent, psychologist, and just about everything other than what a teacher should be. There are three major problems with this. First, given the numbers of students teachers have to work with, it is virtually impossible for a teacher to develop a student's psyche, become her friend and analyze her problems and still have time to teach the skills and knowledge that she needs. What this means, of course, is that therapy ends up replacing academics in school.

The second problem is that teachers are not trained as therapists. Being an effective psychologist or psychoanalyst requires many years of schooling, an internship, and experience—training that few teachers have. Consequently, they translate psychological theories and concepts that they hear in their teacher education courses as well as they can in their classes. The result? Pop psychology dominates schools. In fact, this is one of the ways in which the idea of self-esteem has become so popular in schools. Teachers hear the idea of self-esteem referred to throughout their teacher training but because it is rarely seriously examined or defined, it becomes a catch-all phrase used to defend the most absurd educational policies and practices.

Third, students who do have learning disabilities or other psychological or psychiatric problems could be damaged by teachers who try to "diagnose" or fix their presumed disorders without any real understanding of what they are doing. As we see so often with the self-esteem movement, good intentions can lead to bad consequences.

The Truth: The job of teacher is, or should be, one of the most important in society. Teachers are largely responsible for the intellectual, moral, and physical development of the nation's children. Schools are where we rightly expect our children to acquire the skills and knowledge to become productive citizens. We also expect the moral guidance we give them at home to be reinforced by the school faculty and administration. (And if kids do not receive any moral guidance in the home, the school is likely the only other place where they will get it.) These roles are too important to be set aside while teachers focus on unproven and even dangerous notions of "emotional development."

The Solution: Teachers should try to give students the richest academic education they can. That does not mean that they cannot be empathetic, caring, encouraging, and helpful. They should be. But they should also be demanding and should challenge their students to be curious, adventurous, and skeptical—to never accept what they learn at face value but to examine received knowledge carefully. In other words, there are many other models of teaching than the therapeutic one.

Teachers should be intellectual leaders, researchers, imparters of knowledge—the people who help liberate children's minds. They can include the caring aspects of a therapeutic model in their approach, but it should not be their sole focus. Teachers prepare students to become the leaders of the next generation. But to be effective leaders, they must be politically, socially, culturally and not just *emotionally* literate.

Myth 9: It Is the Teacher's, Not the Student's, Responsibility to Ensure Learning

If any one thing is characteristic of the self-esteem movement, it is its total lack of logic and consistency. Although the movement undermines the role of teacher by reducing her authority, it also promotes the notion that students cannot be held responsible for their learning, which is solely the teacher's job. It is difficult to explain this contradiction, but it arises out of the narcissism that the self-esteem movement creates. Narcissism results not only in neglect of others' feelings and needs but also a neglect of our own responsibilities and obligations. Self-esteem advocates believe it is more important for students to focus on getting in touch with their feelings than to have any responsibility for learning, so it is the teacher's job to ensure that they learn. The other side of this coin is that since students do not take any responsibility for learning, if they choose not to learn, they won't.

The Consequences: What this means is that students are not expected to work hard, turn in their work on time or study for exams unless they want to. Since they are not expected to do anything they don't want, all the responsibility for learning falls on the teacher. Both student and teacher lose here. The student loses by not being expected to learn, and students always live up to our expectations. And the teacher is caught in a catch-22. If she expects Johnny to take some responsibility for his learning, she will be accused of demanding too much of him and damaging his self-esteem; if she expects nothing of him, society (and his parents) will criticize her when it becomes clear he has learned nothing in her class. This entire notion makes a mockery of both student and teacher. And finally, it sets up a classroom environment in which the student is entirely passive—the worst condition for learning.

The Truth: Both teachers and students are responsible for student learning. Although people can learn things on their own, they generally learn much more when they are taught by someone else and in the presence of peers with whom they can exchange ideas. Thus teachers are very important in the learning process. But any teacher will verify that a child who simply refuses to learn won't. No teacher can force a student to learn. So the student also has responsibility for her learning.

The Solution: Students must be taught their responsibilities in the learning process very early on, for habits built early stay late. They should, moreover, be encouraged to be active and not passive learners. This means teaching them that it's a good thing to question the teacher and their classmates, examine their own assumptions, get help when needed with a problem, and always keep their curiosity alive. They need to be taught that they are the cocreators of knowledge with their teachers and that they shouldn't just wait for the teacher to provide them with pearls of wisdom.

The teacher's role is to encourage the development of active learners and stoke the fire of excitement in learning in all students. Children have a natural curiosity about the world that is often destroyed by dull teaching methods, passive learning, and low expectations. Teachers must combat this. They can do so by being prepared in class and by trying to be as responsive as possible to the needs of each of their students—the hardest part of a teacher's job. And finally, they must model the best of intellectual inquiry: honesty, respect for others' opinions, respect for the truth, and an ongoing interest in the world around them. They must themselves be life-long learners and researchers if their students are to be the same.

Myth 10: Feeling Is More Important than Thinking

This statement probably sums up the core of the self-esteem movement better than any other. Theorists from Daniel Goleman and Howard Gardner to entrepreneurs in the self-esteem movement like Jack Canfield have emphasized this repeatedly. Developing reason and critical thinking skills—the foundation of a classical liberal education—is not as important as learning about interpersonal relationships, family dynamics, and personal feelings, and therefore schools should be teaching the latter and not the former.

The Consequences: By putting the idea of emotion before reason, the self-esteem movement has not only threatened the entire structure and process of American education but has confused us into believing that talking about our emotions is, somehow, some form of learning, as Goleman, Gardner, and others seem to be suggesting. Consequently children are not developing their minds and all of us are beginning to lose our respect for the authority of reason in our society. If children are not taught how to reason in school, they will neither be able to reason as adults nor see a purpose in doing so. Schools will cease to exist as we have known them up to now and will become places whose sole mission is the satisfaction of personal desires, whether they be noble and good, or destructive and evil. And teachers will continue to be reduced in importance until their role consists of little more than the poor companion on this dubious journey to self-discovery.

The Truth: Learning is primarily an intellectual and not an emotional experience. Thus it is intellectual capacity that must be developed in order for learning to occur. We all experience emotions when we learn, but they are emotions *about* learning—feeling exhilarated at discovering something new or being happy about a good grade—and not learning per se. Schooling is, or should be, about helping children expand their intellectual capabilities and learn as much about themselves, the world, and their place in it as they can.

The Solution: Teachers must acknowledge children's emotions because emotions can positively or negatively affect the learning process. But they should not be focusing solely on them. Children are allowed freedom to express their emotions outside the school and in the home. Children must understand that school is the place where the important work to be done is intellectual, not emotional, and that therefore they must, when necessary, learn to control their emotions in order to concentrate on the tasks at hand.

As I discuss in the next chapter, emotion has replaced reason as the guiding principle of American society, and the results are catastrophic, both for the individual and for society. The embrace of emotion over reason is the defining step on the slippery slope to barbarism and decadence, something that humanity has been struggling to overcome for centuries. How ironic, and how very tragic, if at the beginning of the third millennium, we should, by embracing this simple idea, erase the most important advances of the first two.

PART THREE

Fighting Back

*Challenging the Consequences
of Self-Esteem*

Too Many Degrees of Separation

Self-Esteem and the Death of Community

They teach you anything in universities these days.
You can major in mudpies.
—Orson Welles[1]

IT IS CLEAR HOW OUR ILLICIT, INDISCREET—and highly inadvisable—affair with the idea of self-esteem has affected our schools. It has transformed school practices to reflect its themes and interests and in the process has threatened the integrity of the curriculum, lowered standards, and undermined the authority of the teacher. School is no longer a place to learn about the world. It has become a place to learn about ourselves. History and social sciences are not taught for the sake of the knowledge alone but are now used primarily to teach kids about their own culture and history. Language and literature is a battleground characterized by the wars over bilingual education as well as the phonics–whole language debate. And every effort is made to inject cultural content into math and science classes in order to appease the demand for "relevant" content—no matter how *irrelevant* such material may be.

As a result, schools have become places for the expression of various kinds of parochial interests. Young people, taught to be self-centered, stick with their own group and grow into adults who are alienated from one another. Students want to learn about themselves and thus self-segregate in ethnic studies classes that foster misunderstanding and promote intol-

175

erance. More than forty years after *Brown v Board of Education* we are re-segregating ourselves and rebuilding the walls of prejudice that *Brown* was supposed to tear down. Walls are being built between communities, as well as individuals, as we buy into what the self-esteem and ethnic studies movements tell us: Identity is the root of self-esteem, ethnicity is the source of identity, and, therefore, to promote self-esteem schools need to teach ethnic studies. Although there can be a role for ethnic studies courses in high school and college, the way they are currently structured and taught only polarizes us further and tears us apart.

It is not my intention to condemn those who have bought into the movement's promises nor to criticize without providing solutions. Unfortunately, the maxim "if it sounds too good to be true, it is" is all too apropos here. As I stated in earlier chapters, the self-esteem movement is seductive, secretive, and highly successful in enticing us into adopting its ideology. Although each of us must ultimately be responsible for our own actions and behaviors, many of us have been brainwashed into believing the empty promises. We *want* to believe in something, and the self-esteem movement looked like something we *should* believe in. The problem is, we didn't adopt the ideas of self-esteem because we wanted to but because we were indoctrinated.

How Good Intentions Can Lead to Indoctrination

When we think of indoctrination, we usually think of some Machiavellian scheme, such as an evil person aiming to control the minds of innocent children. Adolf Hitler's view of education is a prime example of this: "By educating the young generation along the right lines, the People's State will have to see to it that a generation of mankind is formed which will be adequate to this supreme combat that will decide the destinies of the world."[2] This kind of indoctrination is based on myths and lies and is intended to deceive and control people. There is another kind of indoctrination, however that is intended to do good but ultimately deceives people just the same: indoctrination into self-esteem.

Professors of education have no intention of harming their students, but their indoctrination is also built on myths and lies: those of the self-esteem movement. Teacher educators are not evil people. It is safe to say that virtually all of them have the best interests of their students at heart. But there is no question that today's teachers in training are being indoctrinated to believe everything they are told about Johnny's self-esteem. How can this be?

Indoctrination can be defined as inculcating a belief system to get someone to believe something. It is not necessary to show any good reasons for adopting the beliefs, and the beliefs themselves may or may not be true. The only purpose in indoctrination is to persuade someone to accept what one is saying, irrespective of truth or consequence. Thus indoctrination can be motivated by evil or, as in this case, by good. Professors of education *really believe* in the good of the self-esteem movement and work very hard to persuade their students to adopt its premises lock, stock, and barrel. Their intentions are good but the consequences, as we have seen, are not.

Indoctrination is most successful when the idea or belief being put forward is attractive, as in the case of self-esteem. People want to believe it and thus are willing (albeit unwitting) participants in their own deception. Indoctrination is truly successful when the person being influenced is unaware of being indoctrinated and accepts the beliefs unquestioningly. This is what we have with the self-esteem movement. Students simply accept the notion that grading is oppressive, standards cruel, and expectations damaging, and when questioned about these beliefs, are utterly confused. They have been completely inculcated into a system of beliefs that has colored their whole view of what school is about.

Students (either future teachers or their students) who demand an A for effort, won't learn what they don't want to, expect classes to be organized around their interests, do not know how to reason effectively, and treat the instructor and each other badly are the products of an education system that has taught them these things. If students have been taught nothing else, nothing else can be expected of them. That doesn't make it acceptable, but it does help us understand why they have these attitudes about school and about each other. And once we understand it, we will also understand how to change it. But before looking at solutions, we need to look at the effects of the self-esteem movement on our kids and on ourselves.

Narcissism

The narcissism that many young people exhibit is caused primarily by teachers and parents who lead them to believe that they are the center of the universe. Student-centered teaching fosters this, as does the idea of teacher as therapist. Of course Myth 10 (described in Chapter 6), that feeling is more important than thinking, also contributes to a narcissistic outlook, since it is not just feeling per se that is considered important but *my* feelings that count.

This narcissism is expressed in a variety of ways. Students evince little interest in learning about others' ideas because they do not see what they have to do with their own. "I want to learn about myself" is already a very familiar refrain. If school is all about learning about me, why should I care about anyone else? So when they say they don't want to learn something because it doesn't seem "relevant," they are only echoing their teachers. And when they complain about taking tests, they are also expressing what their teachers have told them: that tests are inherently biased and unfair. By definition, tests (apart from the new "personalized" tests I referred to in the last chapter) are intended to measure students against an objective, universal standard and are thus perceived as a threat to student-centered education.

One researcher, in an article entitled "All About Me: Are We Developing Our Children's Self-Esteem or Their Narcissism?" picks up on this prob-lem. The author, Lilian G. Katz, is a professor of early childhood educa-tion at the University of Illinois, director of the ERIC Clearinghouse on Elementary and Early Childhood Education (a national research database in education), and president of the National Association for the Educa-tion of Young Children—clearly an expert in the field. She notes that de-veloping young children's self-esteem "is listed as a major goal in state and school district kindergarten curriculum guides" and that in spite of dis-agreement over how to teach, "the one goal all the approaches agree is im-portant is that of helping children to 'feel good about themselves.'"[3]

Katz is very critical of the common practice among elementary educa-tors to get students to write little stories about themselves, talk about how special they are, or emphasize their abilities, all in the interest of promot-ing self-esteem. She questions whether such exercises really do strengthen children's self-esteem and concludes that "as commendable as it is for chil-dren to have high self-esteem, many of the practices advocated in pursuit of this goal may instead inadvertently develop narcissism in the form of excessive preoccupation with oneself."[4]

What is the remedy to narcissism? Empathy. The only antidote to an "excessive preoccupation with oneself" is to teach kids, from a very young age, that although they are indeed very important as individuals, *so is everyone else*. Self-esteem exercises teach kids that they are special, but they typically leave out the notion that we are special by our actions, be-havior, and attitudes, not just because we exist. They also tend to treat in-dividuals as if each one lived in a vacuum. Kids need to understand that they are part of a community and that in order for communities to flour-ish they must be made up of people who care about each other and not just about themselves. They need to be taught that caring about oneself is fine but that it is just as important to care about other people. As Barbara Wheeler, president of the National School Boards Association, puts it, self-esteem is about making a connection with someone.[5] The ability to enter into the feelings and experiences of someone else (as much as possible) is a prerequisite to the development of connectedness.

The best way to teach this is to ask children who exhibit narcissistic behavior and disregard for the feelings of others how they would feel if someone did that to them. Putting yourself in someone else's shoes is a great way to begin to promote empathy among young kids—who are by nature egocentric. Later on, empathy can be taught as a moral value, that is, as something we should be doing because it's the right thing to do. But in the early years, we can capitalize on children's natural egotism in teaching empathy. Empathy is thus the first step in teaching morality.

I remember my first lesson in this. When I was in first or second grade, my sneakers were stolen from my cubbyhole and, to get even, I took some-one else's (even though I didn't know who had taken mine). I remember very clearly having the distinct feeling that what I had done wasn't right, although I didn't really know why. When my mother realized what I had done, she asked me how I felt having my sneakers stolen. I replied that I felt bad, and then she explained that the student whose shoes I had stolen was feeling bad, too. I knew it couldn't be a good thing to make someone feel bad on purpose, so I knew I had done wrong. She also explained that having someone take something from me did not give me the right to do the same to someone else. Stealing was always wrong. I began to under-stand that too and in learning empathy had my introduction to morality and the all-important lesson that *some things are just wrong.*

The unfortunate postscript to this story is that although my mother brought the incident to the attention of the teacher and suggested that this was a golden opportunity to teach right from wrong, the teacher replied that it wasn't her job to teach morality and refused to get involved. That teacher was wrong. It is always a teacher's job to teach morality and empa-thy. And like parents, teachers should model appropriate behavior. There is no better way for children to learn what's right than to see it practiced in front of them on a daily basis. Lessons learned from practice and experi-ence, like lessons learned from great books, will last.

Empathy goes hand in hand with tolerance. Tolerance means accepting that we can coexist with our neighbors even though we may be culturally or ethnically different. And empathy allows us to move beyond simple co-existence, setting the groundwork for the development of shared values. Although (as I explain in the next chapter) it is possible to have too much tolerance, it is nonetheless necessary for both empathy and connectedness and thus is the first step in improving race relations, for example. Tolerance should be a given; it should not be something we have to work toward creating. But we will not have tolerance while we have separatism.

Separatism

Separatism is a very profound and wide-ranging consequence of the self-esteem movement, infecting both individuals and society. It is a complex phenomenon that comes in several guises and follows quite naturally from narcissism. If each of us is concerned only, or primarily, with our own interests, we tend to isolate ourselves from others. It is ironic that this should result from the self-esteem movement, whose disciples are incessantly proclaiming the importance of cooperation. Cooperation and community can never exist, however, as long as we all perceive that we are alone in the world—or at least its most important inhabitant.

Separatism I: History, Technology, and Alienation

Individual separatism is not a new phenomenon. It has been growing since agrarian societies began to die out with the beginning of the industrial revolution. As labor became more specialized and societies more urbanized, our conception of family and community—as well as work—changed. The extended family that was necessary for the survival of rural and agrarian societies has gradually been superseded by what became known in the 1950s as the "nuclear family"—itself rendered obsolete by a variety of livelihoods and lifestyles that owe more to advances in technology than to any shared vision of what society should be. Although today we speak of the Internet and satellite communications as the route to a new "global village" and a new international, interdependent understanding, I think the jury is still out on just what kind of village these technologies invite. The available technologies have certainly extended our communications capacities beyond anyone's dreams, but communication is not the same thing as community, and information doesn't equal knowledge.

As is always the case with social revolutions, these developments have had both positive and negative effects. On the plus side, the new technologies provide much greater freedom in the labor market, with increasing numbers of people in a variety of occupations now being able to work from home. Rather than commute on our local highways, many of us now "commute" on the information superhighway via the Internet and e-mail as well as fax and phone. This allows people more flexibility in arranging their work and family schedules and permits them to organize their lives to suit themselves rather than their employer. The new face of work also provides more opportunities for those who have been traditionally excluded, particularly the physically disabled, who can now compete more equitably in the labor market by enjoying greater access to it.

However, the downside of all this is that we spend increasing amounts of time alone. The automobile and the television were, prior to the communications revolution, the two major inventions of the twentieth century that, while providing human benefit in terms of mobility and entertainment, also isolated us from one another. Television watching is a solitary and passive experience; educational programming has improved considerably in the last decade or so, but it has limited educational value. And the automobile has become not only a way to get around but a place in which (despite the dangers to ourselves and others) we do business—alone.

Our increasing dependence (*dependence*, not just *use*) on technology has only increased that alienation. We can drive together or watch TV together, but it is pretty impractical and well-nigh impossible to physically work on a computer with anyone else. People will argue that our communications are better than before through Internet chat rooms and e-mail. But these are, or can be, anonymous forms of communication. If you never see the person with whom you are communicating, you can easily hide who you really are. Traveling through Europe with a friend when I was eighteen, the two of us pretended to people that we were nuclear physicists(!?). It was a game—harmless, if silly—but we could (sort of) pull it off because no one really knew who we were, and they were never going to find out. We felt safe; we never had to reveal our true selves.

The Internet lends itself to just that kind of game. It can provide almost endless information (if one knows what to do with it) as well as countless opportunities for discussion, but it is also an effective way to keep distance between individuals. It is thus, in a sense, inauthentic. Marx foresaw the alienation that workers would experience as the products of their labor became the commodities and profits of others during the industrial revolution. What few have foreseen about this technological revolution is that we may experience a more profound alienation than that—an interpersonal alienation created by our collective dependence on these technologies. One thing that is becoming very clear is that the technologies are not freeing us from the constraints of the traditional work environment, as many once envisaged. We are working longer and longer hours and becoming less and less able to free ourselves from the demands of work by the constant attention required by our faxes, phones, and e-mail.

Advances in information technology raise the same kinds of questions as do advances in medical technology. Medical science now allows us to save the lives of very premature infants and very old people. The question of course, is *should* we be doing it just because we *can?* The Internet is no different. Human lives may not depend on it but the human spirit certainly does, and we therefore need to look at the ethical implications of its increasing importance in our lives. We *can* use it, but how *should* we use it? How can we utilize it for social good? For all its *uses,* the Internet has no inherent *virtues:* it does not provide knowledge or intimacy, nor does it demand honesty from its users—the things that are the foundation of meaningful relationships and real community. It is neither good nor bad in and of itself. But its use involves a variety of ethical questions relating to privacy, freedom of speech, conceptions of knowledge, and the protection of children—indeed a whole variety of concerns that should demand our attention.

One of the most important ethical questions is how, and with what intentions, we utilize computers and the Internet in education. In the last five to ten years there has been an explosion in the availability of educational software. Many of these programs can help children solve problems, learn to read or spell, or any number of important skills. But there are a couple of things we need to keep in mind here. First, even when programs are interactive, all the possible directions for the game are preprogrammed into the software and thus the outcomes are always, to a certain extent, predetermined.

Interactive, then, is a relative term. A program is only as interactive as the software designer's imagination. Thus a computer game, no matter how well it is conceptualized, can never be as truly educative as the interaction between a teacher and a student, which, if it is authentic, is not predetermined. Indeed, a good teaching moment will likely have a surprise ending for both teacher and student. Learning through software is kind of like peeking at the last page of a book before reading it: It takes away all the fun and ruins the surprise.

We need to be very careful, then, about how we use computers with our children. I doubt very much that whoever thought up the African proverb "it takes a village to raise a child" imagined that a virtual village would be the one doing the raising. As Hillary Clinton writes, "Technology connects us to the impersonal global village it has created."[6] But as she also points out, we cannot ignore this new village.[7] We have to learn how to incorporate the new technologies into our lives, not the other way around, and ensure that we use them in a way that enhances, not undermines, our existing communities.

Neil Postman, in *Technopoly: The Surrender of Culture to Technology,* writes passionately about our increasing dependence on the various technologies that are transforming not just the way we live but the way we think. He calls this new state of culture "technopoly" and says that it has created

> a world in which the idea of human progress, as Bacon expressed it, has been replaced by the idea of technological progress. The aim is not to reduce ignorance, superstition, and suffering but to accommodate ourselves to the requirements of new technologies. We tell ourselves, of course, that such accommodations will lead to a better life, but that is only the rhetorical residue of a vanishing technocracy. We are a culture consuming itself with information, and many of us do not even wonder how to control the process.[8]

The new technologies are the dream of a narcissistic society, since they are meant to serve our every need. But, ultimately, who is the slave and who is the master? How smart will we be, I wonder, when we succeed in creating technologies that are more clever than we are? As Postman asks, who will have the ultimate control? Since the invention of the atomic bomb many have pointed out how ironic it is that humans are the only creatures in history so "developed" that they can construct the weapons of their own destruction. The killing potential of the A-bomb was clear. But let us beware: The weapons of technology may be more dangerous to the human race than any nuclear arsenal because they are disguised as the tools of our progress.

Separatism II: The Culture Wars

"We gotta learn about ourselves, man." " I want to know about *my* people." "Why should I learn about someone else's history when I don't even know my own?" I have heard these phrases many times from minority students, angry that they have been denied the opportunity to learn about their history and culture in schools. Discrimination against nonwhites in the public school is unfortunately not a new problem. In the early days of the common school, minorities were first excluded and then taught in separate schools and today they often receive an education that is inferior to whites'. Despite state and federal laws requiring equality in funding and access, minority kids are still disadvantaged because until recently they have found their people conspicuously absent from curricula, state frameworks, and textbooks.

In the 1960s and 1970s educators began to acknowledge how alienated minority students were from school. Courses and materials were developed that included the history, language, and culture of African Americans, Chicanos and Latinos, Asian Americans, Native Americans, and other groups, including more recently the physically and mentally disabled. This was the beginning of multicultural education. The rationale for multicultural education is simple: Students need to make some kind of connection with the material they are being taught or they will become disinterested in school, alienated from the curriculum and from their peers, and will end up dropping out or failing. They need to feel that what they are learning is relevant to their own lives because relevance is one of the things that sparks interest in learning. Multicultural education is seen as one way to ignite that interest.

Multicultural education is more than just having a token day on which a certain ethnic group is celebrated, like Cinco de Mayo, for example. It is reorienting all school materials and teaching methods to address the needs of minority students. This could include using history, social studies, and literature texts that discuss the experiences of minority groups. It could involve teaching minority languages as well as English—a controversial idea, as the continuing debate over bilingual education illustrates. It could also mean looking at the different way children from different backgrounds learn. There is some evidence, for example, that African-American children may learn better working in groups than alone, as their socialization in the home is characteristically more community oriented than Anglo-American culture. Multicultural education also includes addressing the learning needs of girls and providing opportunities for them to succeed in areas in which they have traditionally lagged behind boys, such as math and science. Same-sex classes, in which girls can work together and not feel pressured to compete with boys, is a popular solution. But as I discuss a little later, it may do more harm than good.

Multicultural education is thus a very broad education reform that is implemented a little differently in every school. But the ideas behind it are the same everywhere: to help historically disadvantaged students compete on a more level playing field; to promote tolerance and fight racism; to teach about the history and culture of minority groups; to make education more meaningful and relevant to minority students and girls so they can be more active participants in the learning process; to raise the self-esteem of minority students; and to ensure that public education addresses the needs of all students, not just a privileged few. Today this is a widely embraced notion, supported by groups such as the Organization of American Historians, which in 1991 issued a statement affirming the importance of teaching race, class, sex, and ethnicity in the public schools, arguing that because "history is tied up with a people's identity, it is legitimate that minority groups, women, and working people celebrate and seek to derive their self-esteem from aspects of their history."[9] On the face of it this idea seems reasonable, but not everyone is so enthused.

There are different ways to "multiculturalize" schools. One way is to infuse discussion of different cultures into the core curriculum. Another is to teach separate ethnic studies courses, such as Pan-African Studies, Asian-American studies, and so on. Although some celebrate these developments, others, such as historian of education Diane Ravitch, criticize the use of ethnic studies to raise students' self-esteem, arguing that the purpose of formal schooling should be acquiring knowledge, not massaging students' egos and that racism should be fought outside and not inside the academy.[10] Ravitch and others, including Arthur Schlesinger Jr., contend that schooling should be about teaching a core curriculum, not raising self-esteem, and that "multiculturalizing" the curriculum threatens the integrity of that tradition.

The core curriculum typically refers to the Western literary tradition of works from Plato to Joyce and beyond that has historically been the foundation of a classical liberal education. What the core is, or should be, has always been debated, but the debate reached a fever pitch in 1988 when Stanford University officially sanctioned the multicultural movement by reconceptualizing its Western Civilization course, the core of its undergraduate humanities curriculum, along multicultural lines. What had previously been a "great books" curriculum—the books of the traditional Western canon—was changed to a new sequence of courses called "Cultures, Ideas, and Values." The new sequence included more works by women, minorities, and Third World authors in an effort to give recognition to groups that have not historically been represented in the canon.

The argument over whether these works should be taught, and who should teach them, continues to rage more than ten years later. The debate centers over several very important and very contentious issues: What defines a classic? Who decides what is a classic and what is not? Is the Western tradition inherently prejudicial to minorities? Can the Western tradition itself be called multicultural? What is "relevant" literature? Relevant to whom? Should universities and schools be teaching content or self-esteem? Can those two issues be separated? I am not going to try to address all these questions here, as many others have done so at great length. But there are a couple of points to be made.

First, it needs to be emphasized that these debates are about politics and not just literature and history. They serve as an excuse for liberals and conservatives to pontificate about everything from culture to affirmative action. As David Bromwich notes, "Learning itself may have become nothing but a pursuit of political power by other means; a conceit (for those who think this a *good* outcome) which often yields the following polemical deduction: "Since nothing we teach can be altogether isolated from the moral and political views we hold, let us, as efficiently as possible, adopt our own morality and politics as the self-conscious message of everything we teach."[11] In other words, the content of the lesson is lost or at best becomes the mere vehicle through which the instructor gets a chance to indoctrinate his students.

Indoctrinating Your Kid's Teachers: A Case Study.   There is no question that this is a growing trend, at least in higher education. Most professors I know in education make no pretense about it: they are there to let their students know what they think. They feel justified in doing this because they are convinced that they are right (so they don't believe it is indoctrination). But indoctrination is still indoctrination, no matter how prettily packaged and served. And the worst of it is that we are indoctrinating those who have no defenses against us, for our current teachers in training have already been brainwashed by the self-esteem movement in their own K–12 education and therefore do not have the critical thinking skills that are the only defense against indoctrination. They are easy prey.

Just how dangerous this indoctrination can be was forcefully brought home to me one day when I was observing a colleague teach his class. Part of the job of the tenure-track faculty is to observe and evaluate the part-time faculty who teach their course. The instructor I observed was a Latino American (whom I'll call Ramon) teaching a core education course to teachers in training that addresses, among other things, the issues that I am covering in this section: ethnicity, race, multiculturalism, politics and education, the role of the canon, and so on. These are obviously very sensitive issues that must be handled carefully. As far as I am concerned, when dealing with highly personal and political issues with adult learners, the instructor has a responsibility to teach them in a respectful way, offering a variety of perspectives on the issues and then, if appropriate, volunteering his or her opinion, *but making it clear that it is just that.* This young man clearly did not agree.

The class started off with a general discussion of multicultural issues, including the activities of Jesse Jackson and the Rainbow Coalition. The discussion then moved on to bilingual education, and someone brought up the debate over whether, or for how many years, children should be in bilingual education. There are a number of different models of bilingual education, but the most popular among academics and most educators is "maintenance" bilingual ed where children who are nonnative English speakers learn content in both English and Spanish for several years, sometimes through twelfth grade. They do not transition out of Spanish. Not only does the student become fluent in two languages, the idea goes, but also has a chance to become immersed in his or her cultural heritage.

Some students in Ramon's class ventured the opinion that, since maintenance bilingual education is not always successful (as some students never acquire fluency in *either* language), perhaps trying another approach or eliminating it altogether might be advisable. Ramon jumped on these students, saying that not only was eliminating bilingual education the goal of conservatives (and thus to be ridiculed) but no one except left-liberals had the right to even talk about these issues because only people on the left really understand what equal rights and social justice are about!

The students persisted, however, and one pointed out that however attractive bilingual education might be, the priority should be to teach everyone English, since that is what children need to succeed in this society; even new immigrants understood that. Indeed, according to recent news reports, an increasing number of Spanish-speaking parents are fighting to keep their children in English-only classes. In 1996 Latino parents in Los Angeles pulled one hundred kids out of a local school to protest bilingual education. Hispanic parents in Omaha, Nebraska, have also embraced new English-based programs, and in Princeton, New Jersey, parents became so frustrated with the rules governing bilingual education that state legislators were forced to change them.[12] As one New York parent said, "My children know where they come from and who they are. . . . They don't need bilingual education for that."[13]

Common sense tells us that students should benefit by becoming fluent in two languages. The problem is that all too often bilingual programs are hampered by poorly trained teachers, inadequate funds, overcrowded classrooms, and a lack of direction. As a result they may be detrimental to the student's learning, preventing the student from learning subject matter in *either* language. This does not mean that the notion of bilingual education is not worthwhile. Many French immersion programs in Canada, for example, are very popular and quite successful. The situations are not equivalent, however, because in Canada English is the dominant language, not the minority language, as Spanish is in the United States. In Canada, then, learning French is not seen as necessary to one's future but a nice addition to one's education, whereas in the United States learning English is essential.

But Ramon was clearly not interested in debating the finer points of bilingual education. In response to the student who pointed out that some Latino parents may oppose bilingual education for perfectly good reasons, Ramon (who pointed out that he was a *not* a product of bilingual education) said that they didn't know what was good for them or their kids because they had been brainwashed by the rest of society to think that bilingual education is bad. In other words, it's not that they *really don't want* bilingual education, it's that they've been fooled by the powers that be to *think* that they don't want it.

I was speechless by this pronouncement, as were the students. No one dared react to this and, as an observer, I was ethically prohibited from speaking my mind. I don't think I have ever been more angry or upset when observing a class, however. Ramon's paternalistic attitude toward his own people astonished me. According to him, some Latinos are just not clever enough to think for themselves. He insulted his own culture in a misguided, myopic, and arrogant attempt to defend bilingual education at any cost. And he apparently did not see the irony in the fact that he, as a Latino, had become very successful, earning a Ph.D. at a top university and now teaching, despite (or because of?) the fact that he was never in bilingual programs—he learned only English. This was indoctrination pure and simple, disguised as enlightened thinking. Can there be any truer form of oppression than that? And in the ultimate irony, Ramon had adopted the paternalistic and condescending approach toward minorities that he was so bent on exposing. But in the end, he succeeded only in exposing himself.

On Canons and Classics.   In the endless debates over bilingual and multicultural education, rationality frequently gives way to political hyberbole, with the one who can shout the loudest proclaiming victory. I believe, however, that most of us are more interested in trying to improve education than in kicking sand in the eyes of our political opponents. For us, the question is, Can we find a solution to the culture wars that is acceptable to both left and right and, more important, is in the best interests of our young people?

I believe we can. First, we need to ask ourselves what makes a classic piece of literature. A "great work" is a work that speaks to all humanity and addresses themes and issues that all of us experience and are therefore *relevant* to everyone. Great works speak to us about sadness, love, war, jealousy, racism, forgiveness, and other things that all people, and all societies, have known at one time or another. Thus a great work, *no matter what culture it comes from and no matter what ethnicity its author,* cannot, by definition, be contained by that culture but speaks to all of us. Classics stand the test of time. The great works of Goethe, Plato, or Machiavelli are just as relevant to us today as they were to the audiences or readers of their era. That does not mean that all works over a hundred years old are necessarily valuable; it means that works we identify as classics today—if they are true classics—will still be so a hundred or more years hence.

Second, the Western canon, which has historically included works from Western and Eastern Europe and Russia, is, in fact, already multicultural. No one can pretend that Greek culture is the same as British, or Portuguese the same as German. The works that have historically composed the Western canon come from a variety of European cultures and traditions. That said, there is no question that women and minorities are conspicuously absent from this tradition, both as authors and as subjects of history. If they *are* mentioned, it is as objects of others' actions; they are the ones who were raped, enslaved, or otherwise oppressed. But that should not detract from the value of the literature itself. If a writer is racist or anti-Semitic, we can still appreciate the value of the literature while using it to examine how different groups were discriminated against and why racism or anti-Semitism persists.

Third, we need to recognize that there are few works available that were written by women and minorities precisely because they were in subservient positions for most of history. But again, that does not nullify the value of the works we do have. Fourth, a canon of works is, by definition, exclusive. We cannot teach all the literature that exists. That would be impossible as well as self-defeating. Trying to make the canon inclusive reduces the value of the works that it represents. It says that all works are of equal value, which of course they are not, and to suggest otherwise is pure hypocrisy. Recognizing a good piece of literature is similar to recognizing good teaching. We may have difficulty defining it, but we know it when we see it, and so does everyone else.

But even if the canon cannot be totally inclusive, it can be more inclusive, and more multicultural, than it has been. There are other great works that have not been included in the Western canon. Asian, African, and Middle Eastern cultures, for example, have, until recently, been largely ignored in the university humanities curriculum, except as "special topics." Likewise, the contributions of African-American writers, in particular, had, until the last ten to twenty years, been virtually invisible. That is now changing. Today school and university curricula not only include discussion of the experience of African Americans and other groups but, perhaps more important, they include works written *by* African Americans *on their own experience*, as well as other kinds of African-American literature.

But where does this leave us? How can we make sure we have a literary canon that includes "great works" but is also multicultural? Contrary to what one reads in the news articles and academic journals, there is no real obstacle to creating a canon—and a curriculum—that embraces both pluralism and excellence. Why not identify the best of African American, Native American, and other minority literatures and include them in the canon of classic American literature? Each culture has its "great works" that can either be taught as part of that particular tradition or as part of a broader study of American or Western thought. For example, there is now the *Norton Anthology of African-American Literature*, edited by Henry Louis Gates and others. By identifying these works we give needed recognition to the contributions of minority groups and benefit ourselves by having access to literature that we might otherwise never have the opportunity to enjoy.

But again, selectivity is the key. Just because a work is written by a member of an historically oppressed group does not mean it is a great work. Neither the age of the work nor the ethnicity of its author is sufficient evidence of the quality of a piece of literature. This is the point that many people have trouble with: We must be discriminatory in our choices of works in order to preserve the integrity of all of them. Here, being discriminating means identifying the good from the bad, the classic from the fad. But we must also take risks. We do not have to wait several centuries to declare a work a classic; a great work is often evident on the first reading. And if we initially make errors in our choice of works, that is part of the exercise. The canon should not just be the repository of works by dead white men, but a living, changing representation of the best work that humanity—both past and present—has produced.

There are many different ways to group, and to teach, various kinds of literature. One way is as I have suggested: including works from a variety of cultural and ethnic traditions into one broadly multicultural canon. Another is to teach each tradition separately, as is currently done in ethnic studies courses in universities. Although there is nothing inherently wrong with the latter approach, it is the consequences of treating—and teaching—each culture as a separate entity that is problematic. When traditions are separated and taught as distinct ethnic categories, there is a tendency to downplay or even ignore similarities and concentrate solely on differences.   ·

If we teach literature, social studies, or history by emphasizing interethnic conflict and historical injustices, we tend to exacerbate the existing tendency we all have to separate ourselves from others. Separatism is a natural human behavior and may even be an instinctual reaction against perceived biological, social, or cultural threats from others. People tend to want to associate with those with whom they feel they have an affinity of some kind on the basis of things like race, ethnicity, language, or gender. We feel comfortable with people who are like us and naturally seek the security of that familiarity. But what are the consequences of this separatism?

Separatism III: Identity Politics and Its Costs

When we define ourselves as irremediably different from others, we are effectively placing barriers between all of us. When we say, "You and I have nothing in common because we are from different cultures," we are cutting off communication, severing any possible ties that could help us understand each other better. This is what is all too frequently taught in ethnic studies classes, which have largely replaced multicultural classes on college campuses. For many on the left, the purpose of ethnic studies is to accentuate ethnic difference in the hope of empowering minorities.

But empowerment is one thing; mutual alienation is another. Individual empowerment is meaningless unless it is part of a broader social enlightenment about justice and inequality, and that enlightenment cannot develop in a climate of mutual ignorance and mistrust. While there is no question that race and ethnicity are, for many of us, very important aspects of our identity, *they are not the sole determinants of our identity.*

We are complex creatures. For each of us, identity means something different. For some, religion is the most important defining characteristic. For others it is gender or sexual orientation. For still others it is language. When my survey of student teachers asked which part of our identity is most closely tied up with our self-esteem, 63 percent identified family background and socioeconomic status as the most important determinant; the second most popular answer (18 percent) was ability or disability. Race, gender, age, nationality, and ethnicity all scored lower. Clearly ethnicity is important, but it is only one part of who we are. But self-esteem advocates, in their wisdom, having decided that ethnicity and race are the most important aspects of our identity, contend that schools must teach about ethnicity in order to boost self-esteem. The result of this is an overdetermination of ethnicity in the construction of our identity.

This obsession with ethnicity does not improve interracial awareness or tolerance. On the contrary: it merely makes us more suspicious of one another. It suggests that if we do not come from the same racial group, we have nothing in common and nothing to learn from one another. It also creates a kind of cultural arrogance as each subgroup tries to claim superiority over the others in a never ending game of ethnic one-upmanship. Conversely, it can produce a victim mentality, whereby each group tries to outdo the other by proclaiming that its members have suffered more than anyone else. And that in itself is a kind of arrogance that makes a mockery of every group's experiences.

Moreover, many students and professors seem to believe that you have to be of a certain ethnicity to really understand it or teach it. But matching a professor's ethnicity with the course he teaches only undermines his authority, and that of all instructors, because it implies that one's knowledge and experience are irrelevant. Only ethnicity counts. I have been challenged on this point many times by students, and I give them the same answer I gave someone who asked me about this issue when interviewing me for a job. The post was an assistant professorship at a prestigious liberal arts college in the East. The college had traditionally been very white and upper-crust but in recent years had greatly diversified its student population and was looking for instructors to teach multicultural courses.

If I got the job, I would be teaching general classes in culture and education to undergraduates, and the interviewer asked me what I would do if a black student, for example, demanded what right I, a white woman, had to be telling him about African-American history? I didn't even have to think about my response because it seemed so clear to me what the right answer was. First of all, I said, I obviously have no personal experience in what it is like to be an African-American male in American society today. I have not been stopped by police for no reason nor do I often get suspicious looks from store security guards. I have not suffered the countless indignities that many minorities face on a daily basis.

What I do have, I told him, is a background in multicultural education, political theory, and cultural and literary history that gives me an insight into the kinds of obstacles and challenges that minorities, as well as whites, face in America today. The student has experience that I don't, and I have knowledge that he doesn't. My belief was, and is, that we could learn from each other, that our backgrounds complemented each other. They shouldn't be seen as canceling each other out. My academic education does not make his experiences less important, and vice versa. To this day I remain convinced that this is the only logical answer to that question, but I have a feeling that the interviewer didn't agree: I didn't get the job!

This attitude, "if you're not in my group, I don't want to know you," not only creates more mistrust between individuals but leads to a balkanization of courses whereby only white students take English or American literature, for example, and only black students study Pan-African or African-American literature. It also undermines the notion that truth and knowledge are universals—that there are elements of the human experience that speak profoundly to all of us. When we teach Latinos about Latino history and whites about Anglo-American history, there is an implication that only individuals from those groups can understand that history. Experience is all-determining in this point of view; academic knowledge, empathy, or anything else that gives us an insight into another culture is apparently considered irrelevant. In fact, students seem increasingly interested in learning only about their own culture, to the exclusion of others. And as the following example illustrates, some will go to almost any lengths to make it happen.

In June 1993 a group of Chicano students, together with a professor and a parent, went on a hunger strike and camped out at UCLA to pressure university administrators to create a Chicano Studies Department. Chancellor Charles Young at first resisted the pressure but eventually succumbed to what was threatening to turn into a public relations nightmare. An agreement was reached on the twelfth day of the fast for the creation of an autonomous Chicana/o Studies Center.[14] Although the center would not have the campus prestige of a full-fledged department, the agreement allowed the students to end their fast with a modicum of dignity, the administration to breathe a sigh of relief, and both sides to claim victory.

The entire campus had naturally got caught up in the affair—myself included. One day I went over to talk to a member of the group. I asked him why a Chicano Studies Department was so important to him. He replied that he wanted to study himself and learn about his people. I then asked him what he would do if he were the chancellor and had to determine priorities for disbursement of funds for academic programs. How would he defend the importance of a Chicano Studies Department vis-à-vis other programs? Would he be willing to get rid of the History Department, for example, to make way for Chicano studies? What about other ethnic studies departments? He clearly had not examined these questions and, looking somewhat nervous, said again that he had the right to learn about himself. I had the feeling that he thought I was trying to trap him so, rather than pursue the matter further, I thanked him and left.

His sentiments are quite understandable. Many minority students feel, justifiably, that their history, their culture—much of what gives structure and meaning to their lives—has been left out of the standard curriculum.

Their demands for ethnic studies courses are an expression of the desire that we all have to be included in society—to feel that we count. Although the motivation is reasonable, ethnic studies classes may not be the answer because many students seem to think that's *all* they need to know or that they need to understand themselves *before* they understand anyone else. It is important to know about oneself, but in the end it is by understanding others and our social, political, and historical relationships with them that we begin to see ourselves in a context that we may well miss by studying only ourselves. We need to see the big picture.

Clearly, acknowledgment of ethnic identity in education is tied in some ways to an individual's self-confidence. Knowing who we are may help us feel good about ourselves. Therefore ethnic studies classes may have a valuable contribution to make to K–12 and tertiary education. But we need to take care to avoid the segregationist tendencies that ethnic studies seem to promote. If ethnic studies classes are offered in high school, they must not replace the core curriculum but be part of it. These classes should be mandatory for all students, and students must take at least one class in a culture other than their own. And if possible, ethnic studies should be complemented by multicultural studies classes, which should emphasize the commonality of experience of a variety of cultural groups. While the historical details of each group's experience are unique, the human consequences are the same. Everyone has known pain, humiliation, fear, happiness, love, and joy. The circumstances may differ, but the emotions remain the same.

Separate but Equal All Over Again.   Perhaps the first thing to say about deliberately separating ourselves from each other on the basis of ethnicity is that it has been tried before and the consequences are well-known. As I explained in Chapter 4, the history of "separate but equal" is an ugly one; it was a phrase that was defended by racists in order to keep black Americans uneducated, uninformed, and uninvolved in American society. When the Supreme Court ruled against this doctrine in 1954 and ordered that schools be desegregated, it looked like the beginning of a new era of racial equality. Many people—black and white—were relieved to see the end of a doctrine that had perpetuated decades of suffering and misery.

It is important to point out here that "separate but equal" was a notion used with the singular intention of forcibly segregating people in order to control and oppress them. Blacks lived in segregated neighborhoods not because they wanted it that way but because the white establishment wanted it that way. And to some extent, this is still true. Poverty, poor educational facilities, and lack of economic opportunities for young African

Americans still ensure segregation in many communities throughout the country. This is a serious economic and demographic problem that needs to be addressed at local and federal levels. What I am concerned with here, however, is not economic, involuntary segregation but voluntary segregation—self-segregation—in today's schools and universities.

Today "separate but equal" has been resurrected and turned on its head to defend ethnic studies. The argument is that separating kids and teaching them about their history will bring about the equality that they did not enjoy when "separate but equal" was official policy and that they still haven't achieved since the doctrine was quashed in 1954. Desegregation has been a very slow process indeed, and it has not, to date, produced equality. Therefore, some believe that teaching ethnic studies courses to black Americans by black Americans will empower the African-American community and perhaps create the conditions for social justice that desegregation has failed to produce.

This is a new kind of segregation: self-segregation. We need to ask ourselves whether any kind of segregation, no matter what the intent, is healthy for all of us in the long term. Is the idea of separate but equal *ever* defensible, even when it is intended to promote, rather than deny, equality? Can we really construct a healthy society by focusing on our differences? These are questions that all of us must examine because when people self-segregate, it affects everyone. A society is only as healthy as the relationship between its members, and when we segregate ourselves we tend to ignore the political and moral values that tie us together.

If we stop to think for a moment about ethnic separatism and its possible consequences, we can easily see how destructive it can be. Ethnic separatism only leads to ethnic strife, as events in Yugoslavia, Northern Ireland, and the Middle East tell us. Nelson Mandela fought for decades from a jail cell for the end of apartheid, acknowledged as a vicious and inhumane form of ethnic and racial separatism and oppression. The South African experience should tell us that once a people's collective identity and self-esteem are defined purely by ethnicity or race, self-esteem inevitably leads to narcissism and narcissism to superiority. And with superiority comes racism, prejudice, and hatred. Let us not follow in those footsteps but take the road less traveled—the road of tolerance and peace.

The road to tolerance could be a long one, however, for ethnic studies and even ethnic separatism may be a necessary historical moment in the progress of minority groups from a position of subjugation to a position of equality. Because they have suffered such injustice, minorities may need time to learn about themselves before reconsidering and redefining their role in American society as a whole. In this respect, ethnic studies may serve the same purpose as affirmative action. Although both may temporarily produce misunderstanding and mistrust between ethnic groups, both may be necessary at this time. For better or for worse, minorities perceive that they need to group together to fight for their culture and identity.

Separate but equal, then, may be a necessary stop in the long road toward social justice. While separatism may be trying in the short term, in the long term it may be to everyone's benefit. What is to be hoped is that these separatist tendencies will slowly give way to pluralist, community-oriented perspectives that will allow all of us to begin to embrace our similarities as well as respect our differences. It is difficult, if not impossible, to foresee the course of history, but it does not seem fanciful to suggest that sooner or later policies of affirmative action and ethnic studies will have served their purpose and minorities will achieve equality in education and in the economy. When that happens, the need to separate from others may no longer exist. In this respect, equality is the finest form of self-esteem. When everyone enjoys equal rights and freedoms, we have the confidence to let down the social, psychological, and even geographical barriers that keep us apart.

Separatism IV: "Genderizing" Schools

Although many consider ethnicity the primary source of identity and self-esteem, over the last twenty years researchers have begun to take a look at how gender differences and gender roles affect the development of self-esteem. One of the consequences of this research has been a growth in the numbers of girls-only schools and classes. Given that women, like minorities, have historically been the objects of discrimination, this sounds like a promising avenue of research. Unfortunately, it has unfolded in a way that has, I believe, done girls more harm than good.

The move to segregate girls from boys is an outgrowth of developments in the feminist movement, which has taken a number of turns since its birth in the 1960s. Early on the challenge was to wake up the rest of the country (men *and* women) to the ways in which women were economically, politically, and psychologically disenfranchised. But in trying to wake people up, the movement may have exaggerated women's capabilities. In the 1970s and early 1980s the slogan was "I am woman, I am strong," as the song goes. Women could do everything. We could have great careers, be supportive wives and great lovers, take care of the kids, and still have time for the gym and a weekly massage.

Well, women soon figured out that this version of "keeping up with the Joneses" was ridiculous. Who were we trying to keep up with? Ourselves? Martha Stewart? By setting impossible goals, women were oppressing themselves much more effectively than men ever could. So in the 1980s we decided that real liberation was making the choices we felt were best for ourselves as individuals, regardless of whether they were politically correct. Today, mothers working at home with kids, who used to have to defend what they did, are now beginning to get some of the respect they deserve, and women who work outside the home and have decided not to have children realize they don't have anything to feel guilty about.

We have come a long way in terms of employment opportunities, economic empowerment, and lifestyle choices. But the progress in education equity is more questionable. A very popular view among feminist scholars is that schools have traditionally embraced male values, like competition, aggression, independence, and assertiveness, and that as a result girls have become alienated from the schooling process. Gloria Steinem writes how the Western tradition in schools profoundly alienates girls by teaching them history from which they were absent or oppressed, teaching them philosophies that placed males in a superior social position, and generally showing them that they are somehow less important than boys.[15] Researchers point out that girls have suffered the same kind of oppression as minorities: They are called upon less frequently than boys by teachers, are not often represented appropriately in textbooks, and are at a disadvantage when taking standardized tests that assume a male perspective. All of this, the argument goes, is likely to produce low self-esteem.

Carol Gilligan, a professor at Harvard University and a well-known writer on women's psychological development and education, also believes in the oppressiveness of the Western tradition—what she calls "the wall of Western culture"[16]—and believes that girls' identity (remember, the presumed basis of self-esteem) is formed differently than boys'. In reviewing psychological and psychoanalytic literature on the development of both genders, Gilligan concludes that female identity is defined in the context of a relationship in which care is important and that for women "the concept of identity expands to include the experience of interconnection."[17] For boys, however, identity is much more self-contained, as it were; relationships seem less necessary to male identity formation than female. For girls, then, it would seem that self-esteem is more connected to, or dependent upon, their relationships with others (including how they are perceived by others), whereas boys appear to be more self-sufficient and thus more reliant on their own views of themselves for their self-esteem.

The conclusion that Gilligan and others draw from this is that schooling should be reorganized to acknowledge and recognize female values as
well as male values. Female values are believed to include cooperation,
sharing, empathy, and preserving relationships whereas men value autonomy, independent thinking, and assertiveness. Anyone who accepts this
dichotomy would have to agree that schools have indeed typically stressed
male values over female. The Socratic method of teaching is one example
of this. This is the old-school way of teaching whereby the instructor
"picks on" one student and asks the student a series of questions in order
to get her to think more deeply and come to the logical conclusion of her
thought.

Lani Guinier, former Clinton nominee for U.S. Assistant Attorney General for Civil Rights, asserts that the Socratic method discriminates against
women and believes that it should not be used in law schools. In her book
Becoming Gentlemen: Women, Law School, and Institutional Change
Guinier contends that the Socratic method reinforces an aggressive and
combative teaching style that is alienating to women, who function better,
she believes, in a more cooperative environment. According to Guinier "a
standardized, hierarchical, competitive approach to training lawyers inhibits many women *and some men*," and "conventional approaches to legal education do not necessarily educate or evaluate everyone based on
their capacity either to learn or to do the job of a lawyer."[18]

But this belief is based on the questionable assumption that most
women function better in groups and are unable to survive in a competitive environment. There may indeed be a place for more cooperative
learning in law schools and, as all educators know, working in groups is a
great way to brainstorm and exchange ideas. But basing a policy change
on the view that women can't compete is counterproductive to the effort
to give women equality. As Elizabeth Warren, a former colleague of
Guinier's and a professor at Harvard Law School points out, "The conclusion that women are somehow less able to withstand Socratic questioning
is fundamentally insulting to women."[19]

So do we really know for sure that researchers have correctly identified
certain characteristics as "male" and others as "female"? Christina Hoff
Sommers takes on Carol Gilligan and the myth of girls' low self-esteem in
an article entitled "Pathological Social Science: Carol Gilligan and the Incredible Shrinking Girl." She contends that the available research "tends to
disconfirm Gilligan's thesis that there is a substantive difference in the
moral psychology of men and women"[20] and refers to analyses of Gilligan's work as well as a self-esteem study by Gilligan and the American Association of University Women that suggest that the hypothesis of
diminishing self-esteem in adolescence has really not been proven.[21]

We need to examine these studies carefully before making policy decisions based on them. But there is another important question here: If men are more aggressive and women more submissive, is this the result of socialization or genetics? Psychologists, biologists, anthropologists, and sociologists have argued for centuries about which of our behavior and personality traits are biologically determined and which are products of our environment. The pendulum continues to swing on this one; in the late nineteenth and early twentieth centuries many scientists believed that biology was destiny. Researchers in the last thirty or forty years have come to recognize the immense influence of the environment on human development. But in the last fifteen years brain researchers have begun to take a closer look at the organic roots of cognitive and social development, and today the pendulum has shifted back somewhat as we gain more insights into the mysteries of the brain.

This is a particularly important issue in public education because the way we regard the roots of behavior and cognitive (intellectual) development affects how we treat students in school and what we expect of them. For example, if we believe that intelligence is entirely a product of biology and is not at all influenced by environment, then we must believe that intelligence is fixed and unchanging throughout one's lifetime. This sets up a deterministic view of development that can have disastrous effects on kids in school. If Johnny performs poorly in class in kindergarten and first grade, for example, from this perspective we would have to assume that he is of low intelligence. As a result, we expect little of him and, since children almost always meet our expectations (high or low), he would likely improve little in school, further confirming our initial impressions.

Fortunately for Johnny and his colleagues, this is not the prevailing view in schools today. We realize that family background, economic status (social class), ethnicity, peer pressure, and the media, among other forces, greatly influence a student's progress in school. From this perspective, then, taking the same example of Johnny performing poorly early on, rather than decide that he is a lost cause, we would take a look at his home environment or other forces that may be inhibiting his learning. Here intelligence is viewed as something that can be altered through schooling or through the environment. No child is seen as hopeless.

Bearing this in mind, what does the research on gender tell us? Whether they believe that males and females are wired differently or are socialized into their respective roles, many researchers have accepted the notion that men and women are fundamentally different creatures. There is no question that biologically men and women differ, and this biology may cause them to gravitate naturally toward certain social roles, which are then reinforced by the way we are brought up. Any mother who has tried, and failed, to get her daughter to play with trains rather than dolls with the intention of breaking stereotypical behavior can tell us about the power of biology. Given that both biology and sociology are important, we need to ask ourselves what we do with that information. How do we construct schools to ensure that the best interests of girls and boys are represented? And what are the effects on society if we make the wrong choice?

The problem here is that since no one really knows how much of anyone's behavior is determined by his or her genes or by society, we tend to make rash generalizations based on simple observation. But such generalizations can be dangerous. For example, it is now well-known that many standardized tests are often constructed from a "male" perspective, using sports language or athletic metaphors in a math problem that may be quite comprehensible to boys but very confusing to girls. Girls will thus be at an unfair disadvantage when taking such a test. The same kind of problem arises in interest or aptitude tests.

I myself experienced what biased testing can produce when, at about twenty-seven years of age and wondering what to do with my life, I took interest inventory and aptitude tests. The results were astonishing—even shocking—for me and the examiner. Apparently the computer had determined from the results that I should be a *male* lawyer. Thank goodness *female* lawyer was the computer's second choice or I might have had some kind of serious existential crisis! Well, I knew with absolute certainty that I was never going to be a male lawyer, at any rate, and asked the examiner what all this meant.

He looked at the individual characteristics and attitudes that I had identified as being important to me and, lo and behold, there was the answer to our confusion. I had selected independence, autonomy, logical reasoning, and assertiveness along with some other traits as characteristics I admired. The authors of the test had apparently decided that these were male traits and had programmed them as such into the computer. Based on the information available, the computer decided that the test taker *had* to be male and was best suited to be a lawyer. This shows just how misleading gender stereotyping can be. It also shows how, by assuming that girls learn differently than boys or that girls are more interested in caring than in getting the right answer on a quiz, we can be doing both sexes a huge disservice.

By what I call "genderizing" schools—determining educational policies based on sex difference—we are turning back the clock on progress by suggesting that girls cannot learn or compete on the same playing field (oops! another "male" metaphor) as their male colleagues. Researchers are beginning to address this regression and single-sex schooling for girls, which was invented to address their specific learning needs, is being reexamined by researchers. A recent report by the American Association of University Women indicates that single-sex education is not necessarily better than mixed (coed) schooling; although separate schools or classes might be helpful for some girls, they aren't necessarily better for all girls.[22] This is a surprising statement, given that the AAUW in 1995 supported experimenting with separate schools and in 1991 identified gender bias in schools as one of the primary causes for low self-esteem among adolescent girls. The later report found that some single-sex programs help some girls in math and science but that the gains in achievement are not significant and that sexism is found in coed *and* single-sex classrooms—both of which can actually reinforce stereotypes about men and women.[23]

Exactly. By segregating girls from boys in order to boost girls self-esteem, we are basically giving up the fight, admitting that girls just can't hack it in the real world, which is, after all, coeducational. And not surprisingly, gender segregation leads to the same problems as ethnic segregation. Apart from the questionable educational value of such policies, they may actually undermine an individual's chances of success in school or in the workforce because he or she will not have the experience of dealing with others outside his or her group. Part of education should be teaching kids about the real world and preparing them to enter it as responsible, confident adults. It is very doubtful whether segregating kids will help us achieve that.

The good news is that we have considerable evidence indicating that girls are catching up to boys, both academically and socially. According to a recent study by the National Council for Research on Women, *The Girls Report: What We Know and Need to Know About Growing Up Female,* girls are breaking through traditional female stereotypes in a number of ways. In the 1996 National Assessment of Educational Progress, for example, girls performed as well as boys in math and science, and the report concludes that overall "girls appear to be doing considerably better than popular discussions would suggest."[24] Girls are also participating in a much wider range of sports than they used to (and people are paying more attention to women in sports, as the attendance records at the 1999 FIFA Women's World Cup showed), and some of the research cited in the report counters Carol Gilligan's popular view that adolescent girls undergo a loss of self-esteem in adolescence. African-American girls, for example, do not, on the whole, appear to suffer any such loss and have a healthier body image than white and Hispanic girls.[25] In addition, some studies suggest that the reasons girls are sometimes reluctant to speak up in class may be strategic rather than psychological or emotional: If they think their views will be supported they might speak up. If they don't, they might be more likely to keep their own counsel.[26]

Unfortunately, girls are catching up to boys in other ways too. For example, the percentage of girls who smoke, drink, or abuse drugs is growing.[27] In 1991, 13 percent of eighth-grade girls reported smoking; by 1996 that had gone up to 21 percent—a faster increase than for boys, although African-American girls (who suffer fewer self-esteem problems) are much less likely to smoke than girls of other races or African-American boys.[28] In addition, although girls are less likely than boys to be arrested for violent crime, the rate at which they are being arrested increased faster than for boys between 1986 and 1995.[29]

It is probably inevitable, but nonetheless disturbing, that as girls achieve more equity with boys, they adopt some of their male counterparts' less attractive behaviors. Stories of female violence are becoming distressingly common as "little girl" gangs beat up girls and boys, no doubt in a misguided attempt to exhibit "girl power." This is also a problem north of the forty-ninth parallel. In 1997 Canadians, who tend to feel smug about their relatively low rate of violent crime compared to the United States, were shocked by the brutal beating and murder of Reena Virk, a ninth-grade student who lived on normally peaceful Vancouver Island in British Columbia. Eight teenagers (seven of them girls) between the ages of fourteen and sixteen were arrested and faced charges ranging from second-degree murder to aggravated assault.[30] Six of the girls have been convicted of assault charges, one girl faces second-degree murder charges, and the boy involved, now eighteen, was recently found guilty of second-degree murder and was sent to an adult prison.[31]

This is part of a rising trend in Canada and the United States. Since 1986 assault rates for girls in British Columbia alone have more than tripled, from 178 that year to 624 in 1993.[32] Some of the reasons for this growth in female juvenile crime are much the same as those for boys: an abusive home environment, absent father or mother, poverty, and other social factors. But according to Sibylle Artz, author of Sex, Power, and the Violent School Girl, the violent girl also typically sees female–male relationships as very traditional and may have had a mother who was very dominated by her husband. Her views on equality are also likely to differ considerably from that of her peers. She may see equality as a question of power rather than justice, and thus being equal with the boys may mean to her the ability to beat someone up, just as they do.[33]

The experience, both positive and negative, of girls reaching equality with boys is a clear lesson to us to abandon the kind of segregating practices we have adopted and instead educate both girls *and* boys in the values and virtues that we can all support. There is no reason to identify "girl" and "boy" attitudes or aptitudes. We should be telling all children that it's okay to be assertive but that they should also be caring and empathetic. They need to know that being independent is a very important thing (especially for girls, given their traditional dependent role) but that learning to work with others is also important.

We should be encouraging boys and girls to compete on the soccer field, work together in woodworking class, and compete against themselves in school. Girls do not acquire self-confidence by being told that they have to learn math separately from boys; they acquire it by being expected to do just as well in math as the boys. That does not mean that we should not do everything we can to make math and science accessible to girls but that good teaching should reach both sexes.

Fighting Separatism and Constructing Community

The first step in fighting separatism in school is to make sure all students feel comfortable, and included, in the learning process but never to "dumb down" classes or segregate them so they feel a false sense of achievement. This is the most difficult part of a teacher's job: trying to address each child's needs while ensuring that they are learning necessary skills. If we can achieve a balance between both demands, then we will be serving the interests of both equity and excellence, the twin pillars of the public school system. The second step is to teach the curriculum, particularly literature, social sciences, and history from a pluralistic but inclusive perspective. This means recognizing that while each of us is indeed unique, we are, as I discuss in the next chapter, connected by moral, political, and intellectual values and virtues.

We need to teach kids that we are all connected, like it or not, by history. Some say we are all connected to everyone else in the world through ten other people and we may be much more closely connected to each other than that. There is no reason for women to feel oppressed when they read about male achievements. Although historically women have not been allowed the same opportunities as men, learning about that should in itself be empowering, since knowledge is power. Even if history is not what we would like it to be, we can learn from it and resolve not to repeat it. We should be able to share in the accomplishments of our predecessors, no matter what their culture or gender. Whether we were the victors or the objects of someone else's victory, we are involved in each other's history.

Learning the lessons of that history will help foster the tolerance and mutual respect needed to create a healthy society. Denying it helps no one.

Parents have an important role to play in teaching their kids that literature and history can only oppress you if you let them. I was lucky: I was
never taught to feel inferior as a girl. When I was a child my father
brought me wonderful books to read every week: classics of children's literature from Mother Goose's nursery rhymes to C. S. Lewis and
Madeleine L'Engle. Unlike Gloria Steinem, I did not feel oppressed if I
read about the men off fighting the wars while the women stayed home
but reveled in their achievements *because they were achievements of the
human race.*

I was fortunate to be in school in the days before political correctness,
when the classics were taught as the books that reveal the truths of the human experience. No one pointed out to me that this was a man who had
succeeded, and not a woman, or that most books had been written by
men. Consequently the seeds of self-doubt were never planted. If a man
could do it, I could do it. In fact, it was simpler than that: If anyone could
do it, I could do it. End of story. I never felt that girls were less important
or less able than boys. Although I understood that in the past women had
been put down, ignored, persecuted, or worse, I didn't see why I should
follow in their footsteps. At any rate, I decided I would do everything in
my power to avoid it. And by the time I understood that oppression is often something you don't have any control over, I felt confident enough to
take them on. All girls deserve that.

What we see, then, is that gender separation, like ethnic separation, can
reinforce dangerous stereotypes and undermine the possibility of creating
workable communities both in schools and in society as a whole. I am not
trying to promote a kind of communitarian agenda in which individual
rights and liberties might be threatened by a forced allegiance to some
imaginary majority, but something much more straightforward and
much less dangerous: recognizing real links between all of us. By teaching
common values, rather than "girl" values versus "boy" values or "black" issues versus "white" issues, we could bring an end to the kind of alienation
that Steinem and others write about. We need to remember what we have
forgotten in our hurry to separate ourselves from one another: Your
achievements and mine should all be celebrated. The real source of self-
esteem is feeling powerful, optimistic, and courageous because we know
we can achieve great things and being confident enough in ourselves to
embrace the achievements of our fellow man—or woman.

It is often easier to see the problems with one's own society by comparing them to another, and a brief look at the cultural and ethnic experience

in Canada compared to that in the United States tells us much about both. Neither has been entirely successful. The ethnic history of the United States can be characterized by two conflicting ideologies: slavery and the attempted Americanization and assimilation of minorities. Slavery is the most extreme example of the complete disenfranchisement of an ethnic or racial minority group while assimilation is the ideal of a culturally united society.

This contradiction is not lost on minorities, many of whom today reject the idea of society as "melting pot," "mosaic," or even "salad bowl." Having been the objects of oppression for centuries, they are naturally leery about proclaiming allegiance to a society that has, up to now, excluded them. In fact, the more pressure there is to conform, the more likely they are to resist it and the more they will become increasingly alienated from others. Nonetheless, the historical emphasis on being an American has, at least until now, helped foster a very strong sense of national identity and patriotism, at least compared to other industrial democracies.

Compare this to the ethnic experience in Canada. As in the United States, there has been discrimination against native peoples, although Canada does not bear the legacy of slavery. Ethnic minorities have always been encouraged to retain their uniqueness and have been more or less free to express it any way they wish: creating their own communities, celebrating ethnic holidays, and teaching their language and culture in after-school or weekend programs. As a result, a considerable degree of tolerance and trust exists among different ethnic groups in Canada. The downside of this, however, is that there is very little sense of national identity. Regionalism is rampant, in the west as well as in the east, and the country may be torn in two by French separatists in Quebec who want some form of ethnic sovereignty.

Clearly, neither of these scenarios is without problems. What is needed is balance between individualism and ethnic freedom and a sense of community; a society in which all individuals feel free to express their personal and cultural identity but feel just as free to declare their allegiance to a common—or shared—political culture. And that is the fundamental lesson to learn about identity. Despite our many differences, Americans and Canadians of all backgrounds share in their respective political cultures, which emphasize in varying degrees the ideals of freedom, tolerance, democracy, individual rights and responsibilities, as well as a fundamental respect for human rights. And if the citizens of these two societies are to find their individual or collective self-esteem, it will be in a recognition of these common ideals, not in empty proclamations of petty differences.

By fighting separation, we begin to build the foundation of cohesive communities and a civil society. It is at once an enormous and a humble task. As General Colin Powell writes, we need to re-create a civil society "one child at a time"[34] through grassroots organizations, community groups, parent involvement, and other means. What is a civil society? Powell identifies it as a society "whose members care about each other and about the well-being of the community as a whole."[35] And a civil society is tested, writes Michael Walzer, "by its capacity to produce citizens whose interests, at least sometimes, reach farther than themselves and their comrades."[36] The notion of recognizing the rights of others is pretty unpopular these days, but it is necessary to any conception of social justice. None of us has boundless rights; they are constrained both by the rights of others and by the responsibilities that they entail.

In a way thinking about rights and our relationships to others is a lot like establishing the property line around a house. We all know that we have to respect the boundaries of our neighbors' property, just as they must respect ours. But nature doesn't always respect boundaries, and when the neighbor's tree grows roots under our fence or drapes itself over the top of it, we have to sit down with one another and negotiate what to do with it. Do we let the tree grow over our side of the fence in deference to our neighbors and to save a tree? How far are we willing to go? What is more important, our rights to keep their trees off our property or our relationship with our neighbors?

These are the same questions we have to address when our rights to free speech, freedom of movement and association, or other rights start to infringe on the rights of others, as they inevitably will. In a primitive society, power determines who is in control, but in a democratic civil society, public debate and reason should determine where my rights end and yours begin. Mediation and negotiation are always preferable to litigation, except perhaps when negligence or malice are involved. By talking *with* one another instead of fighting *against* one other, we can begin to understand one another, and understanding is the first step toward caring. Seen in this way, caring about others in our community does not imply a restriction of individual liberty or an infringement of individual rights; it simply means recognizing that the health and happiness of each of us is connected to and dependent on the well-being of our neighbors. It is as simple as that.

The Return of Ethics in Education

Answering Emotivism

Real education should educate us out of self into something far finer—
into selflessness which links us with all humanity.
—Nancy Astor[1]

ONE OF THE PRIVILEGES of being a college student is finally getting the chance to choose your classes and arrange your schedule. For those of us who are not morning people, this is what we have been waiting for: no more 8:00 A.M. classes! And those who want to spend sixteen hours at school one day and stay home the rest of the week can usually figure out a way to do it. It takes a little ingenuity and considerable luck, but it can be done.

Time scheduling is not the only advantage of being in college. Students get to select their professors, and word gets around pretty quickly: who's the hard grader in freshman chemistry and who gives all A's in art history. Students rush to get into the classes of the popular professors, and consequently other instructors, particularly if they are part-time or untenured, feel pressure to "sell" their courses to students. Selling might involve minimizing course requirements (always a popular strategy), reducing the reading list, becoming a comedian, or any number of tactics designed to draw in students.

What is more worrying is that this notion of "selling" education to students has trickled down to the public school, thanks to the self-esteem movement. Students have become increasingly demanding consumers of education, forcing professors and teachers to become idea merchants who desperately try to package and sell their courses in a way that will bring in the buyers. Students expect a lot from their instructors—and their schools—and don't believe they have to give much in return.

"Don't Forget: I Pay Your Salary"

These words can send a chill up the spine of any teacher or professor and they reflect the growing sense of entitlement of many of today's high school and university students. Students are very demanding. They expect an A in each course, whether or not they have actually earned it. They believe that it is the instructor's responsibility to ensure that they get their A; all they need to do is say that they tried hard. This a perfect example of entitlement—the feeling that we *deserve* something, whatever it may be, without actually *earning* it. Students also seem to believe that the instructor is there to serve them. They have paid for their courses and they expect to get their money's worth, which they believe entitles them to run the show.

They express this view in a number of ways. Some say outright that they are A students and have never gotten less than an A; others say "I expect to get what I want out of this course" or even "you really work for me." I have heard variations of all of these statements, which were meant to let me know just who's in charge. Given the staggering cost of higher education, particularly at the private colleges, it is to be expected that students want to get their money's worth. That in itself is not the problem. The problem is what they mean by "getting their money's worth." For increasing numbers of students, it seems to mean that they, not the professor, should dictate what goes on in the course. The days when getting a bang for your buck at the university meant acquiring a classical liberal education are gone. Today it means learning something "relevant" (teach me only what I want to know), "useful" (does it get me a job), and "fun" (keep me entertained, or else).

The self-esteem movement is directly responsible for this. If we teach kids that they are the center of the universe and that schools revolve around them, they will come to believe that they are entitled to everything they want in schools, whether that be good grades, easy assignments, no homework, or turning up in class only when it pleases them. While we can debate what college students should expect for their money, there should be no debate about what is expected in the public school. Children are there to learn from their teachers and should respect their authority. Historically, public school students have had little or no choice in their teachers; they were forced to take the good with the bad.

Thanks to the self-esteem movement this is changing, however, and some school districts are considering a plan to allow students to choose their teachers. A couple of years ago, a school district in Virginia was examining the possibility of allowing high school students to pick their teachers. The superintendent defended this notion by arguing that this would allow a match between teaching and learning styles,[2] presumably benefiting both student and teacher. And a principal argued that it would likely result in improved student and teacher performance.[3] A high school in Versailles, Kentucky, began allowing students to choose their teachers several years ago and staff members say it has been successful.[4] But one teacher there notes that everything comes down to salesmanship: "You have to get out and sell your class."[5]

This is exactly what students are trying to promote at my university. The undergraduate student association is now requesting professors to submit to an evaluation of their classes by their students. The evaluation is "proctored" by the "Faculty and Course Evaluations" section of the Associated Students and the results published and made available for students for a small fee. The purpose of these evaluations is not to gauge instructor effectiveness; faculty are already evaluated by students every term, with the results made available to the faculty member and other relevant persons. These public evaluations are expressly intended to let students know which professors can be counted on to give easy grades and which are known as tough graders. In the lexicon of many college students, "easy" means a "good" professor and "tough" means "bad." Let's face it: If you have the option of taking a course with someone who is known to be a hard grader, no matter how brilliant he or she may be, or with someone who gives mostly A's, not very many of us would choose the former.

The wording of the evaluation questions reveals how students interpret faculty quality. For example, two questions that are asked are: (1) whether the course requirements are appropriate and (2) whether class requirements are relevant to the course. But how does a student know if they are or not? "Professor's teaching techniques motivate students to learn material." How about students motivating themselves? "Professor's teaching style facilitates note taking." Isn't that a skill that students need to develop? These questions suggest that the students, not the professor, are in charge, and that they *know* what is "appropriate," "relevant," and "motivating."

The professor is not seen as an authority figure, someone from whom they might learn something, but someone who is there to serve them. That is entitlement, pure and simple.

Entitlement in education comes in a variety of forms, and it's not always about grades or fees. I remember one student, whom I'll call Jim, who was enrolled in my class but did not actually make it to class until the fifth week of the semester. The university's rules on attendance are unambiguous: A student who does not turn up by the second class can be dropped by the instructor (unless there are extraordinary circumstances). Jim, however, hadn't familiarized himself with these details, and when I pointed them out to him he was unimpressed. He said that he had a "right" to be in the class. He had paid for it and he wanted to take it. I explained that not only was that a violation of the rules, but I had already put people in their study groups, covered a fair amount of material, and collected the first assignment. He was just too late.

Jim's reaction to this was to proclaim even more loudly that he had his rights and no one was going to take them away from him. Foolishly, I thought that logic and reason might get through to him where spouting off rules had not. I explained that along with rights come responsibilities and that his responsibility was to turn up in class or, if there was a very good reason why he could not come to the first five weeks of class, to let me know so we could discuss it. Unfortunately, the responsibility argument fell on deaf ears; not only did he not agree, he was clearly confused about the concept of rights involving responsibilities.

Anyway, he said, he couldn't get hold of me because my name wasn't in the course listing. I was shocked to hear that and leafed through my catalog. There I was. "Oh," he said. "Well, I didn't know your telephone number." "It's listed in the campus directory," I replied. "I don't have one." "The department has one." "I didn't know what department you were in." You get the idea. In the end I spent far more time arguing with Jim than was necessary. Nothing I had to say was going to change his mind. As far as he was concerned, the university and I had ripped him off. His rights had been violated; he had been victimized.

The entitlement and victimization mind-set seems to be on the rise. Just a couple of examples from the newspapers give us an indication of the extent of the problem. A former Wake Forest University law student has sued the law school for allegedly allowing professors to harass him in front of his classmates. Apparently he suffered fatigue and weight loss from being subjected to the Socratic method, which he compared to hazing in its effects on students.[6] Apparently Lani Guinier is correct: The Socratic method is oppressive to everyone, not just girls! And in New Mexico a student who flunked out of the University of New Mexico's medical school sued the school in federal district court. His reason? He suffers from extreme test anxiety and claims that school officials made no effort to accommodate what he calls his "learning disability."[7] I guess his institution doesn't offer the new "personalized" tests that allow the test taker to manipulate the difficulty level in order to get a better grade!

There are no doubt endless examples of this kind of attitude, but the lesson from each is clear. Promoting a sense of entitlement among young people is a very bad idea, even some self-esteem advocates take exception to it. Nathaniel Branden, frequently hailed as the father of the self-esteem movement, criticizes this approach to developing self-esteem. In *The Six Pillars of Self-Esteem* Branden writes, "If one examines the proposals offered to teachers on how to raise students' self-esteem, many are the kind of trivial nonsense that gives self-esteem a bad name, such as praising and applauding a child for virtually everything he or she does, dismissing the importance of objective accomplishments, handing out gold stars on every possible occasion, and propounding an 'entitlement' idea of self-esteem that leaves it divorced from both behavior and character."[8]

Precisely. Students need to learn that in life you cannot always have everything (including the teacher) that you want. Allowing high school students to choose their teachers is inadvisable for a couple of reasons. First, as a rule they are not sufficiently mature to objectively determine what makes a good teacher. Most, like their college counterparts, think a good teacher is someone who is an easy grader. Second, the great teacher who is talented but also tough might find herself without students, who also lose by not having the opportunity to benefit from her talents. The pressure on teachers and professors to be "nice," often at the expense of being effective, is enormous. Even popular instructors who end up with waiting lists for their classes have to be on their best behavior because students can turn around and say: "We chose you; you should be lucky to have us in your classes; now give us what we want!" Who could not cave in under such pressure?

If one of the goals of allowing students to choose their teachers is to improve teacher quality, there are far more practical and useful ways of doing that. Student feedback on teacher effectiveness could be one component of an overall teacher evaluation, but it should not be the only component. Teachers should be evaluated according to some generally agreed-upon criteria of good teaching (after all, we all know what bad teaching is when we see it, so we should be able to agree on what good teaching is), how their students progress over time and on standardized tests, how much creativity they bring to their lessons, and a whole host of other variables. Allowing students to choose their teachers or evaluate their professors and then use that information against them degrades the educative process, turning teachers into vendors and schools into malls where the customer is always right.

How Many Diseases Does Your Kid Have?

One of the most troubling consequences of the self-esteem movement is the intertwining quality of its effects. The focus on the self promotes narcissism, and narcissism promotes a sense of entitlement and a lack of a sense of responsibility for learning or behavior. This, in turn, leads to a sense of victimization. Teaching kids that they are "entitled" to things without having to earn them produces a victim mentality that comes to the fore whenever they don't get what they want. And when kids don't seem to be as happy, well-adjusted, or successful in school as we would like, parents suffer an enormous amount of guilt and look for ways to alleviate it. As always, the self-esteem movement is ready with an answer: If your child isn't a star pupil or seems a little distracted, don't worry. It's not because he needs a little more discipline, a little more encouragement, or a little more time with you. It's because he's sick.

The questionable logic runs as follows. Since kids cannot be held responsible for their learning and parents often don't have the time or expertise to examine their children's learning or behavioral problems, the answer from the self-esteem camp is to diagnose them with an illness. That way no one can be held responsible for their deficits, which can presumably be fixed by giving them a pill. Everyone wins: The parents and teachers are relieved that nothing they've done is responsible for Johnny's problems (so *they* can feel good about themselves) and Johnny is told his failures are not his fault, so he feels good too. And the drug companies make a fortune. The pharmaceutical industry makes hundreds of millions of dollars each year from the drugs sold to treat the estimated 1 million children in the United States currently medicated for Attention Deficit Disorder (A.D.D.).[9]

Unquestionably, some learning disabilities (like dyslexia) are real, and early diagnosis is essential to initiate proper behavioral or pharmacological treatment. But the number of students diagnosed with learning disabilities in the United States today is far greater than in the past. In 1977, about 1.8 percent of the student body was determined to be learning disabled; by 1996, 4.3 percent of children were in publicly funded programs for diagnosed disabilities.[10] Some researchers estimate that up to 20 percent of schoolchildren may have some kind of neurological deficit that affects their ability to read and write.[11]

There are a couple of potential explanations for this growth in the numbers of children diagnosed as learning disabled. It is possible that more children have learning deficits today than twenty years ago, but it seems unlikely, particularly given advances in pre- and postnatal care and early childhood education. Another possibility is that there have always been roughly the same numbers of children with learning disabilities but that today we do a better job at identifying them than in the past. This is no doubt true. With advances in brain research, we learn more about the causes and remedies of learning disabilities and are in a better position today than twenty years ago to diagnose them.

But we also tend to over diagnose in our effort to preserve our kids'—and our own—self-esteem. Two of the more popular diagnoses these days are attention deficit disorder and attention deficit hyperactivity disorder (A.D.H.D.). Thomas Armstrong, in *The Myth of the A.D.D. Child*, describes the myth of these diseases. A.D.D. is believed to be a neurologically based disorder that affects between 3 and 5 million American children. It is characterized by hyperactivity, impulsivity, and inattention; children affected by the disorder typically suffer low self-esteem. There are no lab tests to diagnose A.D.D. and there is no cure, but it can be treated with counseling, behavior therapy, and medication, most popularly Ritalin.[12]

However, no one actually knows whether A.D.D. really is the result of some kind of neurochemical imbalance or whether it is what we might call a "socially constructed" disease (more on reality as "socially constructed" in Chapter 9). Armstrong briefly describes the history of A.D.D. in his book and notes that it has had numerous other incarnations, including "restlessness syndrome," "minimal brain dysfunction," and "hyperactive child syndrome" on its "bumpy ride" to full-fledged A.D.D. status.[13] It received a big boost in 1980 when the American Psychiatric Association determined that it was a "real" disorder.[14]

In fact, A.D.D. developed into the hottest childhood disease much as self-esteem developed into the hottest national obsession. Armstrong points out that, like self-esteem, A.D.D. came about not because it was discovered but because political, social, economic, and other influences were ripe for it to appear.[15] In other words, we believe in A.D.D., as we believe in the power and importance of self-esteem, *because we want to*, not because truth and evidence warrant it. It is as if society had engaged in collective self-hypnosis. "You *will* believe in self-esteem/A.D.D., you *will* believe" said the psychologists. When they are repeated often enough to enough people, myths "become" real. Or so we like to think.

The reality, however, is that neither diagnosing kids with imaginary diseases nor medicating them is going to help their self-esteem; it will only convince them of their victimization. Are parents really willing to do that in order to avoid the guilt associated with being an imperfect parent? Apparently so. Production of Ritalin, the drug of choice for treatment of kids with A.D.D., went up from about 3,000 kilograms in 1991 to more than 13,000 kilos in 1997.[16] In 1995 nearly half a million prescriptions were written for controlled substances like Ritalin for children between the ages of three and six.[17]

All this medicating may in fact harm kids' self-esteem. Ritalin may initially help a child feel good about himself because with it he might be able to fit in better with his peer group. But by the time he's a teenager, he may begin to wonder whether he fits in because people really like *him* or *him on a pill.*[18] Would he be popular without Ritalin? The dependence on the drug may be more damaging to his self-esteem than the "illness" itself. In our rush to diagnose we may be damaging our children psychologically by actually lowering their self-esteem. And Ritalin's long-term physical effects on children are unknown.

Whereas once we had to worry about soccer moms and dads getting a little too involved—and a little too competitive—in their children's athletic activities, we now have competitions to see whose kid is on the most drugs or whose child has the most diagnosed diseases. Being labeled A.D.D. or A.D.H.D. has become almost a badge of honor in some circles, although for the child it is purely tragic. Competitive victimization has replaced competitive sports in a very sick game in which the children are indeed victims—not of their diseases, but of society's attempts to avoid its responsibilities for them.

Not Only Are We Not Smarter, We're Not Nicer, Either

The self-esteem movement is full of ironies because it almost invariably has the opposite effect of what its adherents intend. The movement was supposed to help kids do better in schools; it hasn't. It was also supposed to help us be nicer to one another and learn to work more cooperatively together, the idea being that we will all feel better about ourselves if we do. It hasn't. The narcissism and separatism that it produces not only lead to entitlement and victimhood but to incivility as well.

Civility comes from a recognition that, to paraphrase Rodney King, "we all need to get along" and that consideration for others helps pave the way.

Civility may not come naturally, but it can be taught. Respect and consideration for others and for their property is something that all children should learn. It is pretty clear, however, that civility cannot grow from narcissism, for the first requirement for civility is the recognition and acknowledgment of others' needs and desires: the very opposite of narcissism. Neither can it develop from a sense of entitlement, since feeling we are *due* something is very likely to foster incivility when we don't get it.

Lack of civility has become a popular topic in the last couple of years, with newsmagazines and news articles suggesting that it is caused by everything from the continuing breakdown of the traditional family structure to our overly busy lives (i.e., we don't have *time* to be polite) or even our increasing dependence on technology. These may all be contributing factors, but the primary culprit is the self-esteem movement. As William Damon, author of *Greater Expectations: Overcoming the Culture of Indulgence in America's Homes and Schools*, writes, "the pursuit of self-esteem *in and of itself* is a misdirected quest. It is a logical *and* a psychological contradiction in terms. One cannot "find" self-esteem in isolation from one's relation to others because it does not exist apart from those relations."[19]

Likewise, civility cannot exist unless we are ready to acknowledge our relationship with others, even, or perhaps especially, with strangers. Civility requires not only recognition that we live in communities with others but an a priori acknowledgment that in order to coexist in relative peace, each of us needs to extend at least minimal courtesy and empathy toward others. But if we do not recognize the existence of a community and are unconcerned with the emotions, thoughts, and situations of others, there is little possibility for civility. And nowhere is this more apparent than in our schools and universities.

The vast majority of my colleagues in teacher education are consumed with the apparent attractions of self-esteem and promote its academic directives with warmth and enthusiasm; their responses to its behavioral consequences, however, are considerably cooler. While they can wax poetic on the virtues of self-esteem in the classroom, when their own students start to exhibit the self-centeredness and incivility that it invariably produces, they are not happy. At least in this respect we all share the same view: Bad behavior in schools and universities is reaching epidemic proportions.

Virtually all of my colleagues have experienced the following problem: students coming chronically late to class; students interrupting and even ridiculing one another if they don't like what they are hearing, and arguing endlessly about assignments. These are not exceptions to the rule, but daily events. One day in class the extent of this problem was brought forcibly home to me. A group of students that was supposed to be doing a presentation came to class very late and totally unprepared. The students suggested that since they weren't ready, we should all just go home early. A colleague of theirs agreed, lamenting publicly that she hadn't seized the opportunity to escape the class at the break! What struck me was that many in the class seemed to think it a reasonable idea and looked decidedly disgruntled when I indicated that no one was going home early.

Just as children learn their behavior from their parents, college students may be acquiring their manners (or lack of them) from their professors. Elaine Showalter, former president of the Modern Language Association, writes of what she calls the "rampant incivility" in academe.[20] Showalter began receiving hate email (commonly referred to as email "flames") after she published a book on modern types of hysteria that apparently upset a number of people (some of whom admitted that they neither had nor would read it). The communications became so vicious and specific that she was forced to hire four armed male bodyguards to protect her at the 1997 M.L.A. convention in Toronto.[21] (Although they followed her everywhere, no one seemed to notice them in their suits. Showalter surmises that people probably mistook them for English professors[22]—not known, in general, for their fashion flair.)

She ignited another firestorm and further flaming by suggesting that the M.L.A. should address the dwindling job market for humanities Ph.D.s by advising graduates to begin looking outside academia for jobs. Showalter notes that the hostile tone of the communications was no doubt facilitated by the "mechanical impersonality"[23] of e-mail but that "the decline in civility, community, and good humor in academic life has certainly become an issue of the 1990s—and it's not rooted just in electronic communication."[24] The situation reminds me of a joke that I believe can be attributed to Henry Kissinger. Question: "Why are the politics in academia so vicious?" Answer: "Because the stakes are so low." The more trivial the issues, the more bitter the debates.

Incivility is no laughing matter, however, and when supposedly educated people—whether professors or graduate students—turn to anonymous threats to make their voices heard we know we are in serious trouble. Incivility is also the beginning of a slippery slope toward more dangerous behaviors: outright aggression, violence, and racism. A recent article in the Chronicle of Higher Education reviewed this problem, noting that professors at institutions across the country are having their classes "hijacked by 'classroom terrorists'"[25] doing the kinds of things I listed above and more, including bringing portable televisions into class,[26] presumably to keep themselves amused. The article points out that one reason for all this is that college kids no longer respect the authority of professors (or other adults for that matter),[27] and it chronicles the travails of an African-American female professor who experienced not only disruptive behavior in her classroom but harassing phone calls, racist threats, and anonymous letters. She filed grievances against the students involved but little was done.[28]

Many faculty are reluctant to actively discipline college students for bad behavior or for more serious offenses like cheating or plagiarism because they are afraid of being subjected to further harassment by students and suspect that they will not be supported by the university administration. The procedures for filing a formal complaint against a student are often formidable, and the student can easily file countercharges suggesting that the professor treated him or her unfairly. Frequently, the mere suggestion of countercharges is enough to make the professor back off. Administrators, fearing student lawsuits, may be tempted to turn a blind eye to their classroom misdemeanors.[29] Nonetheless, as William Damon has noted, professors should be leading the way, demonstrating what civic-mindedness and civility are all about and not just talking about it.[30]

The problem with classroom hijinks is that they don't stay in the classroom. Students eventually graduate from high school or university and take what they learn with them into the world. If in school they believed that they were victims of their teachers, as adults they are likely to continue to believe that they are victims of some imaginary insult and that society therefore "owes" them something (e.g., money, a job, a house) in recompense. This creates a very fractured and paranoid society. We seem to have forgotten that "civil" society should mean a society not of barbarians but of people who are civil to one another. As Michael Lerner writes in *The Politics of Meaning*, "We learn that everyone else is just out for personal gain, and that we would be foolish to behave otherwise. We assume that no one is going to be there for us when we need help, so there is no point in taking risks for the sake of others."[31] Sadly, many seem to have taken the motto of the self-esteem movement to heart: *Do it to others before they do it to you.*

Society Under Siege

Today a widely recognized expression of entitlement and incivility is road rage. Most of us know, somewhere deep down, that we should drive defensively and courteously. But when we get behind a wheel something happens. It may be the power that we wield. After all, cars are deadly weapons, one might even say "weapons of mass destruction." Or it may be that, as with e-mail, we believe we are sufficiently insulated from others that we can express our rage with impunity. Whatever it is, road rage is becoming a serious problem. Whenever we are willing to risk our own life in order to effect revenge on someone else for a slight—real or imagined—we know that society is getting out of control.

Road rage is only the extreme version of expressions of entitlement and incivility when driving. How many of us have tailgated because we were in a hurry and wanted the guy ahead to get out of the way? How many of us have left the car on a main street in rush hour while we dash to the ATM? What about blocking traffic while we wait for an opening to change lanes? These are things almost everyone does from time to time. We figure if we can get away with it, it's okay and, anyway, we're entitled to do it—everyone else does, right? And that, of course, is the problem.

Road rage has extended beyond the highways and into the not-so-friendly skies as "air rage." British Airways has led a three-year campaign against air rage, which includes everything from drunken passengers, passengers who defy smoking bans, and passengers who start fights or harass the flight attendants.[32] Apparently taking a cue from the world of international soccer, in the fall of 1998 BA began handing out yellow cards to disruptive passengers. These cards are a final notice to passengers, warning them that if they continue to misbehave or flout regulations they may be arrested upon landing or be held liable for costs if the captain is forced to land early to discharge them.[33] Transport Canada has also initiated a campaign to educate and warn travelers about the implications of air rage. Anyone found guilty of dangerous behavior, including refusal to follow crew instructions, physical assault, verbal abuse, or other violations, will face fines of up to $5,000 or imprisonment.[34]

The problem is getting so bad that Bangor, Maine, has now gained the dubious honor of being the favored stop for pilots coming or going across the Atlantic for dumping off violent and disruptive passengers. Where else can people vent their incivility, apart from the skies and roads? Why, the ski slopes, of course. "Ski rage" is becoming a serious problem at many popular ski resorts. Serious injuries are on the rise, with some of the injuries apparently being caused by aggressive and reckless skiers.[35]

A sense of entitlement often accompanies a victim mentality, with increasingly ugly consequences. The Menendez brothers' murder trial is a perfect example of this. Erik and Lyle Menendez were the Beverly Hills siblings who in August 1989 butchered their wealthy parents and then tried to defend their actions by mounting the "abuse excuse": Their father had abused them, so they had to kill him and their mother to escape the misery. Although the facts of the case, which included evidence of premeditation, did not support this defense, the jury deadlocked and a mistrial was declared. It took a second trial to convict the brothers of first-degree murder.

Although Erik and Lyle Menendez were eventually sent to prison, the case illustrates the power of this sense of entitlement and our devotion to the myths of self-esteem. The whole "abuse excuse" defense relies on the notion that abuse survivors are victims who cannot be held responsible for their actions. As we know, children who suffer mental or physical abuse do typically suffer an enormous blow to their self-esteem. But most of them do not go on to kill their parents, and being a victim of abuse does not entitle anyone to kill the abuser. But the fact that, at least for a time, the Menendez brothers were able to evade justice illustrates how ready we are to accept any excuse for criminal behavior and, more important, how deeply the self-esteem movement has become entrenched in the national consciousness.

It is frightening to see how narcissism and separatism can lead to a mind-set that enables the most heinous acts. The murders of James Byrd and Matthew Shepard come to mind. Byrd was chained to the back of a truck and dragged to his death, his body parts strewn along the roadway. Matthew Shepard was brutally beaten, tied to a fence, and left to die. Both killings have been called "lynchings"—the only word that seems to fit these inhuman acts.

One may ask what on earth these terrible crimes have to do with self-esteem. Sadly, quite a bit. Crimes this horrifying are only possible when individuals are completely alienated from each other, and that alienation is one of the effects of extreme narcissism. When we cease to be civil to one another and cease to recognize our mutual humanity and the feelings and experiences that we all share, racism and hate crimes become possible. When I see you as irremediably different from me, so different that I cannot empathize with you, I objectify you and thereby become capable of treating you in ways that should be unthinkable.

Fortunately, however alienated we may be from one another, most of us retain a sense of morality and decency (or at least a fear of the law) and do not commit such acts. But the fact that they happen should make us stop and reconsider the consequences of our regression into ourselves. Perhaps the only way to persuade people to examine these issues is to remind them that any of us could be Matthew Shepard or James Byrd. These murders have been described as hate crimes—one homophobic and one racist— and clearly they are. But they are also crimes against humanity. When one of us commits an unthinkable act we are all affected; our collective humanity is threatened and each of us shares a little responsibility for making such crimes possible.

And finally, in becoming alienated from each other we also become alienated from ourselves because our humanity, decency, and morality only exist in a society of people. Having the right sentiments is meaningless unless they are practised. It is just another in the many ironies of the self-esteem movement, whose purpose is to have us "get in touch" with ourselves. The consequences of this—narcissism, separatism, entitlement, incivility, and alienation—are pretty clear. What is not so evident is what, in our efforts to focus on our feelings, we have failed to keep in touch with or even keep alive: rationality and morality. This is emotivism.

Understanding Emotivism

Emotivism is the third major consequence of the prophet of self-esteem. Put simply, an emotivist is someone who views the world primarily from the perspective of his emotions rather than his intellect. Feelings are what counts, and ideas are simply extensions of those feelings. Emotivists rely on emotion and intuition to make their way in the world; empirical evidence or scientific truths do not impress them. They believe that all ideas are equal and that therefore there is no truth, only opinion.

Emotivism as a worldview is the inevitable consequence of the self-esteem movement. Young children are naturally egocentric and naturally curious about the world. In the first few years of schooling, the ways in which we direct and train these tendencies will affect the child's entire intellectual, emotional, and moral development. If, for example, we begin to teach them moral lessons, encourage them to try to empathize with the feelings of others, and develop their curiosity, we lay the groundwork for them to become responsible, moral adults who are also critical thinkers.

If, on the other hand, we play upon their egocentrism and teach them to think only of themselves, they quickly lose their curiosity about the world outside them and become interested only in their own emotional development. They become obsessed with emotion and fail to develop their intellectual capacities. Eventually they become unable to distinguish between "thinking" and "feeling." When students write personal essays, it is no accident that they frequently write "I feel" rather than "I think," since they view the world through their emotions and not their minds. In its extreme form, emotivism is the inability to distinguish between fact and fiction, good and evil, sense and nonsense; it is total intellectual and moral decay.

Several myths of the self-esteem movement encourage emotivism by fostering anti-intellectual habits. For example, the myths that high expectations are dangerous and that learning is the responsibility of the teacher encourage emotivism, as does the notion of teacher as therapist, which has effectively transformed schools from places of learning to therapeutic clinics. These myths promote emotivism by taking responsibility for learning away from the student and giving it to the teacher and by telling the student that his intellectual work and his intellectual capacities are valued neither by the teacher nor by society.

Consequently, several important intellectual skills, such as the ability to compare points of view, evaluate different arguments, determine relevancy in a discussion, or solve moral dilemmas are casualties of emotivism. There are two principal components of emotivism: first, the belief that feelings are more important than thinking and, second, that all opinions are equal. These two beliefs are closely interconnected. One consequence of them is intellectual relativism, which I discuss in the next chapter. The other is moral relativism.

Why the Self-Esteem Movement Is Amoral

In Chapter 7 I discussed one of the goals of the self-esteem movement—to have people work more cooperatively with one another and to promote tolerance, often through multicultural education. One of the ground rules of tolerance is that no one judges anyone else, since to do so suggests that the person judging believes himself to be in a position of moral authority. Judging others implies being morally superior to them and assuming a "holier than thou" attitude. Today taking a stand makes many of us feel uncomfortable because we have been indoctrinated into the moral relativism of the self-esteem movement, in which there is no conception of moral virtue. Moral relativism means everyone is equal; no one can judge anyone else, and everyone's opinion is just as good as everyone else's.

Being a rational person is a prerequisite to being a moral person; to be a moral person you have to know how to think because acting morally is not an instinctual behavior, but requires conscious deliberation. It sometimes means doing things we don't want to do, which requires the ability to separate ourselves from our feelings and examine a situation as objectively as possible. We need to be able to reason out moral dilemmas, examine consequences of actions, and reflect on our own behavior, all of which are intellectual, not emotional, activities. "Doing the right thing"—

whatever that involves in a particular situation—requires an intellectual awareness of just what that is.

Moral relativism is a natural outcome of the schools' neglect of the intellect. As long as the schools value emotion over reason, our children will acquire neither intellectual skills nor moral values, and without one they cannot have the other. This is why the self-esteem movement is amoral: it actually inhibits the growth of the intellectual capacities, such as critical thinking and logical reasoning, that are necessary for the development of morality. Don Dinkmeyer and Rudolf Dreikurs, in *Encouraging Children to Learn: The Encouragement Process,* explain how a focus on self and ethical behavior are contradictory:

> The self-concept consists of the individual's personal perceptions, the convictions he holds about himself. Any concept that involves the I, such as "I am," "I like," "I do," is part of the self-concept. . . . The environmental evaluation consists of attitudes or convictions about anything that is not the self. Ethical attitudes are the conceptions of what the individual should or should not do. In practice, then, a conflict between a self-concept and a self-ideal could develop inferiority feelings.[36]

In other words, one must never challenge oneself to be a better person nor accept such a challenge from the outside world because doing so could cause irreparable damage to one's self-esteem. Consequently self-esteem advocates construct their own idea of ethics and morality. They identify feeling good with being good, but they are wrong: *Feeling good about yourself does not make you a good person* (although the inverse may be true: being a good person may help you feel good about yourself). It is quite possible to have high self-esteem and be self-centered and narcissistic, even violent, as the research I surveyed in Chapter 5 illustrated. *Feeling* good is not the same as *being* good or *doing* good.

The best that we can hope for as long as the self-esteem movement is controlling our schools is that kids will acquire some of Daniel Goleman's "emotional intelligence"; that they become people who can function in a variety of social environments and learn how to get along with others. But emotional intelligence is a moral void. Having emotional intelligence can include being socially adept or diplomatic, but it does not imply any kind of intellectual or moral *virtues.* In other words, while having good social skills is certainly useful, they are no more than tools to help us get along better in life. Like high self-esteem, emotional intelligence doesn't make us, or society, any better.

Values or Virtues?

One reason that the self-esteem movement has enjoyed such success is that its adherents have cleverly packaged "values" as one of its attractions. Part of "getting in touch" with your feelings includes knowing how you feel about different social and moral issues. Therefore, part of acquiring high self-esteem is knowing your own values, since values are an essential part of identity, and identity is the key to self-esteem (so the theory goes). But there is a big difference between values and virtues. Feeling good about yourself may be a *value* of the self-esteem movement, but it is not a *virtue*.

Values come in a variety of flavors and colors. There are political values, such as a belief in democracy and liberty. There are also moral values, represented, for example, in the Ten Commandments. Moral values are precepts that guide us in our lives. Many of them are derived from religious teachings, but a person need not be religious in order to be spiritual and moral. Political and moral values are the cement that holds society together. Honesty or democracy may mean something a little different for each of us, but there is general consensus on their importance in our lives.

We teach both political and moral values in schools. Political values underlie social studies and history classes, and moral values are found in literature and in the lessons we learn from history. But both are, more importantly, taught by example. Students learn moral values, in particular, when they see them exhibited every day by people they respect. Discussions of values are often confusing because not all values are created equal; not all values are virtues. Values like honesty, integrity, and decency are all virtues; a person who practices them can be called a virtuous or a good person. But feeling good about yourself, for example, or wanting to be in shape, are not virtues. They may be values that are personally important to us, but they do not make us better people. Contrary to what Hollywood would tell us, looking good does not make us good people!

The distinction between values and virtues is something that all children need to be taught, for it is the first step in becoming a moral person. Values are belief systems that vary from one person to another, whereas virtues are moral values that the public deems desirable for our individual and collective well-being. Virtues are the ideals of decency, goodness, honesty, and integrity that used to govern human behavior. As Gertrude Himmelfarb writes, "It was not until the present century that morality became so thoroughly relativized and subjectified that virtues ceased to be 'virtues' and became 'values.'"[37] Children need to understand that their personal preferences are purely individual values that may conflict with public virtues, and that part of becoming an ethical person is learning when to put aside our own values in favor of the public good. They also need to understand a very difficult lesson that many adults have not learned: when being tolerant and nonjudgmental is a good thing and when it is dangerous. They need to learn how to judge and how to be judged.

"Judgment" is a bad word in the self-esteem lexicon, since it seems antithetical to the development of self-acceptance and acceptance of others. Not surprisingly, the self-esteem approach to teaching values is to not teach them at all. A program that began in the 1960s during the heady days of the open curriculum and "discovery" learning is a great example of this. The program was called "values clarification" and presented a radical departure from the traditional ways of teaching virtue, character, or morality. Historically, children were taught moral lessons through direct instruction or were expected to learn them from reading books. But the inventors of values clarification envisioned changing all that. Rather than teach children virtues, they contended, we should encourage them to develop their own personal value systems.

The teacher's role in values clarification is not to guide the students toward the right moral answer but to allow them to express their own values, and refrain from comment. So when the teacher asks little Johnny whether it's okay to steal or use drugs or swear at one's parents and he says "yes, I think it is," the teacher commends Johnny for being clear about what he thinks. She does not correct him or question his values. All she expects is for him to be clear about what he thinks. An excerpt from the bible of this approach, *Values and Teaching,* shows this in action. The value under discussion is honesty.

> TEACHER: So some of you think it is best to be honest on tests, is that right? . . . And some of you think dishonesty is all right? . . . Well, are there any other choices or is it just a matter of dishonesty versus honesty? . . .
> TRACY: You could be honest in some situations and not in others. . . .
> TEACHER: Is that a possible choice, class? . . .
> SAM: It seems to me that you have to be all one way or all the other.
> TEACHER: Just a minute, Sam. . . . we are first looking for the alternatives that there are in the issue. . . .
> GINGER: Does that mean that we can decide for ourselves whether we should be honest on tests here?

TEACHER: No, that means you can decide on the value . . . although you may choose to be dishonest, I shall insist that we be honest on our tests here. In other areas of your life, you may have more free-dom to be dishonest. . . .

GINGER: Aren't you telling us what to value? . . .

TEACHER: I don't mean to tell you what you should value. That's up to you. . . . All of you who choose dishonesty as a value may not prac-tice it here, that's all I'm saying.[38]

This exchange clearly demonstrates the moral relativism of the self-esteem approach to values. The teacher insists on honesty in her class-room but makes no attempt to argue for honesty *as a virtue*. This leaves the students with the impression that all values are equal—that it is quite acceptable for someone to choose dishonesty as a personal value. I think it is safe to say, however, that for most people, dishonesty as a value is *not* equal to honesty. But values clarification does not differentiate between *personal values* and *public virtues*. Since the students are not told that hon-esty is better than dishonesty, they have no understanding of virtue or what it means to be a moral or virtuous person.

It is interesting to note that if we read the passage closely, we can see that Sam had a primitive understanding of virtue: "You have to be all one way or all the other." He was trying to say that people who are honest and virtuous do not lie some of the time, when convenient. They attempt to be honest at all times. Sam was looking for moral guidance and provided the teacher a prime opportunity to explain the difference between values and virtues, but unfortunately she didn't take the hint.

It is easy to see why this approach appeals to self-esteem advocates and why it is still frequently practiced in schools today. It does not require the teacher to judge her students' values or take responsibility for teaching them the "correct" values. It also leaves each child's worldview—no matter how distorted—intact, which of course is considered essential to the preservation of self-esteem. The belief is that if the teacher had used the exchange as an opportunity to teach the virtue of honesty, students would be forced to question their values, which might undermine their self-esteem. This of course is just another myth. It is unlikely that questioning their values is enough to undermine their self-confidence. In fact, it is only through such self-examination that children can begin not only to learn about their own prejudices but learn real moral lessons.

Morality cannot be legislated, and in the end people make up their own mind about what values or virtues they support. But as William Kilpatrick writes in *Why Johnny Can't Tell Right from Wrong*, "a person who has learned something of courage, respect for truth, and concern for others, who has begun to put these ideals into practice, and who cares about doing the right thing is better equipped to reach sound moral judgments than one who has been schooled only to exchange opinions."[39]

Why Moral Education Makes Liberals Nervous

Self-esteem promoters are not the only ones who shy away from the issue of teaching moral values to children in schools. It is a topic that makes many people nervous, primarily because moral education has become associated with conservative—and particularly religious conservative—politics. Part of the reason for this is due to the different ways liberals and conservatives view the purposes of education. Conservatives believe schools should provide young people the tools the need to take their place in society. They support a classical liberal arts and sciences education that inculcates the traditional intellectual and moral virtues of hard work, obedience, development of logic, and so on. The teacher is considered the authority in the classroom and, along with the parents, the primary moral role model for children.

Political liberals, on the other hand, tend to regard schools as instruments of social and political change. Most believe that the liberal arts and sciences (the "core" curriculum) should be taught, but they also believe that students should learn about different cultures and become familiar with issues of poverty, race, and social justice. From this perspective, schooling is about releasing the potential of each individual student and helping all students become aware of a variety of social, political, and economic concerns. Thus for conservatives, the purposes of schooling are primarily intellectual and moral but for liberals, they are social and political.

From a liberal perspective, therefore, the idea of moral education implies the imposition of a set of values that perhaps not all students support. Teaching morality thus may seem to go against the liberal value of tolerance, which includes respect not only for cultural differences but for moral and ethical differences as well. Liberals consequently have tended to shy away from supporting moral education, arguing that the best we can do with sex education, for example, is provide "neutral" information regarding choices and consequences, leaving the students to decide what's right on their own. Conservatives have jumped into the moral void left by liberals and formed their own agenda for character education, which of course includes notions such as prayer in schools and an end to any form of sex education.

Predictably, liberals roundly condemn conservatives for trying to get prayer back into the schools as part of their not-so-hidden moral agenda while conservatives criticize liberals for assuming a totally hands-off approach to the issue. The irony, of course, is that both groups are right. By refusing to become involved in moral education, liberals have allowed conservatives to set the public agenda for it. And conservatives, seeing a golden opportunity to improve their public image and influence education policy, have been only too glad to jump in and claim ownership of moral issues. Conservatives understand something very important that liberals have failed to grasp: The public wants moral leadership and if only one agenda is offered, they'll take it.

The 1995 Phi Delta Kappa/Gallup poll on the public's attitudes toward public education illustrates just how far people will go to support any measure that promises to bring back morality into the public schools. According to the poll, 75 percent of public school parents and 71 percent of all respondents favored a constitutional amendment to bring prayer back into the public schools. This was up slightly from 1984, when 73 percent of public school parents and 69 percent of all respondents supported the idea.[40] (The most recent poll from September 1998 shows 73 percent of public school parents and 67 percent of all respondents supporting such an amendment.)[41] At first glance, the responses would seem to indicate considerable support for conservative views on education. However, the picture is considerably more complex than that. When asked whether they believed that the introduction of spoken prayer would improve student behavior, more than half of the respondents, *including those who opposed public school prayer*, said they believed it would.[42]

These results should serve as a wake-up call to liberals. Clearly, moral education is an issue parents care about. If even parents who oppose school prayer are willing to consider it to improve student behavior, then parents are truly desperate for some leadership in the area of moral education. And clearly, parents are willing to examine a variety of options. In the 1995 poll, when asked whether prayers should be Christian or whether they should reflect all major religions, an overwhelming 81 percent supported the latter. Seventy percent indicated a preference for a moment of silence, while only 24 percent voiced support of spoken prayer.[43] The results speak for themselves. Parents want some kind of moral education in schools but do not favor Christian prayer or any kind of prayer, for that matter. They are only willing to consider it because they don't see many other options. Most parents clearly want moral education that includes tolerance of others and respect for different religious and cultural practices. But if that isn't offered, they will take what is.

If liberals do not like the kinds of moral education their children are being served up in schools, they will have to get involved in the debate. They may see this as a dilemma because they fear that supporting any version of moral education will threaten their commitment to cultural diversity and tolerance. But liberals cannot have it both ways; they must either define a liberal moral agenda as an alternative to conservative moralizing or they must accept whatever the conservatives put forward. In other words, they either have to put up or shut up.

What We Believe In

Liberals have made two errors in assuming that supporting moral education in school violates civil liberties or somehow threatens social justice. The first error is the belief that there are no moral values supported by everyone and that therefore any kind of moral education will necessarily be oppressive or offensive to someone. Now if we believe that moral education consists only of what conservatives make it out to be—prayer, no sex education, and homilies against homosexuality—that does seem pretty sure to offend someone. But there are many other values, what I call "generic" moral values, that the vast majority of citizens can support.

The 1993 Phi Delta Kappa/Gallup poll on the public's perceptions on education surveyed what values, if any, the public believed should be taught in public schools. Ninety-seven percent of respondents cited honesty and 93 percent supported teaching democracy and acceptance of people of different races. Patriotism, caring for friends and family members, moral courage, and the Golden Rule were supported by 91 percent of respondents and 87 percent agreed that we should teach acceptance of people who hold different religious beliefs.[44] Even more significant is that the level of agreement was much higher than the respondents themselves had anticipated. When asked if they thought it possible to agree on a set of basic values such as honesty and patriotism that would be taught in the public schools, only 69 percent of all respondents answered in the affirmative.[45]

Clearly, most of us are skeptics. We do not believe that we could possibly reach agreement on a set of values to be taught in schools, but the facts tell us otherwise. There is close to universal agreement on several values. Some observers will of course object that it is not that simple; that my definition of "responsible" or "respectful" may not be the same as yours and that any one of these moral values could be taught in a way that furthers someone's political agenda. That is always the case. Moral values do not exist in a vacuum and only have meaning within a particular political and social context. There is no such thing as "pure," unadulterated moral values, just as there are no pure, unadulterated humans who practice them. We are all subject to a variety of pressures, political and otherwise, but that does not mean that we should therefore give up trying to teach character in schools.

Indeed, lack of discipline, drug use, and violence and gangs are, along with financial constraints, the three issues that the polls show the public is, year after year, concerned about in the schools. In the 1995 Gallup poll, when asked about the causes of student violence, 24 percent of parents identified lack of parental control and discipline, and lack of values, and 20 percent believed that lack of family structure, family problems, or poverty are to blame. Drug problems were cited as the third most important cause, while lack of self-esteem was cited by only 6 percent of respondents nationally.[46]

Educational researcher and commentator Alfie Kohn writes that "exhorting students to be 'respectful' or rewarding them if they are caught being 'good' may likewise mean nothing more than getting them to do whatever the adults demand."[47] He worries that this kind of character education is much more likely to produce compliant, unthinking individuals than independent-minded, thoughtful persons. Kohn refers to a reader's letter in the *New York Times Magazine* on character education and wonders whether moral education could lead to the kind of mindless obedience that allowed the Nazis to assume power in Germany in the 1930s.[48] He suggests that we might consider teaching empathy and skepticism as an alternative to traditional character education with its focus on patriotism and obedience.[49]

Empathy I have already discussed at length as the necessary cure for the epidemic of narcissism that the self-esteem movement has spread. I address skepticism in the next chapter as the antidote to cynicism and to the kind of indoctrination of which teacher educators are guilty. I disagree with Kohn that demanding students be respectful threatens their ability to think for themselves, but I agree that empathy and skepticism are probably two of the most important moral values we could teach to children. But again, doing so requires those of us who do not agree with the religious conservatives to be courageous enough to speak up about it, and let the American public know that there are alternatives. Character education, moral education, ethics—it can be whatever we want to call it and whatever we want it to be. No one person or one group "owns" morality in this country; it belongs to us all.

What we need is a public conversation regarding these values, a conversation that includes liberals, conservatives, and everyone in between. Liberals may never be able to convince religious conservatives that homosexuality and abortion are not sins, and there may always be issues that divide. But we must talk to one another. Moral education is a public, national responsibility that should not be left to one political interest group, no matter who it is. It is far too important to all of us.

What's Good Isn't Relative: When Tolerance Can Be a Bad Thing

The second error that liberals make regarding moral education is to posit tolerance as a virtue above all other virtues. At first glance, it would seem that tolerance is a good thing for children to learn. They need to understand the importance of accepting differences or personal preferences in music, dress, language, and so on, and learn that judging others arbitrarily because of how they look or talk is not acceptable in a civil society.

But tolerance is not always a good thing. We have to ask ourselves how much tolerance is too much. For example, it is one thing to tolerate cultural differences. Why shouldn't we? Just because others dress or act differently than we do is not a reason to judge them. But there are definitely times when we should judge others. What if we are confronted with a horrific crime, such as the dragging death of James Byrd or the lynching of Matthew Shepard? Are these acts tolerable? If we answer yes, then we are saying that our society will tolerate other heinous acts. But I believe that the vast majority of people believe that those are acts that should never be tolerated. We condemn them—judge them—as evil.

Tolerance, then, is not a virtue like honesty, something that is always a good thing, but a value that has its place. It must therefore be tempered with other moral principles. In the cases above, it is clear that respect for human life must outweigh tolerance. Too much tolerance can lead to a tacit acceptance and thereby implicit approval of acts that should not be tolerated—acts that should be judged unacceptable. If we were to become accustomed to tolerating anything, we would lose our ability to recognize that which is wrong.

In a recent article in the *Chronicle of Higher Education* one observer writes about a problem that she experienced in her creative writing class.[50] The class was reading a short story that included a description of human sacrifice. Over the many years she had taught the course the responses had always been the same: shock, horror, and surprise. But this time, things were different. The students were blasé; not only did the human sacrifice not shock them, it didn't even seem to interest them. She pushed them, trying to get an authentic response of outrage or anger at such acts, but was met with a variety of responses, all of which indicated the students' unwillingness or inability to actually admit that they were against human sacrifice.

Finally, she turned to a fifty-something student, a nurse, who seemed to be a sensible person. But the nurse said, "Well, I teach a course for our hospital personnel in multicultural understanding, and if it's part of a person's culture, we are taught not to judge, and if it has worked for them. . . ." (I have heard this same kind of discussion many times, and it is the same questionable logic (as well as questionable ethics) that underlies Western women's defense of practices like female circumcision, more properly called genital mutilation.) At this point, the instructor gave up. Clearly, her students had been taught that we must have tolerance at all costs, even if that means the loss of our individual moral principles and collective moral outrage.

Putting tolerance on too high a pedestal merely reinforces moral relativism. Too much tolerance renders us incapable of identifying what is honorable, moral behavior and judging what is evil. And if we lose the ability to judge good from bad, we lose the moral foundation of a civil society. Ironically, the total absence of moral guidelines has the same consequences as the character indoctrination that Alfie Kohn and others worry about. Moral relativism renders us unable to differentiate good from evil, and moral indoctrination—moral absolutism—renders us unable to act for good, even if we wanted to. Either way, society loses.

But if conservatives do not see how character indoctrination can become character assassination, liberals do not see the dangers of too much tolerance. They worry that judging someone, even someone who has committed a heinous crime, makes them not a nice person. Unquestionably, judging others is likely to make one unpopular. But what is more important, being good or being nice? In our efforts to promote self-esteem at all costs, we seem to have confused the two. It bears repeating that *feeling* good is not the same as *being* good or *doing* good.

Another thing that worries liberals about teaching morality is that somehow teaching virtue is not democratic; that it sets up standards that no one can meet and therefore discriminates against certain groups. But the virtue of virtue, as it were, is that it is precisely the opposite. It does not discriminate. If we expect all students to be honest, decent, responsible, and courageous, how can that possibly be called discriminatory? It is not as if working-class parents are less interested in these values than middle-class parents. African Americans do not care less about their children's upbringing than Asian Americans or Latinos, for example.

Establishing different moral criteria for different groups *would* be discriminatory, but setting the same standards for all students is not. Although the method of teaching values in each cultural or social class group may be slightly different, clearly there are values that cut across all class and ethnic lines. In this sense, the teaching of virtue—simply put, behaving according to accepted principles—is profoundly egalitarian. It says we believe that all students can and will uphold these common virtues.

Clearly, parents understand the importance of moral education. So the challenge in front of us is not primarily to convince parents of the wisdom of teaching virtue but to convince teachers. In general, teachers are notoriously reluctant to teach morality, not only because it sometimes involves debating contentious issues or examining moral dilemmas, but because it might make them unpopular with students, and they want to be liked. But as a friend of mine—an experienced teacher—told me before I started teaching at university, "It doesn't matter if they like you; they only have to learn something from you." And she was right.

The same goes for public school students. Contrary to what the self-esteem movement has taught us, they are not in school to become best friends with their teachers but to learn something from them. And ethical principles and behavior is one of the most important things they will learn. William Kilpatrick writes in *Why Johnny Can't Tell Right from Wrong* that when given the option of teaching character education as either "values clarification" (getting students to be clear about their own values) or the conscious inculcation of certain values, parents will almost invariably choose the second, while teachers are likely to choose the first.[51]

Who has it right, the parents or the teachers? I'll throw my lot in with Kilpatrick, who concludes that

> parents and teachers in America have been on different wavelengths for quite some time, but I don't think it's necessarily the parents who need to make an adjustment. I believe they prefer character education over the experimental model not because of some knee-jerk conservatism, or because of their limited knowledge of theory, but because they have a better grasp of what is at stake, and because it is their own children who are in question.[52]

Parents today need all the support they can get because their natural instinct to guide and discipline their children has been so undermined by self-esteem dogma that many have lost faith in their abilities and even their motives in parenting. Having been told for over twenty years that setting ethical and behavioral standards for their children will destroy their self-esteem, some parents are experiencing a crisis of confidence in their parenting skills. Most parents probably have the right instincts, but they have been seriously undermined. What they need right now is a little reinforcement.

"Raise Your Children Well":
Morality and Other Lessons for Parents and Teachers

In some ways this book is all about moral values and how we need to resurrect them in order to fight the amorality and immorality of the self-esteem movement. I have proposed empathy to replace narcissism, a sense of community or connectedness to stem separatism, and now rationality and morality to counter the relativism of emotivism. I discuss intellectual relativism and rationality in the next chapter, but here I offer a few suggestions on how moral and intellectual values are best preserved.

I have already referred to moral values and political values, but now I would like to propose another category of values that schoolchildren need to be taught: intellectual values. These are the principles that should underlie all student learning and behavior in schools. Intellectual values are those values that everyone should acquire in school: understanding the importance of hard work; good study habits and organization; a respect for the ideas of others; a respect for the truth and a healthy skepticism of what is often packaged as "the truth"; the development of critical thinking and logical reasoning; taking responsibility for one's learning (including doing required assignments and being prepared for class); and a general understanding that success is earned, not given.

Basic civil behavior, which includes allowing others to express their views in a respectful environment, acknowledging the authority of the instructor, and arriving in class on time, is also an intellectual value. These are not revolutionary ideas, but they are very important. Without them classrooms degenerate into chaos, teachers lose their authority, and children fail to learn. Fortunately, these attitudes and behaviors can be taught without much difficulty, but only if they are introduced at the very beginning of a child's educational experience. Middle school or high school is far too late to be developing study habits and critical thinking. But once a student acquires them, she has them for life.

Intellectual values must be taught hand in hand with moral values, and the two complement one another. A student who respects the opinions of others (an intellectual virtue) can understand the virtue of courtesy, for example (a moral virtue). And the student who respects the concept of truth can easily be taught the importance of honesty. Intellectual values thus provide the mental scaffolding that helps prepare the student to learn moral lessons. Like the concrete foundation or wood beams supporting a house, they may not be sexy but they are certainly necessary. Without them, the house cannot stand. And now, some specific suggestions for teaching morality in schools and in the home.

Lesson 1: Actions really do speak louder than words. Set an example.
Nothing speaks more profoundly to a child than the example set by her
parents and teachers. Moral lessons mean nothing unless the child sees
them modeled by people she respects. For parents, this means monitoring
your own behavior in the home or anywhere you are with your child, including the language you use and the attitudes you have toward others.
For teachers, it means doing that and more: treating all your students
equally and with respect, and letting them know that you also expect respect from them.

Lesson 2: Make the values and virtues you believe in explicit. While setting an example is essential, it is also important to convey to children just
what being a "good" person means. Young children in particular need
ideas explained in concrete ways. Use stories from your own childhood to
explain what you learned about honesty, for example, and why that is an
important virtue. Use their natural egotism to ask them how they would
feel if someone did something bad to them. This will help them develop
empathy and get beyond their own feelings to consider the feelings of others—the first step in moral education.

It is a little more complicated with teenagers. They may flout your rules
and say they don't care about "virtues" just to act out and express their independence. Parents and teachers need to understand the adolescent desire
for individual expression while making it clear to young people that they,
the adults, are still the moral authorities in their lives. But this can also be
an interesting time. Teenagers are fully capable of abstract thinking, and if
they have been taught the basics of ethical behavior, this could be a time to
debate the virtues of honesty or other values. Engage them, if you can, and
ask why they disagree with you. This kind of discussion not only helps
teenagers work through their own ideas but can open other useful avenues
of communication between them and the adults in their lives.

**Lesson 3: Monitor what children read and see on TV and use that ma-
terial to discuss moral and ethical concerns.** There are many wonderful
books for children as well as teenagers that address moral issues without
hitting the reader over the head with them. Any book that is worth reading includes some kind of moral tension, concern, or dilemma simply because they are part of life. Take time to read the books yourself and then
read them with and to your children. Nothing has been proven to be more
important as a gauge of academic success than early literacy, and the best
way parents can encourage it is to read to their children. By reading good
literature themselves, children absorb moral lessons in a very natural way.

Monitoring television watching is equally if not more important than
monitoring reading because, unlike reading, watching television is pas-

sive. Today American children watch on average an unbelievable seven hours of television a day. This is time that could be far better spent doing sports, talking with the family, reading, or doing any number of other activities. Try to limit the number of hours your children watch TV and make sure you know what they are watching. Although a lot of television is pretty worthless, there are some good programs for children and teenagers. Watch them with your kids (if you can convince them to let you!) and discuss some of the issues that come up. And don't rely on the new TV rating system to decide what is and is not appropriate for your child. You are the only censor that counts.

Lesson 4: Get children involved in the rule-making process. Remember: principles precede practice. This is one area in which the teachers may be ahead of the parents. A very useful trick that elementary and middle school teachers often use when establishing rules of behavior and comportment is to get the kids to brainstorm good rules. There are a couple of advantages to this. First, the students feel involved in the decision-making process and feel that their opinions count. Second, they are more likely to adhere to rules that they feel they had an investment in creating, so the very act of rule making helps teach them responsibility and consequences for actions. Although the teacher really controls the process by directing the students toward appropriate rule making, she is relieved of some of the pressure and does not seem to be unilaterally imposing sanctions.

I am not proposing here some kind of "values clarification" approach to behavior but am encouraging parents and teachers to allow their children some input when making household or classroom rules. The parent or teacher, however, is the one in charge and reserves the final authority when it comes to rules. A final benefit of this approach with teenagers is that it allows an opportunity for debate over moral issues. The teenager might think she is just bargaining for a later curfew; that's fine—let her think that. But the bargaining process will help her start thinking about what is appropriate behavior and what is not—and that is ultimately the goal. Teenagers need to know why we have rules, and what the principles underlying them really mean.

Lesson 5: Ask children what they think, not feel, about political, moral, and social issues. Your children get enough talk about feelings at school. Use your time with them to ask them what they think about issues. It doesn't matter whether they know anything much about a topic—just get them to exercise their brains. Ask them about things they are interested in, even if it's basketball or video games. Get them thinking; it's a skill that needs to be developed like anything else. And for teachers who are fed up with the emphasis on feelings: Lead the way!

I remember being at a friend's house when I was only six or seven. The whole family ate dinner together, and while they ate they discussed various political issues. I didn't understand any of it, and when my friend's father asked me my opinion I don't think I had much to contribute, but the fact that I was asked stuck in my mind. Two things occurred to me that day: first, that there was a whole world out there and maybe I should learn about it, and, second, that maybe my opinion on that world mattered. That is a wonderful basis for developing self-confidence. And remember: We have to be thinking beings in order to be moral beings.

Lesson 6: Know how ethics are dealt with at your child's school. I say "dealt with" rather than "taught" because you may very well find that they are not taught at all. Talk with the principal and the classroom teachers. What responsibility do they believe they have as moral authorities? Do they believe children need guidance in developing a sense of ethics or do they think children should be left to make up their own minds, without any moral grounding? If they believe the latter, that is a clear sign that some version of "values clarification" is going on in your child's school.

In addition to examining the approach toward ethics, find out what the specific classroom rules are. If there are few rules or if they are very vague, chances are your children are not getting a clear picture of right and wrong. If they are explicit, with clear consequences for infractions, you can be confident that your child is learning within a defined moral structure.

Lesson 7: Make sure you know who your children's friends are. Schools have a very strong socialization influence on children, and nothing influences them more than their peers. In the early grades the authority of the teacher may overshadow the authority of one's peers, but by middle school and high school students are much more concerned with the opinions of their colleagues. All parents of course have to decide for themselves the kinds of friends they feel comfortable with their child having, and there are no hard-and-fast rules here. But the more you know about your children's friends and their families the better able you will be to deal with any problems that may arise.

And do not jump to conclusions. Just because your child brings home someone of a different race or class is no reason to think that he or she is not an appropriate friend. Morality crosses all boundaries. Invite your children's friends over and call up their parents to introduce yourselves. If you want to be sure that your child is associating with people who share the same kinds of values as you, you need to take the time to get to know them.

Lesson 8: Show your child that she is a member of a community. We are all members of a variety of communities. A community could be made up of neighbors, people who speak the same language, people of the same ethnicity, or people who attend the same house of worship. We may even form communities with people we see at the gym. The point is, in one way or another, we are all connected.

Understanding that we have meaningful relationships with others is very important for children to learn, and a first step in becoming ethical persons. Part of being in a community means coming to care for others in it, and that caring—empathy—helps us come out of ourselves and think of others. Being an ethical person means acting honorably toward people we don't know, as well as to those we do, but giving of ourselves to a friend or a neighbor is a good first step. Again, this is not something that should be shoved down a child's throat. Getting your children involved in community activities like the local softball league or dance lessons or volunteering together at an old people's home or an animal shelter are all great ways to open up the world to the children and help them see how much they have to give.

Lesson 9: Encourage your children to set high personal standards for themselves in every area of life. Becoming a good person, like becoming a successful person, can only happen if we set high standards for ourselves. If we teach children to be the best they can be intellectually and morally right from the start, they keep those habits as adults. And having high expectations in one area usually transfers to another area. This is why students who excel academically frequently succeed in sports or the arts as well.

Setting high standards for ourselves becomes a way of life. If children are accustomed to trying hard in all areas of their lives, becoming an ethical person will seem very natural. Although we all fall short of our expectations in one way or another, we need to teach our children one very important lesson: *There is no shame in failing; there is only shame in failing to try.*

Lesson 10: Be involved in your child's school. My teacher-education students have frequently joked with me about the parent from hell—the one who is always in class, checking up on things, volunteering, asking questions, and generally getting in people's hair. Well, nothing will ensure that your child gets a good education better than your becoming that parent. While most teachers do welcome parental involvement, some see it as infringement on their "territory." But wherever your child's welfare is at stake, that is your territory too. Do not be intimidated by your child's teachers. Remember, you are the first and most important educator in your child's life. So get involved, and if something doesn't smell right to you, ask questions and don't stop asking until they are answered to your satisfaction.

There are hundreds of questions that you may want answered about your child's education. But there are very specific questions you need to ask that will tell you how much the self-esteem movement is influencing your child's education. Below are some questions that will help guide you in identifying and addressing problems in your child's education related specifically to the self-esteem movement, and red flags that indicate a potential problem.

Questions *You* Need to Know the Answers to About Your Child's Education

Question 1: How are reading and writing taught in elementary school? Are children actually instructed in specific skills? Is there a variety of interesting, quality literature available for them to read?
   Red flags: Children expected to "pick up" reading skills when they are "ready." Children always reading in groups. Children not reading by second grade.
Question 2: Are students expected to master material before going on to the next grade?
   Red flags: Children passed on irrespective of knowledge or achievement (social promotion). No discussion of such policy with parent. School downplaying student's lack of knowledge or achievement. Little school interest in student progress.
Question 3: How are students evaluated? Are they given a variety of measures, including tests, essay work, individual and group projects? Are they evaluated continually?
   Red flags: Infrequent evaluations. Evaluations based primarily on group work. Teachers referring to evaluation/grading in negative terms. Excuses made for poor student performance.
Question 4: Are your children being challenged by their work?
   Red flags: "Dumbed-down" material, such as "children's" versions of classic literature with "easy" language. Children not being allowed to advance at their own pace. Boredom.
Question 5: Are high school students taking a solid core of courses and being prepared for college?
   Red flags: Students with too much time on their hands. More than one or two elective courses. Vocational rather than academic courses. Courses that you do not see the need for. Little college and career counseling available; your child is unclear about her postsecondary educational or employment options.

Question 6: Do your children receive regular homework assignments?

    Red flags: No homework; negative teacher attitude regarding home-work; child insists she always finishes her homework at school.

Question 7: How does your child's teacher define his or her job?

    Red flags: Teacher sees himself as therapist rather than intellectual leader. *Giveaways:* Too much discussion of "caring" and how children "feel" and too little of academic achievement or standards.

Question 8: How are computers used in your child's education?

    Red flags: Computer-assisted instruction replaces much of live teacher–student interaction. Teacher lets students work on comput-ers with little instruction, guidance, or input. Child reluctant to read; wants to only play with computer. Child will read *only* on computer. Child watching too much TV.

Question 9: Are your children learning how to manage information as well as the principles of research? Are they required to do a variety of writ-ing assignments?

    Red flags: Little or no writing assignments (sadly, very common). Students never go to the library or do research on the Internet. Too much reliance on Internet. Kids never ask for your help in doing re-search assignment (means they probably aren't doing any).

Question 10: Is your participation as a parent welcomed?

    Red flags: You feel pressure from faculty and staff to stay clear of school. Few school involvement opportunities. Teachers/administra-tion reluctant to answer any of your questions.

It may be that you don't find any of these red flags at your child's school. If so, you are fortunate. Your child has the opportunity to obtain the maximum benefit from her education. But parents must always be vigilant. While the tide is beginning to turn and educators are starting to question their commitment to self-esteem, its effects are likely to linger. Ending emotivism and its consequences is not something that will be ac-complished in a day. It requires an ongoing commitment from parents and teachers together. The measure of our success will not only be whether our sons and daughters grow up to be the decent, responsible, and honest citizens we know they can be, but whether they will end our dependence on the myth of self-esteem when they become the parents and teachers of the future.

Back to the Future

From Cynicism to Skepticism and Hope

> *Toto, I have a feeling we're not in Kansas anymore.*
> —Dorothy, in *The Wizard of Oz*

WHEN O. J. SIMPSON WAS ACQUITTED of the murder of his ex-wife, Nicole Brown Simpson, and her friend Ronald Goldman, the American public was divided over whether this was a just verdict or a travesty of justice. The most obvious fault line appeared to be race, with many African Americans exulting that for once a black defendant had enjoyed true justice. White Americans, however, argued that the black members of the jury had used this high-profile case to help settle the score for all those black Americans unjustly imprisoned. Only O. J. Simpson knows the truth of what happened that day in June 1994. He has repeatedly proclaimed his innocence.

Whether race was in fact an issue in the murder investigation, as the defense contended, it clearly colors how we regard its outcome. But there was something else going on there too: how the evidence against Simpson was perceived by the jury. The blood evidence that he was at the crime scene seemed overwhelming; there seemed little question that Simpson had been there. The defense tried to explain away the physical evidence by arguing that (1) Simpson, the great football star, would simply never do such a thing and/or (2) Simpson was the victim of a police conspiracy to frame him for the murders and/or (3) the police were incompetent in their handling of the evidence, the blood samples were tainted, and the physical evidence unreliable. It was a brilliant strategy. Being offered a smorgasbord of defenses, each juror could pick whichever one he or she liked best and thus sufficient doubt would be raised to acquit Simpson. And that, of course, is exactly what happened.

Critics of the verdict argued that defenses (2) and (3) were intellectually dishonest, based not on facts but on imagination and conjecture; whether or not Judge Ito should have permitted them is open to debate. But what should really concern us is how the jurors were sufficiently swayed by these doubts that they were apparently able to discount the blood evidence. Two issues: (1) that there was no logical reason why the police would have framed Simpson and (2) that even if the blood evidence *was* tainted, that did not mean it was not *his* blood did not hold water with the jury. Once the seeds of doubt were planted, nothing could uproot them.

My point here is not to argue the facts of the case but to illustrate the fragility of our reasoning powers and the ease with which they can be supplanted by conjecture, opinion, fantasy, and myth. In retrospect, it is not surprising that the jury delivered the verdict that it did—there was just too much emotional baggage attached to this case. None of us knows what went on in the minds of the jury members, but it seems very likely that two issues—race and celebrity—shaped the trial in such a way that, for these individuals (and perhaps for many of us), no other verdict was possible.

What ties race and celebrity together is that they both play on our emotions. Race is a political, economic, and social issue, but it is also highly emotional for both whites and blacks. No matter what the reality of a situation may be, many of us react emotionally, rather than rationally, when it comes to race. And many of us, particularly in California, where the trials and tribulations of celebrities are daily features on the local newscasts, are very impressed with celebrities, especially sports heroes. In essence, the jurors were unable to extricate themselves from these emotional issues and thus apparently rendered a verdict based on emotion rather than reason or even common sense. This lack of rationality is another consequence of emotivism.

"You're Not Using Your Brain!"

How often have we heard this said or how often have we said it to others, trying to get them to understand something that to us seems obvious? All of us are emotional and intellectual beings, but when deciding issues of law, or even difficult issues in our private lives, be it finances, children, or the in-laws, it always pays to rely on your head, not your heart, because your heart can so often lead you astray. Women in abusive marriages, for example, frequently need lots of encouragement *and* logical argument to convince them that even though they may love their husband, abuse is never an expression of love. They *feel* love, but it is a *wrong* love, if we can put it that way—it is love misplaced. Only reason (and time) can help them understand that it is usually in their best interests to leave their husband. If we left these women to decide their fate based on emotion alone, it is certain that we would see an increase not only in the numbers of women who stay with abusive men but an increase in the numbers murdered by them.

This is just one example of the innumerable ways in which "putting our thinking caps on" (as my teachers used to say) is critical for our social, economic, and intellectual survival. But the thinking cap seems to have gone out of fashion, at least with some professors of education, who are trying to replace it with a dunce cap, knit from the yarns spun by the self-esteem movement. Myth 6, for example, encouraging social promotion (discussed in Chapter 6), fosters anti-intellectualism because it says to kids that we don't really take their intellectual endeavors very seriously. If they don't do well or work hard, it doesn't really matter; they'll be passed on to the next grade just the same. Myth 8, that teachers should be therapists, also dumbs down schools, since it suggests that the historic role of the teacher as an intellectual leader is no longer valued. And finally, of course, Myth 10, that feeling is more important than thinking, just sums it all up.

The message that children absorb from this is that being an intellectual, that is, someone who knows how to think clearly, reason logically, and analyze purposefully, is not just nerdy but is a waste of their time. What they learn from the self-esteem movement is that being a thinking person is no longer valued, which is of course not true for the vast majority of the public. Just try to find a parent who doesn't care if his or her children learn how to think. Apparently the only ones who are ready to put questionable emotional "skills" above intellectual skills are professors of education and educational psychologists and, sadly, their protégés—our kids' teachers.

As a teacher educator I have witnessed countless examples of poor thinking skills, and one assignment I give them always seems to amplify this problem. The assignment is to review an academic article of their choice on almost any topic in education. I set out the guidelines in writing and review them with the class, explaining that although they should briefly summarize the article's content for my information, I am primarily interested in their analysis of it. What was the author's main point? Was there an obvious political bias? What did you learn from it? Was the writing clear and concise or did it obscure the main points (a big problem with academic writing, particularly in the humanities and social sciences). How could it have been improved? Although some reviews are first-rate—concise, clear, probing, and even witty—the vast majority are typically simple recitations of the article. They can do a fair job of *summarizing*, but there is little *analyzing*. And when there is analysis, it is *emotional* rather than *intellectual*. They are able to describe how they *feel* about the article but not what they *think* about it.

This lamentable inability to critically analyze a text or take apart an argument is not their fault. It is a skill they were never taught. And as always, there is a distinct difference in the skill and comprehension levels between most of the younger students (under age 30) and the "mature" students who went through public education before it fell under the spell of the self-esteem movement with its "discovery" learning, "invented" spelling, and other associated fantasies. The older students also understand the importance of trying to be objective when discussing an issue in class.

In the section on multiculturalism, for example, in an effort to give the students as broad an understanding as possible of the topic, I provide an overview of three distinct perspectives on it. During the discussion I volunteer my personal opinion on which of these perspectives I prefer and why, since I believe it is important to let the students know that there are a range of views on the topic. The mature students clearly understand the value of objectivity and fairness when covering such contentious issues, but the younger students either want to know which is the "right" answer (so they don't have to think about it) or why they need to know what other people think (because only their *feelings* about the issue matter).

This may sound like simple laziness, but it is actually much more serious than that. The whole basis of liberal education is critical thinking; getting out of ourselves to learn about the world around us. If we no longer care what others think or even what *we* think, only what we *feel*, the very bedrock upon which our education system rests is in danger of disintegrating. The self-esteem movement has caused an intellectual earthquake of such magnitude that its aftershocks will continue to reverberate throughout our schools for some time unless we take swift action to stop it.

One of the major problems with emotivism, as I explained in Chapter 8, is that it elevates feelings over thinking and thus is amoral. If we are not able to think clearly, we cannot become truly moral persons. Being moral means understanding ethical norms and principles and acting in accordance with them. Determining the right course of action in a given situation requires the ability not only to prioritize issues but to arbitrate between competing moral claims and find a way out of moral dilemmas. Without these skills we become moral relativists—obliged to accept all moral claims as equivalent and thus pretty much abandon the notion of right and wrong.

Emotivism also promotes an intellectual relativism—the view that all ideas, and all actions, are considered equal or that no one argument, for example, is a better, a more logical, or a more coherent argument than another. This is practically heresy for philosophers, who spend their lives trying to determine which statements are inherently nonsensical, which lead to irrational or immoral outcomes, and which are logically coherent. It should be heresy for all of us. Again, look at the Simpson trial. Perhaps if the members of the jury had been practiced in critical thinking, they would have been able to ferret out the truth and discard the lies and innuendoes. But they were unable to see the logic and power of the physical evidence and thus were left vulnerable to the claims of the defense, no matter how fanciful.

The fact is, *truth matters*. But if, for lack of intellectual training, we are unable to differentiate between fact and fiction, the very concept of truth and notions like justice, civil rights, democracy, and freedom are also at risk. These are not just abstract ideas that only scholars have to worry about but the moral and political ideals that are the foundation of American society and, indeed, of all civil societies. The classic, horrifying example of what happens when ideas (and ideals) become supplanted by myth and propaganda is the persecution of Jews, gypsies, and others in Germany during the 1930s and 1940s. The reality of anti-Semitism and the camps illustrates how massive propaganda campaigns can very successfully make the inconceivable conceivable and the impossible come true.

Historian Eric Hobsbawm describes how Hitler initiated his anti-Jewish and anti-intellectual programs as soon as he seized power, and how his book burning and other activities symbolized his hostility to the values of what most us would consider a civilized society.[1] Hobsbawm notes, however, that in the 1930s, when the concentration camps were used primarily as deterrents for potential communist subversives, a surprisingly large number of people saw the camps as unpleasant but, at worst, "limited aberrations."[2] How easily they became transformed into killing machines for millions. We may say to ourselves today, "Oh, that could never happen again." But if we do not preserve the ideals that prohibit such atrocities, they will indeed be repeated, as they were recently in Rwanda and once again in Yugoslavia.

Many of us may believe that as moral, right-thinking people we are immune to the propaganda and myth making that creates the conditions in which such acts become possible. That is a conceit in which we can no longer afford to indulge. We are all vulnerable to propaganda and indoctrination. As Jacques Ellul wrote in his classic work, *Propaganda: The Formation of Men's Attitudes*, "propaganda must be based on some truth that can be said in few words and is able to linger in the collective consciousness."[3] Successful propagandists use fragments of truth to lure us into believing what is in essence not truth. As Ellul points out, "Propaganda is necessarily false when it speaks of values, of *truth*, of *good*, of *justice*, of *happiness*."[4] The only defense against propaganda—and the descent into barbarism—is a disciplined mind and a good heart, which neither "emotional intelligence" nor the self-esteem movement can provide.

The reader may object that just because today's kids can't read or write as well as their parents doesn't mean that they're on the verge of committing some terrible atrocity. That is true, as far as it goes, because most of us preserve some basic moral sense that prevents us from crossing the line. But let us put it this way. It is much easier to convince someone to believe something amoral, or to do something amoral, if they have no conception of what that really means. We see this problem in young boys who have committed murder but seem somehow dissociated from it, as if someone else had done the killing. If we have a very specific and clear intellectual understanding of right and wrong, we are likely to at least pause to reflect before acting on the side of wrong. That does not mean, of course, that bright or educated persons are not capable of committing heinous crimes (Ted Bundy comes to mind) but rather that there is at least a possibility that they will be deterred from such action if they understand the basic premises of moral action and responsibility, as well as the consequences for violating those premises.

By not teaching children how to reason, we have left them vulnerable to all kinds of propaganda and, as Ellul points out, the real point of propaganda is not just to convince people of ideas but to get them to act in accordance with those ideas—however heinous they may be.[5] He writes:

> The aim of modern propaganda is no longer to modify ideas, but to provoke action. It is no longer to change adherence to a doctrine, but to make the individual cling irrationally to a process of action. It is no longer to lead to a choice, but to loosen the reflexes. It is no longer to transform an opinion, but to arouse an active and mythical belief.[6]

In fact, our collective indoctrination by the self-esteem movement is the paradigmatic example of this whole problem. We did not stop to examine it before inflicting its ideas on our children. We should have asked what it means, how it works, where is the evidence for it, and, perhaps more important, who is telling us about it and what is their investment in its success as a concept? But we didn't. We unthinkingly accepted its tenets and reorganized our conceptions of teaching and learning in accordance with its ideology—with tragic results. The consequences for our children I have already documented. But our continued commitment to the myths of the self-esteem movement has much more profound and far-reaching implications. It is not going too far to say that the self-esteem movement has been so successful in its objectives that it threatens the very essence of rationality and progress. Emotivism is antirational and therefore antiprogress, for reason is the instrument of progress whereas emotion is the club of barbarism.

Constructing Reality: Science, Pseudoscience, and the Future of Progress

Philosophers tell us that knowledge is defined as "justified true belief." Thus a belief is only true and can be called knowledge if it is supported by evidence. Beliefs alone are not knowledge, then, if they are neither true nor defensible on scientific grounds. Although we often use "belief" and "knowledge" interchangeably, they are not at all the same thing. It is important to understand the difference between knowledge and belief because that distinction is what allows us to differentiate between what is true and false. It is what allows us to make sense of the world.

We have all had the experience, at one time or another, of finding out that something we had accepted as true was really false, that it was not knowledge but merely an erroneous belief. One of the most famous historical examples of this was the belief that the earth was flat. When it was discovered to be round, humanity was forced to rethink an entire belief system, since what we thought we knew turned out to be false (although not everyone is convinced; the flat-earth society is still going strong). People said that they *knew* the earth was flat, but in fact they did not *know* it but merely *believed* it.

Indeed, the revelation that previously held beliefs were wrong is what scientific inquiry is all about. As Stephen Hawking writes in *A Brief History of Time,* "Ever since the dawn of civilization, people have not been content to see events as unconnected and inexplicable. They have craved an understanding of the underlying order in the world."[7] Science is ultimately concerned with trying to satisfy that craving. And every day in medicine, astronomy, physics, biology, and chemistry, we make discoveries—small or large—that help us either confirm the truth of previously held beliefs or provide evidence to disprove them. In either case, we learn something and build on our knowledge base, which gains both from the growth of new knowledge and from the elimination of myths and falsehoods.

But that craving for understanding, which provides the impetus for scientific advances, also makes us vulnerable to claims made by *social* science researchers that we should be cautious about accepting. In Chapter 2 I explained that professors of education tend to suffer from professional low self-esteem, since schools of education are generally not held in very high esteem on college campuses. In addition to this burden, education professors also suffer the same insecurities as their colleagues in other social science disciplines like sociology, psychology, or anthropology because social science research has not typically been considered as "rigorous" as research in the physical or biological sciences. They thus tend to take their research *very* seriously, as if that will prove that what they are engaged in is meaningful. But as one observer put it, "A bit more humility, perhaps, and a lot less arrogance from the men with science envy, will go further to make a better world for us all."[8]

In their efforts to be taken seriously by the public, as well as the academic community, social scientists tend to obfuscate their arguments by using language that is virtually unintelligible to anyone else (and perhaps even to them!). Many social science and humanities writers need to learn the value of economy of phrase and clarity of thought, as evidenced by their success in the 1998 Bad Writing Contest, sponsored by the editors of the scholarly journal *Philosophy and Literature*. The editors explained the winners' success by noting that all were "well known, highly paid experts who have doubtless laboured for years to write as badly as this. That they must know what they are doing is validated by the fact that, as always, the winning entries were published by reputable university presses and scholarly journals."[9]

More seriously, however, social researchers present their findings as objective scientific research that provides us universal truths about the human condition. The only problem with this, as Neil Postman has observed, is that "the quest to understand human behavior and feeling can in no sense except the most trivial be called science."[10] Postman contends that social researchers, like many of us, have fallen under the spell of what he calls "scientism": the belief that methods in the natural sciences can be used to study human behavior; that social research can produce not only knowledge but perhaps universal laws about human behavior; that such research generates principles which can be used to organize society; and that science (and the products of science) can even serve as the moral foundation of society.[11]

Postman argues that social research is not really scientific because it cannot provide universal laws regarding the human condition and because "there are almost no experiments that will reveal a social-science theory to be false."[12] This is one reason that it has been so difficult to dislodge the concept of self-esteem: because it is so vague and empty a concept that it is very difficult to refute. So, ironically, the lack of rigor in studies purporting to show the importance of self-esteem protects the concept from being seriously examined. However, where virtually *no* data exist that explain the importance of self-esteem, the sheer volume and consistency of the data from the meta-analyses I presented in Chapter 5 showing its *lack* of meaning should be sufficient evidence to show just how false the claims made regarding its importance really are.

Here the politics in which the research is embedded are as revealing as the research itself. If the data on self-esteem had not been found to refute its supposed importance in education and society, the California Task Force on Self-Esteem would not have gone to such lengths to undermine its own research. Although a popular concept in social theory can hide behind its own vagueness and be elusive to either confirmation or disconfirmation, a theory that is truly scientific must be amenable to testing that will either prove or disprove its validity. But as Postman dryly points out, "Theories in social science disappear . . . because they are boring, not because they are refuted."[13] What Postman's analysis suggests to us is that the "truths" we believe we are "discovering" through social science research are, instead, either commonplaces we already know or falsehoods masquerading as truths (as in the self-esteem movement).

I remember the precise moment when this became patently clear to me. I was a member of a faculty group reviewing other faculty applications for research funding. After we had individually rated each application according to agreed-upon criteria, we met as a group and discussed our ratings to make final decisions. One of the applications to me seemed absurd, and I said so. It was a request for funding to continue a long-term research project that was attempting to prove that children who have parents who are actively and positively involved in their education do better in school than those whose parents are not involved.

I looked around the table to see if anyone found anything unusual about the proposal, but they all said very seriously that it was a very worthwhile project. Realizing that I would have to be explicit, I said that parental involvement was certainly an important issue in education, but didn't we all already know that the hypothesis was true? This was not something that required time and funding to prove; everyone knows that, generally speaking, kids whose parents are involved in their education do better than those whose parents are not. It is obvious and a matter of simple common sense. A couple of my colleagues reluctantly admitted that, yes, there had been a lot of research to prove the hypothesis but that it was still a worthy project, and so it was funded. The fact that other proposals asked important questions to which we did not already know the answers was ignored; much better to provide funding for something that we know we can prove and thus enhance our individual and collective standing— our *esteem*—in the research community.

Historian of education Diane Ravitch writes about the sad state of educational research in a recent article in the *Chronicle of Higher Education*. On a trip to California she suddenly became ill with what turned out to be a pulmonary embolism—a potentially life-threatening condition. Lying on the examining table and listening to the physicians discuss her condition, she came to a realization: "I was deeply grateful that my treatment was based on medical research, and not education research."[14] She began to imagine what would happen if physicians dealt with illness as educators deal with problems in education. She envisioned professors arguing over whether or not she really was ill, some saying that she indeed had a problem while "others scoffed and said that such an analysis was tantamount to 'blaming the victim.'"[15] She imagined others challenging the very concept of "illness," suggesting that it was merely a social construction, with others contending that the whole discussion merely diverted attention from other, more important social injustices.[16]

Her discussion, while amusing, also tells us something important about the problems inherent to research in education and the social sciences. Physicians, she notes, "have canons of scientific validity to protect innocent patients from unproven remedies and specious theories."[17] Educators can make no such claims. But we have an obligation to make clear just how tentative our research findings are while working to make educational research as rigorous as possible. As Ravitch concludes, "In our society, we rightly insist upon valid medical research; after all, lives are at risk. Now that I am on the mend, I wonder: Why don't we insist with equal vehemence on well-tested, validated education research? Lives are at risk here, too."[18]

How a Lie Repeated a Thousand Times Becomes "The Truth"

Postman believes that "unlike science, social research never discovers anything."[19] I believe that social research does have some value, primarily through telling the story of the human experience in a new or innovative way. And it could be argued that even scientists don't "discover" things but merely piece together knowledge that already exists. As Alan Gross writes in *The Rhetoric of Science,* "Discovered knowledge is certain because, like America, it was always there."[20] Gross prefers to call scientific discoveries "inventions," arguing that scientists employ rhetorical devices to convey their ideas.[21]

Our analysis of that rhetoric can tell us much about the "invention," its author, and the era in which any particular scientific "story" was told. For example, the rhetoric in the foreword to the report issued by the California Task Force on Self-Esteem revealed a deliberate attempt to deny the research results that the task force had itself commissioned. Social science researchers and scientific researchers engage in forms of storytelling, some of which are more compelling than others. The stories scientists tell about the universe are akin to histories, biographies, and even poetry: sometimes hard to get through, but ultimately rewarding, revealing truths about ourselves and the world we inhabit. Social science researchers are, on the other hand, much more adept at writing romance novels—easy reading and with invariably a happy ending. Not surprisingly, the vast majority of the public are drawn to the latter. And no recent story has been more compelling, and better reading, than the story of the self-esteem movement. But how, exactly, did such a piece of fiction sell itself as the truth?

It is not, perhaps, surprising that at the end of a millennium we find ourselves asking the big questions: Why are we here? and What does the future hold? We move away from science, which can never give us totally definitive answers, and back toward traditional religion, New Age mysticism, or any number of other accounts of the human experience to help us make the transition into the new era. But what we would not expect is that science and the progress it has brought us would be so casually discarded and so readily replaced by willful ignorance and hysterical irrationality.

A recent article describing the development of the concept of self-esteem notes that "over the last one hundred years the concept of self-esteem has grown from a fragile idea used to ground the newly emerging discipline of psychology to a basic truth about human experience and motivation."[22] In the article the author, Steven Ward, explores the history of the concept of self-esteem and explains how it has insinuated itself into not only the fabric of social science research but the fabric of our daily lives. According to Ward, the first reference to self-esteem in psychology was in William James's *Principles of Psychology,* first published in 1890.[23] In the 1940s and 1950s the first comprehensive clinical studies of self-esteem appeared, with Abraham Maslow, among others, leading the way. Carl Rogers made self-esteem important to psychotherapy, and between the 1940s and 1970s the concept outgrew its marginal position in psychology and psychotherapy and assumed a more central role, with self-esteem being considered important to success in therapy.[24] Researchers began to explore the role of self-esteem and psychopathological disorders, such as schizophrenia, as well as the relationship between self-esteem and social class, ethnicity, anxiety, motivation, and leadership potential, among other variables.[25]

Empirical research on self-esteem exploded in the 1960s, which typically focused on parenting and education and their effect on a child's self-esteem. By the early 1970s, the concept "was so interwoven into psychological thinking that nothing short of declaring an end to psychology could stop it."[26] Up to this point the use of the concept of self-esteem had been largely confined to academia, but beginning in the 1970s it entered common parlance through the self-help movement, which had unofficially begun in 1952 with the publication of Norman Vincent Peale's *The Power of Positive Thinking*.[27]

According to Ward, three factors were responsible for the transformation of the concept of self-esteem from an obscure psychological construct to a generally accepted truth. First, self-esteem moved from being a tangential concept in psychology to an accepted term in both clinical and experimental psychology. Second, the term began to be used in daily clinical practice, which set the stage for its acceptance by those working outside of psychology. Subsequently, self-esteem began to seep into the public consciousness and thus the self-help industry began to grow.

Finally, during the years between 1940 and 1970 researchers attempted to "objectify" self-esteem by developing scales designed to measure it. As Ward notes, the fact that these scales are only approximations and have problems with what is called "construct validity" (in other words, they don't actually objectify much of anything) is conveniently forgotten once they are put into use.[28] The result of all this is that self-esteem has spread from psychology to the other human sciences and into everyday experience. It is considered indispensable for parents, children, corporate executives, and all who have drinking problems, eating problems, drug problems, marital problems, depression, or insecurity, and even those who have problems with their pets—in other words, just about everyone.

What we have here, according to Ward, is a "fragile concept"[29] that has been transformed into a strong statement that "dominates many discussions of the self within the human sciences, as well as psychological testing measures, therapeutic techniques, psychology textbooks, self-help manuals, and public discourse."[30] How self-esteem came to be so embedded in the American culture and psyche would not be worth noting if it had been a concept proven to be of import in education. But as the evidence shows, it isn't. Another observer points out that "cultural beliefs regarding self-esteem and its influence on individual behavior provide a powerful counterbalance to academic knowledge claims on the topic. This cultural commitment leads to widespread support for self-esteem despite the consistent failure of sympathetic researchers to demonstrate a causal connection between it and various forms of prosocial behavior."[31]

John P. Hewitt, in *The Myth of Self-Esteem: Finding Happiness and Solving Problems in America*, gives a slightly different but complementary explanation of how the concept of self-esteem became so important to us. He attributes the explosion in the popularity of the idea of self-esteem to what he calls "conceptual entrepreneurs" who develop and promote ideas regarding solutions to various individual and social problems (the California Task Force again).[32] Hewitt characterizes the activities of conceptual entrepreneurs as follows.[33] First, they make claims designed to persuade others of the importance of their discoveries. Second, they refer to science, or what they claim to be scientific evidence, to argue the truth and legitimacy of those claims. Third, they promote specific programs or activities based on the central concept, often modifying it to fit their own agenda. And, finally, they stand to gain financially or socially as a result of these entrepreneurial activities.

These characteristics are all part of the academic community's and the self-help gurus' approach to self-esteem. The claims regarding self-esteem have been made for about forty years now and do not even have to be defended; they are just accepted as fact. Nonetheless, just to keep interest alive, academic articles purporting to demonstrate the importance of self-esteem in our lives number in the thousands while popular articles and books on self-esteem and self-help fill up the shelves in our bookstores. Each article and book offers a slightly different slant on how self-esteem can be used or defined. Of course the only way to sell a self-help book is to claim that *yours* provides the *real* truth and the *real* insights into the power of self-esteem. What can these conceptual entrepreneurs expect to get out of their marketing efforts? Plenty, including tenure and prestige for academics, huge profits for publishing houses, and fat royalty checks for authors. It's a win-win venture; a no-brainer in more ways than one.

What is fascinating, as I have already noted, is that our obsession with the self-esteem movement and our current practice of diagnosing kids, whenever possible, with A.D.D., A.D.H.D., or some other fashionable "disease" have developed similarly. Indeed, as Hewitt points out, self-esteem entrepreneurs "tend to claim the status of victim for those whose lives they seek to improve."[34] Telling a child he has a disease or an impairment is a great way to invest him with victim status, providing the opportunity for psychologists to make their academic careers writing about it and pharmaceutical companies to make millions of dollars profiting from it. (The fact that the collection of symptoms that are called A.D.D. can also be used to describe intellectually gifted children is apparently not of interest to these companies—unless, of course, we can turn being really smart into a disease too. Now there's an idea. ...)

We should not be surprised that many people have used these myths to become very rich. That is, after all, the American way: Where there's an opportunity to make money, you can be sure that someone will grab it. And why not? If we have such a disregard for the truth and for scientific evidence that we are willing to accept a myth as true just because it claims to make us feel good, then we deserve everything we get. Our readiness to believe is an example of both American naïveté and the trend toward anti-intellectualism. Anti-intellectualism is not solely an American affliction, however. It reaches across the Atlantic as well. One observer, Oliver James, writing in the *Manchester Guardian Weekly* argues that the whole concept of schooling and exams is just too oppressive for kids and makes the tired argument that because people like entrepreneur Richard Branson don't have degrees, that proves higher education is a pointless exercise.

The fact that people like Branson, or Bill Gates for that matter, are the extremely rare exception rather than the rule is ignored. The suggestion, of course, is that they are successful *because* they don't have degrees. The reality is that they are successful *despite* that fact. Indeed, Bill Gates has demonstrated his belief in the importance of schooling by donating millions to various educational projects around the country and around the world. And taking a novel approach toward the self-esteem issue, James contends that kids in school, whether they do well or not, suffer low self-esteem just from being there. The only answer to this, he says, is an overall lowering of exam standards to "improve Britons' mental health."[35]

This is all part of a global move away from a reliance on science and even common sense in our lives to a dependence on anecdotal evidence and our emotions—a trend that was in large part caused by the self-help movement. Conventional ideas of truth and knowledge and even science are being discarded in favor of postmodern and New Age paradigms that either ignore or actively reject the idea of progress. I am reminded of a recent television commercial for a headache remedy that is a perfect example of this anti-intellectual attitude. The actor is talking to the camera about his experience with headache remedies, saying how none of them has done much good. Now that he has found this product, of course, his headaches are much improved. But the point he stresses, and clearly the selling point, is that he knows the product works *not* because of the clinical studies that prove it, but because of his *own* experience, which he *knows* he can rely on.

What is striking about this commercial is that the manufacturer is willing to downplay its own research in order to sell its product. The manufacturer and its advertising agency, having presumably researched the best selling approach, decided that playing on emotion and personal experience would sell more product than stressing any scientific evidence. And if they are right, why should selling self-esteem be any different? As John Vasconcellos, former head of the California Task Force on Self-Esteem, recently said when challenged about all the evidence indicating that self-esteem may not mean very much: "All the research in the world won't change my mind about it."[36]

This is another serious problem with education and social science research. Not only is the research itself often of poor quality and of limited use, but truth and integrity of research seem to be less valued than they once were. One of the more disturbing examples of this is the recent furor in the academic community regarding the veracity of Nobel Peace Prize winner Rigoberta Menchu's autobiography, *I Rigoberta Menchu*. In her 1983 book Menchu describes herself as a poor Indian peasant whose family was persecuted by Guatemala's right-wing military and who suffered greatly in her struggle against oppression. In the years since the book's release, some scholars have questioned the veracity of her tale, and a recently published book by David Stoll, a professor at Middlebury College, reveals that although the very broad outlines of her story are more or less accurate, Menchu appears to have filled in the details, using considerable "poetic license." For example, Menchu writes about the horrible living conditions on Guatemala's plantations where she says she was forced to work when she was growing up, but, according to Stoll, she never set foot on the plantations as a child.[37]

Now if Menchu were, say, an aspiring actress who embellished her c.v. to land an audition, we wouldn't worry about a little exaggeration. But her autobiography has been held up as a symbol of the fight for human rights the world over. Scholars and human rights activists everywhere have referred to her work as the paradigmatic example of the struggle for justice and liberty. But the real scandal is the response of many in the academic community to these allegations. Few are contesting the truth of the evidence in Stoll's book, which appears to have been very thoroughly researched. But some scholars argue that it doesn't really matter if Menchu fabricated the actual details of her life because its real value is as testimony and witness to the kinds of atrocities that occurred in Guatemala and other countries. The solidarity it created outweighs its lack of veracity.

The ends justify the means, in other words. That is a very frightening conclusion. Menchu's memoir helped bring attention to social, political, and economic concerns in South and Central America, but that does not excuse fabricating the details of those concerns. But because Menchu has become an icon of ethnic strife and struggles the world over, scholars believe she should be spared the criticism that most of the rest of us would (justifiably) receive were we to make up a story for effect. One observer even claims that those criticizing her exaggerations are discriminating against poor people. Allen Carey-Webb, a professor of English at Western Michigan University, says that "we have a higher standard of truth for poor people like Rigoberta Menchu" and that "if we find a flaw in her, it doesn't mean her whole argument goes down the drain."[38] (It's interesting to note that Carey-Webb coedited a book of articles on how Menchu's book is used in school classrooms.)

In some ways this debate parallels the culture wars. A radical multiculturalist argument about the literary canon and the oppression of minorities and women is that most of the books of our Western heritage were written by men, many of whom were misogynists, racists, classists, anti-Semites, and so on. The response to that, of course, is that the literature produced by such flawed individuals is not worthless. Can we apply the same lesson here? Well, yes and no.

Yes, in the sense that Rigoberta Menchu has probably done some good in getting the world to focus on the plight of those who without her might be a lot worse off. No, in the sense that the good does not negate the deception and fabrication. If on the one hand we celebrate her victories, or those of her people, then on the other we must reject her methods. And if her work is going to continue to be taught in schools and universities, it must be taught in an honest way, one that shows her achievements but pays close attention to the way she pursued them, which leaves a lot to be desired. Remember the outrage that erupted when pop sensation Milli Vanilli was discovered to have lip-synched its Grammy-winning album and was ultimately forced to return the award? (I wonder if the Nobel Committee is familiar with that story?)

The problem with this anti-intellectual and antiscience mind-set is that we do not always know when it is benign and when it might be dangerous to ourselves or others. Believing in some things that cannot be scientifically proven is often harmless or even helpful. After all, religions are based on faith. "Suspending disbelief" can be a source of hope and an inspiration in difficult times and can leave us open to ideas that we might otherwise dismiss out of hand. But as the events like the Jonestown massacre, for example, tell us, blind faith in something evil can have devastating consequences. And sometimes, even when presented with evidence on a particular issue, we continue to believe what has been disproven and deny the science, just because it feels good. We simply don't want to accept the truth because it will involve accepting something unpleasant or disturbing. This is what is called "truth making."

Is It Truth-*Making* or Truth *Finding*? A Reality Check

Truth-making is the process by which an idea becomes common parlance irrespective of its inherent veracity, validity, or utility. Steven Ward, in his study of the concept of self-esteem, notes that through "truth-making" advocates of self-esteem "are able to recruit and mobilize enough allies to forge a network of truth so strong and encompassing that the concept becomes a self-evident matter of fact and fades into the background of accepted knowledge."[39] Ward describes truth-making "as an ongoing process involving the mobilization of human and non-human actants and the construction of an encompassing network of truth."[40] He writes that "it is possible to conclude that some people do have self-esteem" but that it is "only possible within the confines of a particular associational network."[41] What he is saying is that he believes the concept of self-esteem only has meaning within a particular context, namely, the context of psychology and psychoanalysis. Self-esteem became a "truth" because researchers who had a vested interest in keeping the idea alive were able to create interest in it in other disciplines as well as in the public domain.

That may sound a little strange to most of us who are accustomed to believing that things are either true or not true. We think that either things exist or they do not. Throughout this book I have been referring to "the search for truth" in that way, what we could call the "realist" perspective. In fact, however, there are number of different ways in which social scientists define reality, according to the particular model, theory, or paradigm that they support. Briefly examining and comparing them will help us make sense of what seems nonsensical: the overwhelming popularity and influence of the concept of self-esteem despite all the evidence against it.

When we refer to truth in everyday conversation, we usually assume that there are truths to be found (whether or not we ever find them). But scientific research is neither a neutral nor an objective enterprise. The investigator has a relation to what he is investigating and, try as he might to be objective, the results of his research, and in particular the way he frames them, will always reflect his research paradigm or methodology, his political views, or other aspects of himself. After all, none of us lives in splendid isolation from the world; we are all inevitably mixed up with it, like it or not.

Even the "realist" view of truth, then, recognizes that our perspective affects how we portray the world through research. But in this view there is, nonetheless, a world out there, and there are truths about the world that it is our task to discover. The realist perspective is shared by most investigators in the hard sciences, but in social science, including educational research, two other paradigms predominate: constructivism and postmodernism. Volumes have been written on these theories, and I cannot claim to do them justice here. But a few words on each will help us understand the conundrum of self-esteem.

The main purpose of psychology is to examine how individuals view themselves and the world around them. Each individual has a different perspective, leading to the inevitable conclusion that there are as many realities as there are people in the world. This is constructivism: the view that knowledge is not just "out there" in the world in a vacuum, waiting for us to find it, but is created through the interaction of individuals in a given context. In constructivism "reality" is a function of our interactions with others; together we "construct" the world. The main difference between this perspective and the realist perspective is that constructivists do not believe there is a world that exists independently of our perspective, whereas the realist would say that there is indeed a world out there but that it is merely *affected* by our perspective.

So if you are a psychologist, you are likely to be a constructivist. This may explain why professors of education, most of whom are psychologists, are not concerned if the concept of self-esteem is not meaningful in the terms that most of us would like it to be *because they are operating on different terms than the rest of us.* Indeed, *it is only if you are a constructivist that you could be convinced of the importance of self-esteem.* For if you take the realist view, you must accept the overwhelming evidence against it (even taking into consideration the limits of social research). But constructivists might respond to my criticisms of self-esteem by contending that although the evidence might seem clear from my perspective, from theirs, self-esteem still makes sense; therefore they are not convinced. And indeed the test of how strongly the education establishment is committed to constructivism will be whether or not educators disown self-esteem after this evidence is shown to them or whether, like Vasconcellos, they continue to defend it no matter what.

If constructivism seems a little confusing, it is straightforward compared to postmodernism. Postmodernism, or poststructuralism, is currently the dominant research paradigm among philosophers and sociologists of education and is a very complex theory. Like constructivism, it rejects the notion that truth is out there separate from us, waiting for us to discover it. It goes much further than constructivism, however, positing that there *is* no reality apart from our reading of it. Even interpretations are only illusions of themselves, and everything is corrupted by political and economic realities.

Thus a postmodern response to my criticisms of the self-esteem movement might go something like this: "You are against the promotion of self-esteem as currently understood because you have a particular agenda to promote and have been indoctrinated by the oppressive ideology of modernism, which has fooled you into thinking that research can tell us the unvarnished truth about the human condition." From a postmodernist perspective the only reality is the reading we choose to give our interpretations of life, which are constantly changing. I use the term "reading" intentionally here, for postmodernism in the social sciences developed both from post-Marxist ideas of cultural and economic reproduction and from poststructuralist and psychoanalytic literary criticism.

Thus a postmodern, or poststructural, interpretation of reality is, like constructivism, an almost purely rhetorical construct. Let us imagine that we are trying to understand and explain the effects of late-twentieth-century capitalism on the working class through a postmodern lens. Whereas a Marxist analysis would describe the worker as oppressed or alienated by capitalism, a postmodern analysis would treat the worker as the silent subject of a cultural and economic text authored by multinational corporations in which market forces symbolize the control these companies have over the "story" of workers' lives.

If this is beginning to sound rather too esoteric, it is, and that is one of the main drawbacks of postmodernism. If a theory is to have meaning, for my money it also has to be useful, and no one has ever used postmodern theory to help us resolve any of humanity's more pressing concerns. Another problem is that postmodernism leads to a very radical relativism (although that phrase itself strikes me as contradictory) because it is essentially nihilistic. It views humanity as trapped in the here and now, dismissing progress as the colonialist fantasy of redundant modernists.

As paradigms for academic research, neither constructivism nor postmodernism is really of much use. If reality is only a product of experience, as constructivists claim, or if there *is* no reality, as the postmodernists believe, what would be the point of doing any research? What would we be discovering? Mere opinions? More theories? Why bother? Educational and social science research would be nothing more than navel gazing, which it is already dangerously close to becoming. The purpose of research in any field is (or should be) to discover or better explain truths about the human condition. As long as we believe there are things to discover, we must reject both constructivism and poststructuralism. While we must acknowledge that the search for truth is *influenced* by experience and social context, we must also reject the constructivist conclusion that therefore truths are *dependent* upon experience and the world is only a reflection of it. Likewise, we must reject the postmodern conclusion that progress is an illusion and that there is therefore no possibility of improving the human condition.

The reason for this brief detour into research paradigms is that they are very influential in academia and tend to seep out into society and affect how all of us view educational issues. Understanding their influence helps us understand how we, as a nation, came under the spell of the self-esteem movement. What happened is that a community of persons—educational psychologists and others—presented self-esteem as a meaningful concept to society. But most of us did not realize that constructivists' view of "truth" and "reality" is a little different from the norm. They were not telling the truth but engaged in what Steven Ward calls truth-making. And truth-making is virtual proof of Neil Postman's argument that social science research is really not science at all because for scientists evidence, not fantasy, is what counts.

Another example of truth-making is the furor in the early 1990s over silicone breast implants. In 1992 the Food and Drug Administration banned silicone gel–filled breast implants, on the suspicion that they greatly increase a woman's risk of developing connective tissue disorders like lupus. Women with the implants filed suit against the implant manufacturers, who in April 1994 agreed to the largest class-action settlement ever in the United States: $4.25 billion.[42] In November 1998 Dow Corning made another $3 billion settlement as part of a bankruptcy agreement. Few of us shed any tears over this, feeling that women's lives had been put recklessly and needlessly at risk and that therefore the manufacturers—large pharmaceuticals—should pay.

The only problem, according to a recent book by Marcia Angell, M.D., current editor in chief of the *New England Journal of Medicine,* is that before the settlement, there had been no epidemiological studies to demonstrate causation or even correlation between the implants and autoimmune disease, and studies undertaken after the settlement failed to demonstrate such a link.[43] Subsequent studies have shown that autoimmune disease is as, but not more, prevalent in women who have silicone implants as in those who do not. In other words, the manufacturers paid, even though their products have not been found responsible for causing connective tissue disease in women with the implants.

Now when we are dealing with potentially serious health issues it may be prudent to hold the implant manufacturers to a high standard and demand that they demonstrate unequivocally that silicone-gel breast implants do *not* promote connective tissue or other disease in women before marketing them. Nonetheless, the story is a perfect example of the dangers of truth-making. Many of us immediately accepted the story that the implants were dangerous and cheered women who were brave enough to take on the powerful pharmaceutical industry. But the construction of reality in this case was wrong. There is no truth to it, yet we continue to believe it because we want to. After all, the protagonists in the story—women suffering serious health problems—are more sympathetic characters than drug companies. But no matter how much we may sympathize with these women, by supporting their cause we are denying science. As Angell notes, "There is nothing wrong with postulating apparently unscientific hypotheses, but there is something wrong with failing to put them to the test."[44] She concludes that "the best reason for women not to turn against science is the same as it is for men: The scientific method works."[45]

The bottom line is that we should care what science tells us and should be willing to put aside our prejudices (no matter where they fall) and rely on the research to help us *find* the truth, not *make* it. In the case of breast implants, ignoring the science is only hurting drug companies and, frankly, most of us won't lose any sleep over them. But with the self-esteem movement, we are damaging our children's minds, bodies, and souls, and that is something that should keep all of us awake at night. And as Christina Hoff Sommers writes, "Pathological science is expensive. The public will soon be spending countless millions to address a fake self-esteem crisis."[46] Again, the test of whether we are willing to accept the myths of the self-esteem movement will come when, after being told the truth about self-esteem, we either bury our heads in the sand and continue to support it or stand up and say "enough!" Given what we now know about the self-esteem movement, the educational establishment's continued insistence on its importance is beginning to sound sadly like desperate claims of the earth being flat. Let us hope it does not take as long for us to accept the reality about self-esteem as it did to accept the reality about the earth or we are in for a long fight!

The good news is that there is no doubt the tide is turning. Recent articles in both the academic and popular press have begun to question the accepted wisdom regarding self-esteem, but many in the education establishment still support it, and constructivism and anti-intellectualism still exert a considerable hold over our collective psyche. The effects of post-modernism are not as immediately obvious as the effects of construc-tivism, but it too has become part of the national consciousness, demonstrated in the increasing cynicism that we see in society as a whole and particularly in young people. It is the fourth and final symptom of our addiction to self-esteem.

Cynicism

Cynicism, like relativism, is a natural outgrowth of emotivism. Together they constitute two sides of the same coin. Emotivism, by deemphasizing the intellect, leaves us vulnerable to either extreme: accepting any and all ideas (relativism) or accepting none (cynicism). In both cases the intellect is left to atrophy and with it our ability to analyze the world around us, leaving us bereft of both ideas and ideals. Cynicism is the principal char-acteristic of the postmodern condition because ideals are seen as nothing more than the myths we use to deceive ourselves about the possibility of progress. The true postmodernist insists that there is nothing to believe in and no point in believing (another statement, which, upon reflection, sounds contradictory). He is, by definition, a cynic and, having made his ideological bed, he must now lie in it.

But do we really want to accept the postmodernist's very gloomy pic-ture of the human condition, accept, as Gertrude Stein once said, "there's no *there* there?" If that is the case, it does make one wonder why, for exam-ple, the nation got so caught up in the space program in the 1960s, why we cheer when a seventy-seven-year-old man goes up (again) in space, or why we are fascinated with the Hubble pictures of Mars and the possibil-ity of human travel to the red planet. The answer, of course is simple. It is because we want to know more about the universe in which we live *be-cause we believe that there are truths to be discovered, revealed, invented, or interpreted and that our lives will be enriched by knowing those truths.* When it comes to the big picture, most of us remain optimistic. We be-lieve in progress and we believe in the future, and most of all we believe in our children's future. And we need those beliefs and that faith because they are what will sustain us into the next millennium—and help us fight the cynicism of the self-esteem movement.

It may sound absurd to suggest that something as well-meaning as the self-esteem movement could cause cynicism. After all, it's all about feeling good, and surely *that* can't promote cynicism, right? Wrong. It is possible to be cynical about any number of things, but the roots of cynicism are always the same. Cynicism is the end product of a process of disillusionment after we find out that what we thought was true or right turns out to be false or wrong. The more important the thing we believed in, the more cynical we become when it turns out to be false. And the more often we are disillusioned the more cynical we become, as our children are finding out.

When children enter school they almost invariably exhibit a natural enthusiasm and curiosity about learning. As five- or six-year-olds they are in a state of wonder about the world and, if encouraged, will absorb almost anything they're taught. In fact, it's pretty hard to find a cynical five-year-old. But when they discover that no one really cares about their achievement, that they can go on to the next grade without even mastering their current curriculum, and that acting out in class is viewed almost with approbation, the seeds of cynicism are sown.

Most children know by the time they get to school that they need to work hard, behave, and respect their teachers. They understand that school is a serious enterprise and they know what is expected of them. That does not mean that they will not try everything to break those rules—they will. But they know what the rules are. But when they encounter teachers who give them an A just for turning up in class, or for *not* fighting with their neighbor, they have no choice but to become cynical about the educative process. At the early grades this cynicism usually manifests itself behaviorally, through tardiness, lack of attention to work, or boredom. Later on, however, the real meaning of the self-esteem movement becomes more obviously apparent to them, and teenagers will react by becoming not only apathetic but perhaps aggressive, developing poor behavioral and academic attitudes.

What children really learn from the self-esteem movement is not self-respect, but the opposite: that they are not valued. They are taken seriously neither as students nor as individuals. This is the most tragic of all the consequences of the self-esteem movement. For all that it preaches respect of students and the importance of the individual, what the self-esteem movement really says to students is that their achievement is not important and their minds are not worth developing. Nothing is more likely to produce cynicism than that.

The myth that high expectations are bad for kids fosters cynicism, as does the idea that performance doesn't matter. When children realize that little is expected of them, they stop trying, internalize the concept, and decide that doing well is a stupid idea and school is a waste of time. And they can hardly help but become cynical when they realize the opportunity af-

forded them when teachers tell them it's okay as long as they tried. Kids
know that no one else can know whether or not they have really tried, so
they can fool the teacher (and the system) by claiming that they have tried
when in fact they have not.

In addition, students know that teachers are against evaluation in principle, believing it damages kids' self-esteem. So even though they know
they must be evaluated eventually, they also understand that teachers will
go out of their way to grade as generously as possible. They know they literally cannot fail. Again, this is bound to promote cynicism because the
students realize that grading, like discipline, is not taken seriously. Another policy that leads to cynicism is, of course, social promotion. The
very idea of social promotion suggests that educators no longer value the
educative process or, more important, children's intellectual abilities. It
says, in essence, "We don't care enough about Johnny to ensure that he
knows what he should before going on to the next grade. And we don't
think he's a strong enough individual to withstand the social difficulties
he may encounter as a result of being held back." What does the student
learn from this? That even teachers don't take school—or them—seriously. So why should they? What could be more disappointing than to
find out that the entire system of schooling is a farce?

Students also feel angry, deceived, and cynical when they realize that
they are not able to get into the college they want. And if because of receiving grades they did not deserve (grade inflation), they *do* get into college
but then end up in remedial classes, just how good are they going to feel
about themselves? I can tell you, because many of my teacher education
students have found themselves in just that situation. They feel embarrassed, stupid, and angry at their schools for not ensuring that they were
college ready when they graduated from high school. If anything shows a
fundamental lack of respect—and lack of "caring," self-esteem advocates'
favorite word—for students, it is social promotion. These kids *should* be
angry at the school system because it has cheated them out of the education they deserve. How much better they would have been served if they
had been held back in school early in the primary grades if necessary so
that they acquired the skills they needed early on. The necessity for social
promotion would be largely removed if we ensured that kids attained the
appropriate knowledge and skills in the first three years of schooling.

There are three levels to students' cynicism. First, they are bereft of
dreams. William Damon, in *Greater Expectations: Overcoming the Culture
of Indulgence in America's Homes and Schools*, writes that "even at early
ages, children need something beyond themselves to believe in."[47] As I
have argued throughout this book, education in its true sense should in-

volve learning about the world and our role in it, not just learning about ourselves. Discovering the world allows our imaginations to flourish and our hopes to blossom. But centering schools on the internal lives of children deadens their curiosity and denies them the opportunity to imagine the infinite possibilities that lie before them. It deprives them of hope, and that is unforgivable.

Second, students who may have the intellectual imagination to make their own dreams lack the skills to pursue them. Again, because we develop emotionalism rather than intellectualism, many kids are not acquiring the critical thinking, creative, or organizational skills that they need to make their dreams come true. The difference between those who succeed in their endeavors and those who fail is not necessarily innate intelligence (however we define it) but how, or whether, that intelligence has been developed. Successful people know how to get the most out of their skills and knowledge. We are not all blessed with the same abilities and aptitudes—that's life. But it is a crime to not help children develop the skills they do have to the utmost.

Third, kids become cynical when they realize that schooling has become something of a joke in the ways I described above. We have to remember that kids still have their common sense; they have not been completely indoctrinated into self-esteem but, being kids, are going to take advantage of it if it suits them. Initially they may be confused about the fact that they apparently don't need to work to get promoted to the next grade, but they certainly aren't going to argue the point. After all, the teachers must know best, right? And if it doesn't make sense, well, a lot of things grown-ups do don't seem to make sense. This must be just another one.

The overall consequence of cynicism with respect to education is a general disinterest in the learning process. This is probably the most damaging aspect of the self-esteem movement, since the fundamental purpose of education should be to help individuals develop an intrinsic love of learning. Without that, we are left with only force-feeding and memorization, which is training and indoctrination, not education. I have encountered this apathy and disinterest many times, but it is always disturbing to find it among future teachers.

I invariably encounter it when students do the article review paper I described earlier in this chapter. The project is to review an academic article of their choice on any topic in education connected in any way to the content of the course. Since my course covers political, economic, historic, social, and multicultural issues in education, the choice is almost limitless. I encourage them to find an article on something they're interested in or something they don't know much about but would like to know more about, or anything that in some way piques their curiosity. Despite the latitude given them, many students have told me that they just can't find an article that grabs them. There are no issues in education that they want to read about, let alone write about. I find myself wondering why they want to become teachers, since no educational issue captures their imagination. But I have to remind myself that their curiosity has been dulled and their intellectual energy sapped by the relentless manipulations of the self-esteem movement. They don't remember how to be curious and thus, sadly, will not experience the thrill of discovery.

Political Correctness: The Disease of a Cynical Society

Cynicism is not limited to schools, of course, but pervades contemporary society as well. One very insidious example of it is political correctness (PC). Political correctness is a number of things, including a kind of terrorism of the majority by the minority (whoever that may be on any given day). But it is also a clear indication of the value we put on truth in contemporary society. Being politically correct involves either outright lying or using euphemisms to describe people or events in an attempt to avoid controversy, discussion, or any kind of authentic communication.

Media coverage of the 1992 Los Angeles riots is a perfect example of this. The riots are referred to as a "civil disturbance" or "civil unrest"—indeed anything with the word "civil" in it— as if that word can deny the extreme incivility that actually occurred. And if you lived through it, you knew exactly what was going on; it was much more than just a few unhappy people venting their frustrations with the criminal justice system. At the time of the riots I was living in a somewhat dilapidated apartment complex across from a rundown department store. I remember sitting on the roof of the building trying to get a glimpse of what was going on, and what I saw—far from the intersection of Florence and Normandie, the epicenter of this "unrest"—I will never forget.

I saw youths careening down Wilshire Boulevard in trucks, brandishing machine guns; people running through the streets screaming and shouting apparently just for the adrenaline rush; my landlord dressed in his Vietnam flak jacket, fondling his sidearm; and a couple of teenagers breaking the plate glass windows of the store across the street, leaving the mannequins strewn about in a grotesque tableau, silent witnesses to the pillaging taking place within. I remember being stopped in my car two blocks from my home in the middle of an intersection while two police officers stuck their guns in the car windows and demanded to know what

I was doing (five minutes) after curfew. Curfew! No, there was nothing "civil" about this; it was a riot, pure and simple.

The reason we prefer to call it something other than what it was is so that we don't have to face the ugly truth about race relations, the justice system, and our own anger at each other. If we can deceive ourselves that it was really just some kind of neighborhood squabble, we don't need to examine the serious social, economic, and political questions it raises. But calling it "unrest" rather than a riot is more than just an exercise in collective self-deception; it means we don't care what the truth about it really was. And when we stop telling the truth, we stop valuing the truth. Soon we will not even recognize it. And not caring about the truth is the very essence of cynicism.

The irony about political correctness, is, of course, that it fails to do what it was apparently invented for: protecting the most vulnerable members of society. By dressing up the riots in the clothes of "civil unrest," we shove L.A.'s problems under the rug of relative normalcy and therefore don't have to address the needs and concerns of those most affected by them: the citizens of south-central Los Angeles. By refusing to speak the truth about the events of that April, we are also refusing to deal with their aftermath. In this case, political correctness allowed white, middle-class Angelenos—like me—to alleviate their guilt about their role in perpetuating economic disparities and a corrupt justice system while continuing on as though nothing had changed. And of course, it hadn't.

It is easy to comprehend the motivation behind political correctness in regard to the L.A. riots, however damaging it may ultimately prove to be. But in other cases it seems absurd, until we remember the principal tenet of the self-esteem movement: We all have the right to feel good about ourselves, no matter who we are or what we've done. My favorite example of this silliness is a change at the Oscars that I can only assume is the result of the self-esteem movement. Award presenters now say "and the Oscar goes to" rather than the traditional "and the winner is," presumably to preserve the self-esteem of the losers. By not mentioning the word "winner," we can all pretend that there are no losers, either. Not that anyone is confused, as the closeups of the losers' faces reveal!

But the award for the most dangerous use of political correctness must go to the person who invented the phrase "disgruntled postal worker" to describe people who have mowed down dozens of their colleagues and customers at postal stations across the country. "Disgruntled" is how you feel when someone has fifteen items in the ten-item-only line at the grocery. "Disgruntled" is the feeling you have when someone takes your parking place. Indiscriminately firing on innocent people in a post office must merit more than a "disgruntled"; it is evil, unacceptable, amoral, and un-thinkable, and the victims of such violence deserve to have their killer called what he is. The point here is that if we keep calling those who com-mit such crimes "disgruntled," eventually we will believe that's all they are. We will forget their atrocities and forget the truth of the pain of their vic-tims. By avoiding the truth of postal station massacres, we undermine the awfulness of the event, which also leads to cynicism.

The first thing we need to do to combat cynicism is to join those who consistently fight political correctness in the interests of revealing the truth. Bill Maher, comedian and host of *Politically Incorrect*, comes to mind. On the surface he appears the archetypal cynic, but my guess is he's much more a skeptic. If he were truly a cynic, he would not care about re-vealing the lies and stupidity of political correctness. A cynic doesn't care, since he doesn't believe in anything. Nothing is worthwhile and therefore nothing is worth standing up for. But a skeptic is a different breed.

From Cynicism to Skepticism—and Beyond

As I note in the preface, the reader may sense my anger throughout this book—anger not at our children, who are the victims of the self-esteem movement, but anger at the stupidity and hypocrisy of professors and teachers who should know better than to teach such rubbish. This anger and indignation caught the attention of one young reviewer, who suggested that the book seemed cynical. Referring to my suggestions that teachers need to assume some of the burden for teaching morality, he pointed out that many teachers are not very virtuous themselves and that most adults know that dishonesty, deception, and subversion are necessary survival tools in contemporary society. His final comment regarding morality was "Why bother?"—the ultimate comment of a cynical generation.

The answer, of course, is that if we care about the future of our children and our children's schools, we *must* bother. The world may very well be a hard and cruel place, as Ebenezer Scrooge claimed, perhaps even more now than during Dickensian times. But where does that get us? *A Christ-mas Carol* showed us where cynicism and bitterness leads: to isolation, unhappiness, miserliness, and a whole host of other ills. The happy ending to Dickens's story came not because the world changed but because Scrooge changed his attitude toward the world. He discarded his cynicism in favor of hope and decided to make the world a better place by becom-ing a better man. It is a simple message that is as true today as it was then.

So although I may be angry, I am not bitter and I am not resigned to the idea that schools must be what they are today. If I were indeed a cynic, I would not have bothered writing these pages describing what the self-esteem movement has done to our kids and how we can fight it. I am, rather, a skeptic, and an optimistic one at that. The difference between skepticism and cynicism is simple. Whereas the cynic believes in nothing and will always ask "why bother?" or "who cares?" the skeptic retains his or her ideals and believes that there is still good in the world while remaining realistic about the difficulties of contemporary life. We have confused skepticism and cynicism because skeptics, like cynics, are often critical of those who are naive about the bad things that happen in this world. Unlike the cynic, however, the skeptic always keeps hope alive.

Skepticism is the first step to wisdom and is, as French philosopher Denis Diderot writes, "the first step on the road to philosophy."[48] Indeed, a healthy skepticism is, or should be, the foundation of any good education. Anyone who has any experience in the world, a good education, or a critical mind will find it difficult not to be a skeptic. In practice, being a skeptic means not always accepting what is presented as the truth but examining it carefully, asking questions, demanding evidence, analyzing a situation or concept, and then coming to conclusions about what the truth of a situation really is. Critical thinking, which I have emphasized throughout this book as an essential aspect of public education, should lead to a healthy skepticism. Critical thinking means respecting evidence and logic, and demanding both before arriving at a conclusion regarding the rightness or truth of something, not just accepting at face value what is presented.

There is no contradiction between being curious and being skeptical; in fact, the more skeptical a child is about something, the more her curiosity is likely to be piqued and the more likely she will be to study a topic to determine the truth about it. In schools we can help develop skepticism by getting students to ask questions about everything they do not understand. If something does not make sense to them, we need to encourage them to analyze it, study it, and work on it until it does. Teaching good research skills is another way to develop skepticism, both about others' views and the limitations of our own. The more we investigate a topic, the more familiar we become with different views on it, and the more skeptical we become about seemingly simple answers. In research, as in life, if it looks too good to be true, it usually is.

We also need to teach children that they should respect the authority and knowledge of their teachers but that teachers are not infallible and they should not be afraid to question what they learn from them. For their part, teachers must become comfortable with the notion that students can and should question their wisdom, and they need to be prepared to give as much explanation as possible when teaching a new subject. Humility, in both instructor and student, is something that skepticism promotes, since it's pretty hard to be arrogant when you realize how little you really know and how fallible you really are.

Children also need to learn to be skeptical and critical "readers" of television. Children, like the rest of us, don't like being used. We may be surprised to find out just how independent-minded they are when they realize the extent to which they are being manipulated by clothing manufacturers, the music industry, and other groups. Manipulation is the stock-in-trade of the tobacco industry, and with evidence that current antismoking ads of the "just say no" variety aren't working, states and antismoking groups are turning to the kids themselves for ideas on how to encourage their peers to kick the habit. Florida, for instance, has organized the "Truth" campaign, designed in part by teenagers, which accuses the tobacco industry of distorting the truth about cigarettes. The state has also commissioned specialized antismoking curricula in schools, and in just one year, adolescent smoking rates in Florida dropped 19 percent, the largest drop in the United States since the 1970s.[49]

The ads that the kids have developed show the tobacco industry plotting to deceive teens to demonstrate just how far the industry will go to make more addicts. Kids know how bad smoking is for their health but, unfortunately, given the youthful belief in immortality, that sometimes isn't enough to get them to stop. However, being told that they are being indoctrinated by a bunch of cynical tobacco industry executives into thinking that smoking is cool just might get to them, the teens say. Teens' skepticism about the tobacco industry may be their only defense against the onslaught of advertising and may save their lives. The truth—and a healthy skepticism—will set them free.

Skepticism, then, is a defense against both the nihilism of cynicism and the dangerous optimism of naïveté. It is about preparing for the worst while always hoping for the best. And perhaps most important, skepticism helps protect us from being indoctrinated into accepting harmful myths (like self-esteem), ideologies, and lies. In fact, if we had all learned to be skeptics, we might have questioned the wisdom of the self-esteem movement before it took over education in America. We might then have said, "Wait! Hold on a minute!" and asked professors and teachers to explain just how social promotion or lowering standards was going to make our children feel better about themselves or become better people. We would have asked for the evidence and would have discovered that there is none.

There is reason to be hopeful that we can turn this pessimism and cynicism into skepticism and hope by resolving to put an end to our addiction to self-esteem and doing the kinds of things I have suggested throughout this book. There is also reason to be hopeful because Americans are not by nature a cynical people. But sometimes optimism masks an undercurrent of cynicism. How, for example, are we to understand the existence of Celebration, Florida? Celebration is a residential town constructed in 1996 by the Walt Disney company in an effort to create the mythical safe, clean, perfect towns that we think we remember from the 1950s.

This is social engineering on a grand scale. Street plans are designed to foster relationships among residents, and a thick handbook of restrictions governs everything "from the color of the front door to where to store a canoe."[50] Owners must reside at least nine months of the year in their homes and can only sell their property during the first three years in case of extreme hardship, and then any profits must be turned over to a Disney foundation.[51] Houses have white picket fences and porches, and trash cans are kept neatly out of public view in service alleys behind houses: A perfect Disney life. And the idea is catching on. In British Columbia, a similarly perfect town, Auguston, is being constructed, which builders presumably hope will attract families fleeing from the real or perceived evils of city life.

There are two possible reactions to this. The first would be to contend that North Americans must be so cynical about real life that they prefer to live in a corporate fantasy. The other would be to say that if they are willing to give up essential liberties to live in such a community, they must want to connect with others very badly, and so it is a sign of hope. Perhaps both are true. Many of us want to escape the gritty reality of daily living, but if we were true cynics we would not be attracted by such an Eden. So although many of us may be skeptical about both the motivation for such a project and the apparent attraction to it, perhaps we should regard it as a sign that people really want things to be better and, like Ebenezer Scrooge, consider an attitude adjustment.

Like Dorothy in *The Wizard of Oz*, we are all attracted by something that looks new and perfect and promises much. But Celebration, Florida, Oz, Auguston, B.C., and the self-esteem movement are all mirages. As Dorothy discovered, plain old dusty Kansas was, in the end, a lot more appealing and had the added bonus of being *real*. As the Wizard himself said, "Pay no attention to the man behind the curtain." He's just pulling the strings.

Hope: The Final Frontier

Space travel may be the paradigmatic example of our desire for a better life. Although some Americans, particularly media gurus, were cynical about the real purpose of John Glenn's final flight into space (more public relations than science, they said), most of us found it wondrous that such a thing could be achieved. We are similarly conflicted about the Olympic Games. In the past couple of years they have been rocked by bribery scandals and for many years have been tainted by revelations of drug use by athletes, for whom sprinter Ben Johnson became the unwitting poster boy. Nevertheless, for many of us the Olympics remain, like the space program, a symbol of what is best in humanity—and of what the human spirit, body, and mind are capable.

These events, however tainted by human frailty and corruption, capture our imagination and instill us with hope. It is hard to be cynical when we witness a (drug-free) athlete, after years of training, break a world record. Although most of us have little chance to ever reach such heights, we are truly inspired by the athletes' efforts and we also admire those who try but fail to win a medal. We recognize that by identifying a goal, working to achieve it, and doing our best—no excuses—we learn something about ourselves and others, and we become better people. This is probably the most important lesson we can give our children: Aiming for excellence is the best foundation for self-esteem.

The fact that we admire the pursuit of excellence, whether intellectual, artistic, or athletic, is evidence that we have not succumbed entirely to cynicism. There is reason to be hopeful and there are things to hope for. This is the message we must pass along to our children. This is why we need to encourage, not downplay, competition while simultaneously instilling a sense of fair play and mutual respect. This is why we must encourage all kids to literally reach for the stars and ensure that we give them the tools to get there. Aiming for mediocrity, which could be the slogan of the self-esteem movement, only ensures that that's all we'll get. We must reject the kind of early labeling of "intelligences" that Howard Gardner proposes and assume that all children possess the whole spectrum of intelligences, skills, and abilities.

For a long time we have suspected that there is a much greater connection between the mind and the body than traditional medicine has historically entertained, and research into the sources and cures for everything from autoimmune diseases to cancer continues to investigate that relationship. Today we know that having a positive, optimistic outlook helps boost the immune system and promotes the creation of more antibodies to help us ward off disease. It performs exactly the same function in schools. It has been proven many times over that if we expect children to do well, they will. If we teach them that aiming high is important and that the universe is within their grasp, they will continue to surprise us with their achievement. Hope—balanced with a healthy skepticism—is the best cure for the diseases caused by the self-esteem movement. Balance is the key here. Being hopeful gives you energy and purpose; being skeptical makes you reflective and helps develop good judgment. With those attributes we are all in a good place to achieve our dreams—with our head in the clouds but our feet on the ground.

The good news is that the self-doubt, the cynicism, and the low expectations that the self-esteem movement has engendered in our children can easily be turned around by having high expectations; demanding respectful behavior; encouraging effort while rewarding achievement; ensuring that children possess the skills and knowledge they need before they graduate from high school; letting all kids know that they can be "college material" if they just work for it; ensuring that those who really don't want to go on to higher education have employment counseling, training, and experience so they are "job ready" after high school; encouraging parents to be involved in their children's education and letting them know that they are the most important educators; teaching moral virtue and the Golden Rule; and, finally, reminding teachers that their role is intellectual and moral leader, not babysitter, counselor, mother, or even friend.

The most important thing for all of us to remember is that we must model for our children the kinds of virtues—civic, moral, aesthetic, or intellectual—that we wish them to uphold. I hope that my earlier comments on teacher education may help instigate some changes in the way we educate our teachers, but we cannot wait for academics to decide what is best for our children. All of us must take responsibility for the education of this nation's children and fight the destructive addiction to self-esteem. We will need commitment for this enterprise and we will also need patience, since what I am proposing is nothing short of a revolution—a paradigm shift—in the way we view education.

Remember that child-centered education has been around for about a century. Through the Progressive era, the 1960s and "open learning," and finally the full-blown self-esteem movement, the idea of school as clinic, teacher as therapist, and child as "diseased" has slowly but inexorably insinuated itself into the national psyche. We have become accustomed to thinking that schools should be cultivating "emotional" intelligence rather than intellectual or moral intelligence, and it will take time for us all to return to a paradigm of education in which the intellect, not the emotions, is paramount. As Thomas Kuhn explains in *The Structure of Scientific Revolutions,* no paradigm is abandoned for another until a preponderance of the members of a particular scientific community determines that the new paradigm has better explanatory properties than the old. We need to keep that in mind, since we have become so accustomed to psychology-driven theories of child development and learning, which are themselves based on the notion of deficit or disease, that it will take some time to develop a disease-free achievement model of schooling in which the only sickness that needs to be addressed is the one created by the self-esteem movement.

Kuhn notes that when members of a scientific community convert to a new research paradigm, "there are always some men who cling to one or another of the older views, and they are simply read out of the profession, which thereafter ignores their work."[52] Scientific or not, the education community functions in exactly the same way. As I discussed in earlier chapters, so many academics, policymakers, teachers, and educational "consultants" have invested so much in the myths of the self-esteem movement that many will cling to this Titanic of educational fads and go down with it, even when a lifeboat in the form of a new paradigm is offered them. We see this already with the backlash against the failures of the whole language movement and Ebonics. The public and policymakers are beginning to realize what catastrophic failures they were, but academics continue to defend them in an effort to preserve the paradigm—and their careers.

It is to be expected that the self-esteem ideologues won't go down without a fight because they take themselves so seriously. That in itself should have been a dead giveaway. Although we should all take the *concept* and *purpose* of education seriously, the *practice* of education should be exciting and funny, and full of irony. An appreciation of the ridiculous and a recognition of the ironies of life are two of the more felicitous consequences of being a skeptical person and, dare I say it, a truly educated one.

If we are merely socialized and trained and not educated in school, we never develop metacognition, the ability to stand outside oneself, as it were, and appreciate how absurd life can be, despite our best efforts to control, organize, and rationalize it. Through metacognition we realize that we are all fallible, both important and insignificant at the same time, strong as well as powerless, and that ultimately we have only limited control over what happens in our lives. In fact the ability to step outside one's own cognitive framework, if only briefly, is what can help get us through difficult times. That sense of suspended reality, that such and such "isn't really happening to me" can be a very useful temporary survival technique.

After all, that's what got Alice through her adventures in Wonderland: trying to analyze the absurdities of what she experienced as she lived it. Of course, if someone today were to write a book along the lines of Lewis Carroll's masterpiece, he or she would probably be accused of promoting child abuse, or the heroine would be sent swiftly off to a clinic to cure her of the psychoses she doubtless acquired as a result of her trauma. And Alice, *had* she been a contemporary schoolgirl, *would* no doubt be traumatized because she would lack the tools of critical thinking, logic, and humor that helped Carroll's Alice get through her adventures more or less intact. I can see it now: a whole sector of the self-help industry devoted to "victims from Wonderland."

The self-esteem movement has caused us to take our own problems so seriously that, as with A.D.D. and A.D.H.D., we invent diseases as if by doing so we can excuse or somehow mitigate the inherent difficulties of childhood and the necessary responsibilities of parenthood. The movie *Patch Adams* illustrates the power of humor in healing, as did *One Flew over the Cuckoo's Nest*, in a different way. Humor, empathy, connectedness, rationality, morality, skepticism, and hope are all the tools we need to help heal our children and rid our schools of this addiction to self-esteem.

Empathy can easily replace narcissism if we recognize that our individual struggles are unique in circumstance but universal in effect. Understanding the universality of the human experience is the source of connectedness and the answer to separatism. Often when we experience tragedy or loss, we find that the only way to survive it is not to wallow in our own sorrow but to lessen it by giving something or teaching something to others. A sense of connectedness is both essential and simple; it is the knowledge that we are all in this struggle—for better education, better schools, and a better life—together. And although emotivism, that tendency to simply *feel* everything from the emotions rather than *see* and *think* them clearly through the intellect, is still a very dominant tendency in contemporary society, we will have to return to rationality if we wish to preserve a civil society. The heart is important, but it should not rule the head. It is reason, after all, that protects civil society from deteriorating into barbarism and chaos.

But teaching children to use their minds, developing the skills of thinking, is not enough. We must teach them how to use their minds in a personally and socially productive way. By learning moral lessons through literature, seeing the example set by teachers and parents, and being expected to act in honorable ways, children will develop the moral sense that gives the intellect its foundation. If a mind is a terrible thing to waste, a mind used for selfish rather than selfless purposes is an even greater shame—in both senses. If you'll pardon the grammar, it is not enough to *think* good; we must *be* good and *act* good.

Finally, what gets us through life, apart from skills and attitudes, is hope. Benjamin Barber, author of *An Aristocracy of Everyone: The Politics of Education and the Future of America,* writes that "to pessimists and determinists and nihilists—there are plenty around as we approach the next millennium—hope is the fatal flaw in modernity's project of liberation."[53] But Barber contends that hope is a necessary condition for a democratic education.[54] When things go so wrong that we cannot believe they are really that bad, we say "well, things have to improve eventually." We look to the future. That is what we need to preserve for our children: hope for a better future. We need to restore the dreams that have been shattered by the self-esteem movement by letting children know that they are capable of great things—more than they can ever imagine. Hope is not an irrational concept; on the contrary, you might say that rationality is skepticism plus hope. The rational person is aware of the dangers and obstacles that lie between her and her dreams but does not let that deter her from pursuing them.

If, as a society, we embrace these ideals, rather than the ideals of the self-esteem movement, they will not only guide us into the future, as they guided us in the past, but will prevent us from becoming vulnerable to other kinds of dangerous fads that threaten public education. Our children deserve no less.

Epilogue

Education for a New Millennium

WITH THE POSTMODERNISTS telling us that there aren't, and never were, any truths to be discovered about the world and observers like Christopher Lasch marveling that we should still believe in liberal ideals and progress, it is hardly surprising that some of us regard the new millennium with foreboding and doom.[1] Although the millennium does not officially begin until January 1, 2001, academics seem bent on lamenting it a year early. Of course, forecasting death and destruction is a great way to sell books on topics ranging from the general—why it's going to be the end of the world and how to survive it—to the downright bizarre—how to build a bunker in your backyard. How such an edifice might protect anyone from possible millennium dangers escapes me, but perhaps I'm just not sufficiently into the apocalyptic spirit.

Curiously, in contrast to some researchers, the public at large seems to view this new age with optimism, planning New Year's celebrations with great gusto. The prevailing wisdom seems to be that if you happen to be around for the start of the new millennium (whenever you decide that is) you may as well celebrate it. Clearly, how you view this event depends on how you view the world. Academics and writers hasten to point out the gloom and doom in order to give themselves something to write about (and vent their own angst), while most of us probably just want an excuse to act even more silly than we usually do on December 31. Personally, I think the academic community could learn something from the public, and so in a spirit of cautious optimism I herewith offer a few comments on how we might rescue public education from the ravages of the self-esteem movement and help make it something that even academics can cheer about before the next millennium rolls around.

While the doomsayers can no doubt list many things worth being gloomy about, I think our era is most accurately characterized as one of extremes of good and evil, as historian Eric Hobsbawm explains in his history of the twentieth century, *Age of Extremes*.[2] Historian Clive Ponting also develops this idea in his recent work, *Progress and Barbarism: The World in the Twentieth Century*. Ponting contends that the twentieth century has been delineated by both progress and barbarism, with the vast majority of the world's population living under barbaric conditions while a tiny minority enjoys the fruits of progress.[3] And although he believes that this trend will persist over the next few decades,[4] he also notes that making long-term predictions is a pretty futile exercise.[5] He points out that although some of this century's technological developments, for example, might have been foreseen, most of them were unimaginable.

Our use of the Internet, for example, changes so fast that even those developing it cannot predict its future more than a few months ahead. These changes may affect interpersonal communication, our conceptions of knowledge, and indeed the very structure of society in ways that we cannot even begin to understand. Education is already being greatly influenced by the communications revolution, and there is considerable debate amongst educators and neuroscientists as to how the increasing use of new technologies in schools will ultimately affect not only the teaching and learning process but the very structure and functioning of our brains.

Those particular issues will have to be debated elsewhere. What can be said here is that, at least up to now, the self-esteem movement has had more impact on how we conceptualize schooling than the information revolution (although I don't know whether to be relieved or worried about that!). Our biggest concern with any innovation that affects education should be to decide how we want to utilize it to further our stated goals regarding public schooling. We should not allow technology, the self-esteem movement, or indeed any other "innovation" to dictate those goals but should determine as a culture our own philosophy of education and then incorporate technologies and methods to promote it. As historian of education David Tyack suggests, perhaps what we need are good "conservationists" who will "defend endangered species of good schools."[6]

In our rush to ensure that our children are up-to-date on all the latest technology, we need to step back and decide whether that technology furthers our goals in education. Advances in technology are like advances in medicine; just because we *can* use them does not necessarily mean we *should*. The same principle applies to the self-esteem movement in schools, which we hastily adopted with little thought. But it is not too late to remedy the situation. In earlier chapters I identified the myths associated with self-esteem as well as the means to remedy our addiction to it.

Fortunately, our addiction to self-esteem is, unlike an addiction to food, for example, one that we can learn to live very well without.

The practical steps we need to take as individuals to fight the consequences of the self-esteem movement should by now be pretty clear. But if, as I suggested in the last chapter, we are looking at a fundamental paradigm shift in our view of education, in order to implement these steps we need to begin to engage in public discussion regarding the very goals and purposes of education. Not only does each of us have to educate ourselves about what is going on in public schools, we need to educate academics and teachers—the so-called experts in education—about what we want our schools to teach and how we want them to teach it. We also need to accept our responsibilities as consumers of education to be aware of new educational innovations and, as parents, to question teachers and administrators when a new teaching method or pseudophilosophy is introduced that claims to be the "newest" and "best" way of teaching something.

Most important, we need to publicly define the purposes of education because public schooling can only serve a limited number of masters at one time. We cannot serve both the god of self-esteem and the ideals of liberal education. The good news is that although the self-esteem movement has, over this century, slowly changed the *practice* of schooling to reflect its ideology, all the evidence indicates that the public has never changed its *philosophy* of schooling. The ideals of a classical liberal education survive.

The common school was created primarily to educate an informed citizenry that shared common values, was prepared for the world of work, and, perhaps most important, was capable of participating in the democratic process. These original purposes of education remain valid, although schooling is also seen as a way for individuals to express themselves and a means for us to learn about our diversity as well as our commonalities. We may have different cultural and historical experiences but we share common political and moral values. And we believe that every child has a right to an education that is equal in quality to that of all other children. Cynics remind us that we have not yet achieved that very basic goal, but that failing should not be a reason to decry the goal but a reason to work even harder to reach it.

If, in the next century and in the next millennium, or even in the next decade, we want to modify those purposes to fit our present needs, let us do that through informed discussion, not through ignorance or because of perceived technological imperatives. What we need is a national dialogue on education, perhaps like President Clinton's "dialogue on race," which addresses not just policy initiatives, reform agendas, and financial concerns but the real meaning, content, and purpose of public schooling. Education is too important to be left to technocrats and educators. As Marian Wright Edelman, head of the Children's Defense Fund notes, "parents have become so convinced that educators know what is best for children that they forget that they themselves are really the experts."[7] Education is a venture that requires the conscious deliberation of an informed populace. After all, schooling should be first about philosophy and second about method, something we seem to have forgotten.

If education is fundamentally about creating individuals who value democracy and who possess the tools to practice it, it must be conceptualized, organized, and practiced in a democratic way. The classroom itself, for both practical and philosophical reasons, cannot function as a democracy, but schools as a whole must reflect the wishes of the public it serves. Thus the days of education by fiat, whereby the wisdom regarding education is delivered down from professors of education to their obedient servants—we, the people—must end. As citizens we must reclaim public education for ourselves; take it back and let the "experts" know that we are willing to accept their input but that they do not unilaterally decide what is best for our children. People know what self-esteem and self-confidence are really about: recognizing and working on one's limitations and strengths, taking responsibility for one's actions, identifying a goal and taking steps to achieve it, and acknowledging that while each of us is unique, we are also members of communities, and it is that membership that gives meaning, structure, and purpose to our lives.

I can perhaps best describe what authentic self-confidence should be about by sharing an experience I had a couple of years ago. In the summer of 1997, I, along with 160-odd "future leaders" from around the world, spent two months in Jordan as part of a leadership program sponsored by the United Nations University. We had been invited to Amman to study and learn from present world leaders who gave lectures on a variety of topics related to leadership and international relations, including peacekeeping, human rights, business, telecommunications, the role of the United Nations, and the personal aspects of leadership. It was an absolutely amazing experience, combining intellectual, interpersonal, and cultural learning.

We heard from and met King Hussein of Jordan and his wife, Queen Noor, Jordan's prime minister (who initially proposed the forum), former Israeli prime minister Shimon Peres, President Yasir Arafat of the Palestine National Authority, Simone Veil, former president of the European Parliament, several U.S. congressmen, and many other world figures. Just as exciting was the opportunity to meet with other people from around the world, most in their thirties, who were active in academia, government, human rights organizations, law, medicine, journalism, and many other fields. One woman was working with the Truth and Reconciliation Commission in South Africa; many worked with the United Nations, and one attendee, Andres Pastrana, is now president of Colombia.

The opportunity to meet such interesting persons from around the world, both leaders and participants, was extraordinary, and I learned much about the politics and practice of leadership in different cultures. But what I most learned from the experience was a feeling that if I set my mind to it, I could do just about anything. It was not what I expected to feel because frankly I was pretty impressed with many of the participants and initially felt that they were made of more "leadership material" than I was. But sitting down and talking with them, in seminars or over lunch, I learned the real lessons of leadership and self-confidence. I was humbled by the experience of some of the participants, who came from very poor countries and had few resources but continued to fight for basic human rights for themselves and for others. I realized how fortunate I was to be born in a country—Canada—with a standard of living and quality of life unrivaled in the world, and where basic human rights were something I always took for granted.

I also realized that however much we differed linguistically, culturally, and even politically, we all shared a passion for something and wanted to know how to better use our individual skills and knowledge to make a difference in the world. I saw that (almost) everyone had self-doubts, but what kept us all pursuing our respective enterprises was a belief that if something is worth doing, it is worth doing well and it is worth fighting for. By becoming, as it were, leaders in our own lives and in our own communities, we were also "world" leaders. Only a very few will become presidents or prime ministers, but all of us make a difference by taking responsibility for our own piece of the world. This is not a new idea, but it is an important one and something that one needs to experience to know. The confidence came from the experience. That is the basis of true self-esteem: knowing what is possible and achieving it. And that is the highest gift of education.

Notes

Introduction

1. Derek Bok, quoted in James Charlton, ed., *A Little Learning Is a Dangerous Thing: A Treasury of Wise and Witty Observation for Students, Teachers, and Other Survivors of Higher Educaton* (New York: St. Martin's, 1994), 43.

2. See Daniel Goleman, *Emotional Intelligence* (New York: Bantam, 1997).

Chapter 1

1. Tallulah Bankhead, quoted in James Charlton, ed., *A Little Learning Is a Dangerous Thing: A Treasury of Wise and Witty Observations for Students, Teachers, and Other Survivors of Higher Education* (New York: St. Martin's, 1994), 27.

2. See, for example, Robert Nozick, *Anarchy, State, and Utopia* (New York: Basic, 1974), 239–246.

3. John Rawls, *A Theory of Justice* (Cambridge: Harvard University Press, 1971), quoted in Joseph Kahne, "The Politics of Self-Esteem," *American Educational Research Journal* 33, no. 1 (1996): 6.

4. Matthew McKay, Ph.D., and Patrick Fanning, *Self-esteem*, 2d ed. (Oakland, Calif: New Harbinger, 1992), 1.

5. See David D. Burns, M.D., *Feeling Good: The New Mood Therapy* (New York: Avon, 1992), 309.

6. John P. Hewitt, *The Myth of Self-esteem: Finding Happiness and Solving Problems in America* (New York: St. Martin's, 1998), chap. 1.

7. Andrew M. Mecca, "Letter to the Governor and the Legislature," in *Toward a State of Esteem: The Final Report of the California Task Force to Promote Self-esteem and Personal and Social Responsibility* (Sacramento: California State Department of Education, 1990), vii.

8. Jana S. Eaton, "The 'Excuse' Schools: Accommodating Ourselves to Death," *Education Week*, 10 March 1999, 33.

9. Richard Keshen, *Reasonable Self-esteem* (Montreal: McGill-Queen's University Press, 1996), 8–14.

10. Christopher Lasch, *The Culture of Narcissism: American Life in an Age of Diminishing Expectations* (New York: Norton, 1978).

11. Thurgood Marshall, quoted in Charlton, *A Little Learning*, 30.

12. "Quality Counts," *Education Week*, 11 January 1999, 5.

13. Ann Bradley, "Confronting a Tough Issue: Teacher Tenure," *Education Week*, 11 January 1999, 50.

14. Linda Sax, Alexander Astin et al., *The American Freshman National Norms for Fall 1998* (Los Angeles: UCLA Higher Education Research Institute, 1998), 19.

15. U.S. Department of Education, cited in the *Chronicle of Higher Education Almanac*, 28 August 1998, 26.

16. U.S. Census Bureau, "Educational Attainment in the United States: March 1997," quoted in Julie Blair, "Blacks Close Gap in High School Graduation Rates," *Education Week*, 8 July 1998, 3.

17. "Demanding Results," *Education Week*, 11 January 1999, 5.

18. Ibid.

19. Patricia H. Berne and Louis M. Savary, *Building Self-esteem in Children* (New York: Continuum, 1981), 50.

20. Charles W. Anderson, *Prescribing the Life of the Mind: An Essay on the Purpose of the University, the Aims of Liberal Education, the Competence of Citizens, and the Cultivation of Practical Reason* (Madison: University of Wisconsin Press, 1993), 72.

21. R. S. Peters, introduction to *Leviathan*, by Thomas Hobbes (New York: Collier, 1962), 11.

22. See Daniel Goleman, *Emotional Intelligence: Why It Can Matter More Than IQ* (New York: Bantam, 1997).

23. Arthur Schlesinger Jr., *The Disuniting of America: Reflections on a Multicultural Society* (New York: Norton, 1992), 93.

24. William James, quoted in Charlton, *A Little Learning*, 99.

25. R. S. Peters, "Education as Initiation," in R. D. Archambault, ed., *Philosophical Analysis and Education* (New York: Humanities, 1965), 110.

26. Lasch, *Culture of Narcissism*, xv.

27. Matthew McKay and Patrick Fanning, *Self-esteem: A Proven Program of Cognitive Techniques for Assessing, Improving, and Maintaining Your Self-esteem*, 2d ed. (Oakland, Calif.: New Harbinger, 1992), 270.

28. Robert N. Bellah et al., *The Good Society* (New York: Knopf, 1991), 113.

29. Alasdair MacIntyre, *After Virtue: A Study in Moral Theory*, 2d ed. (Notre Dame, Ind.: University of Notre Dame Press, 1984), 11–12.

30. Harvey Siegel, *Educating Reason: Rationality, Critical Thinking, and Education* (New York: Routledge, 1988), 58.

31. *A Dictionary of Philosophy*, 2d ed., ed. Antony Flew (New York: St. Martin's, 1984), 314.

32. Lynn Olson, "The Career Game," *Education Week*, 2 October 1996, 33.

33. *Chronicle of Higher Education*, 31 March 1995, A24.

34. Peter Sacks, *Generation X Goes to College: An Eye-Opening Account of Teaching in Postmodern America* (Chicago: Open Court/Carus, 1998), introduction.

Chapter 2

1. Arthur Powell and Theodore Sizer, "Changing Conceptions of the Professor of Education," in James Counelis, ed., *To Be a Phoenix: The Education Professoriat* (Bloomington, Ill.: Phi Delta Kappa, 1969), quoted in Joel Spring, *American Education*, 7th ed. (New York: McGraw-Hill, 1996), 45.

2. Elliot W. Eisner, *The Educational Imagination: On the Design and Evaluation of School Programs*, 2d ed. (New York: Macmillan, 1985), 177.

3. Hillary Rodham Clinton, *It Takes a Village and Other Lessons Children Teach Us* (New York: Simon & Schuster, 1996).

4. Uniform Crime Report, 1990–96, cited in Beth Shuster, "Living in Fear," *Los Angeles Times*, 23 August 1998, Sunday final, A1.

5. James D. Koerner, *The Miseducation of American Teachers* (Boston: Houghton Mifflin, 1963), 33.

6. Ibid., 35.

7. Ibid., 39.

8. Association of Teacher Educators, *Restructuring the Education of Teachers*, Report of the Commission on the Education of Teachers into the Twenty-first Century (Reston, Va.: Association of Teacher Educators, 1991), 12.

9. Ibid.

10. Jessica L. Sandham, "N.Y. to Require Accreditation for Ed. Schools," *Education Week*, 5 August 1998, 21.

11. Kit Lively, "States Move to Toughen Standards for Teacher-Education Programs," *Chronicle of Higher Education*, 31 July 1998, A27.

12. Sandra Feldman, "Ignoring Standards," *Education Week*, 5 August 1998, 54.

13. Koerner, *Miseducation of Teachers*, 48.

14. See, for example, Dan Lortie, *Schoolteacher: A Sociological Study* (Chicago: Chicago University Press, 1975) or Powell and Sizer, "Changing Conceptions."

15. Koerner, *Miseducation of Teachers*, 34.

16. Rita Kramer, *Ed School Follies: The Miseducation of America's Teachers* (New York: Free Press, 1991), 33.

17. Ibid., 100–101.

18. Ibid., 116.

19. Ibid., 117–118.

20. Ibid., 120–121.

21. Peter Sacks, *Generation X Goes to College: An Eye-Opening Account of Teaching in Postmodern America* (Chicago: Open Court/Carus Publishing, 1998), xi.

22. Richard Lee Colvin, "Suit Challenges Basic Skills Test for Teachers as Biased," *Los Angeles Times*, 5 February 1996, A17.

23. Ibid.

24. Ibid.

25. Jeanne Ponessa, "Calif. Basic-Skills Test for Teachers Upheld," *Education Week*, 25 September 1996, 5.

26. Ibid.

Chapter 3

1. Maria Montessori, quoted in James Charlton, ed., *A Little Learning Is a Dangerous Thing: A Treasury of Wise and Witty Observations for Students, Teachers, and Other Survivors of Higher Education* (New York: St. Martin's, 1994), 95.

2. John Dewey, *Experience and Education* (1938; reprint, New York: Touchstone/Simon & Schuster, 1997), 17.

3. Ibid., 17–18.

4. Ibid., 19–20.

5. Lawrence Cremin, *The Transformation of the School: Progressivism in American Education, 1876–1957* (1961; reprint, New York: Vintage, 1964), viii.

6. Lynn Olson, "Tugging at Tradition," *Education Week,* 21 April 1999, 25.

7. Ibid., 26.

8. Ibid., 26–27.

9. Ibid., 27.

10. Bernadette Baker, "Child-Centered Teaching, Redemption, and Educational Identities: A History of the Present," *Educational Theory* 48, no. 2 (1998): 163.

11. Ibid.

12. Joel Spring, *The American School, 1642–1985* (New York: Longman, 1986), 133.

13. Cremin, *Transformation of the School,* 274.

14. Progressive Education Association, Committee on Experimental Schools, *What Schools Are Doing* (New York: 1937). Quoted in Cremin, *Transformation of the School,* 276.

15. Cremin, *Transformation of the School,* 297.

16. Ibid., 234–235.

17. Erich Fromm, *Man for Himself: An Inquiry into the Psychology of Ethics* (1947; reprint, New York: Holt, Rinehart, and Winston, 1961), 156.

18. Norman F. Cantor with Mindy Cantor, *The American Century: Varieties of Culture in Modern Times* (New York: HarperPerennial, 1998), 168.

19. Ibid., 215.

20. Robert E. Slavin, *Educational Psychology: Theory and Practice,* 4th ed. (Needham Heights, Mass.: Allyn & Bacon, 1994), 57.

21. Cantor with Cantor, *American Century,* 216.

22. Ibid.

23. Slavin, *Educational Psychology,* 57.

24. Cremin, *Transformation of the School,* 338.

25. Ibid., 343.

26. Ibid., 352.

27. Spring, *American School,* 294–295.

28. Cantor with Cantor, *American Century,* 207.

29. Ibid., 224.

30. Abraham Maslow, *Toward a Psychology of Being,* 2d ed. (Princeton, N.J.: Van Nostrand, 1968), 193.

31. Ibid., 198.

32. Carl Rogers, *Freedom to Learn* (Columbus, Ohio: Merrill, 1969), 5.

33. Ibid.

34. Ibid.

35. Ibid.

36. Ibid., 26.

37. Ibid., 17.

38. Ibid., 303.

39. Ibid., 279.

40. Rita Kramer, *Ed School Follies: The Miseducation of America's Teachers* (New York: Free Press, 1991), 195.

41. Wilbert J. McKeachie et al., *Teaching Tips: Strategies, Research, and Theory for College and University Teachers* (Toronto: Heath, 1994), 351–353.

42. Ibid., 356.

43. Ibid., 207–208.

44. Ibid., 144.

45. Alison Schneider, "Jane Tompkins's Message to Academe: Nurture the Individual, Not Just the Intellect," *Chronicle of Higher Education,* 10 July 1998, A8.

46. Ibid.

47. Ibid.

48. Jane Tompkins, *A Life in School: What the Teacher Learned* (Reading, Mass.: Addison-Wesley, 1996), 121.

49. Ibid., 122.

50. Ibid., 123.

51. Ibid., 137.

52. Alison Schneider, "Jane Tompkins's Message to Academe: Nurture the Individual, Not Just the Intellect," *Chronicle of Higher Education,* 10 July 1998, A8.

53. Ibid.

54. Hank Vandenburgh, letter to the editor, *Chronicle of Higher Education,* 14 August 1998, B3.

55. Marjorie Perloff, letter to the editor, *Chronicle of Higher Education,* 14 August 1998, B3.

Chapter 4

1. Will Rogers, quoted in James Charlton, ed., *A Little Learning Is a Dangerous Thing: A Treasury of Wise and Witty Observations for Students, Teachers, and Other Survivors of Higher Education* (New York: St. Martin's, 1994), 87.

2. H. Warren Button and Eugene Provenzo Jr., *History of Education and Culture in America,* 2d ed. (Englewood Cliffs, N.J.: Prentice-Hall, 1989), 146.

3. Ibid.

4. Diane Ravitch, *The Troubled Crusade: American Education, 1945–1980* (New York: Basic, 1983), 115.

5. Ibid., 127.

6. Ibid., 128.

7. Joel Spring, *The American School: 1642–1985* (White Plains, N.Y.: Longman, 1986), 302.

8. Ibid., 302–303.

9. U.S. Congress, House, Committee of the Judiciary, *Hearing on Civil Rights Bill,* 88th Cong, 1st sess., 1963, 2144; quoted in Ravitch, *Troubled Crusade,* 142.

10. Ravitch, *Troubled Crusade,* 251.

11. U.S. Department of Education, National Commission on Excellence in Education, *A Nation at Risk* (Washington, D.C.: U.S. Department of Education, 1983), 11.

12. U.S. Department of Education, *The Nation Responds* (Washington, D.C: U.S. Department of Education, 1984), 15–16.

13. National Education Goals Panel, quoted in *Education Week,* 13 January 1999, 29.

14. Public Agenda, "Given the Circumstances: Teachers Talk About Public Education Today," quoted in Jeanne Ponessa, "Teachers Agree Stress Needed on 'the Basics,'" *Education Week,* 21 February 1996, 1, 17.

15. Ann Bradley, "Survey Reveals Teens Yearn for High Standards," *Education Week,* 12 February 1997, 1, 38.

16. David C. Berliner and Bruce J. Biddle, *The Manufactured Crisis: Myths, Fraud, and the Attack on America's Public Schools* (White Plains, N.Y.: Longman, 1997), xiv.

17. Douglas Lederman, "Persistent Racial Gap in SAT Scores Fuels Affirmative-Action Debate," *Chronicle of Higher Education,* 30 October 1998, A36.

18. Berliner and Biddle, *Manufactured Crisis,* xv.

19. Howard Gardner, *Multiple Intelligences: The Theory in Practice* (New York: Basic, 1993), 6.

20. Ibid., 9.

21. Ibid.

22. Ibid.

23. Ibid., 10.

24. Ibid.

25. Ibid.

26. Ibid., 11.

27. Howard Gardner and Thomas Hatch, "Multiple Intelligences Go to School: Educational Implications of the Theory of Multiple Intelligences," in Robin Fogarty and James Bellanca, eds., *Multiple Intelligences: A Collection* (Palatine, Ill.: IRI/Skylight, 1995), 156.

28. Ibid.

29. Ibid., 157.

30. Ibid., 163.

31. Gardner, *Multiple Intelligences,* 11.

32. Daniel Goleman, *Emotional Intelligence: Why It Can Matter More than IQ* (New York: Bantam, 1997), 36.

33. Ibid., 29.

34. Ibid., 37.

35. Ibid., 44–45.

36. Ibid., 232–233.

37. Ibid., 259.

38. Ibid., 262.

39. Ibid., 268.

40. Ibid., 295.

41. Ibid.

42. Ibid., 296.

Chapter 5

1. H. L. Mencken, quoted in James Charlton, ed., *A Little Learning Is a Dangerous Thing: A Treasury of Wise and Witty Observations for Students, Teachers, and Other Survivors of Higher Education* (New York: St. Martin's, 1994), 100.

2. For a more complete discussion on this point, see Steven Ward, "Filling the World with Self-esteem: A Social History of Truth-Making," *Canadian Journal of Sociology* 21, no. 1 (1996).

3. Joseph Kahne, "The Politics of Self-esteem," *American Educational Research Journal* 33, no. 1 (1996): 5.

4. Cynthia G. Scott et al., "Student Self-esteem and the School System: Perceptions and Implications," *Journal of Educational Research* 89, no. 5 (1996): 292.

5. Ibid.

6. Ibid.

7. Ibid.

8. Mary Ann Scheirer and Robert E. Kraut, "Increasing Educational Achievement via Self Concept Change," *Review of Educational Research* 49, no. 1 (1979): 131.

9. Ibid., 132.

10. Ibid.

11. Ibid.

12. Ibid., 145.

13. B. C. Hansford and J. A. Hattie, "The Relationship Between Self and Achievement/Performance Measures," *Review of Educational Research* 52, no. 1 (1982): 124.

14. Sue K. Grimes, "Underprepared Community College Students: Characteristics, Persistence, and Academic Success," *Community College Journal of Research and Practice* 21, no. 1 (1997): 47.

15. Elliot Aronson and David R. Mettee, "Dishonest Behavior as a Function of Differential Levels of Induced Self-esteem," *Journal of Personality and Social Psychology* 9, no. 2 (1968): 121. Part 1.

16. Jerome Kagan, "The Misleading Abstractions of Social Scientists," *Chronicle of Higher Education,* 12 January 1996, A52.

17. Kim A. McDonald, "Study Finds Adults Happier as They Age," *Chronicle of Higher Education,* 4 December 1998, A18.

18. Jason W. Osborne, "Race and Academic Disidentification," *Journal of Educational Psychology* 89, no. 4 (1997): 731–733.

19. Jerome Kagan, "The Misleading Abstractions of Social Scientists," *Chronicle of Higher Education,* A 52.

20. Roy F. Baumeister, Joseph M. Boden, and Laura Smart, "Relation of Threatened Egotism to Violence and Aggression: The Dark Side of High Self-esteem," *Psychological Review* 103, no. 1 (1996): 5.

21. Ibid.

22. Ibid., 26.

23. Ibid.

24. Ibid., 29.

25. State of California, California Legislation on Self-esteem and Personal and Social Responsibility, Assembly Bill no. 3659, sec. 1, chap. 3.2, para. (g), in California State Department of Education, appendixes to *Toward a State of Esteem* (Sacramento: California State Department of Education, 1990): 102.

26. Ibid., para. (o), 103.

27. John Vasconcellos, "Message from John Vasconcellos," in *Toward a State of Esteem: The Final Report of the California Task Force to Promote Self-esteem and Personal and Social Responsibility* (Sacramento: California State Department of Education, 1990), ix.

28. Andrew M. Mecca, "Letter to the Governor and the Legislature," in *Toward a State of Esteem,* vii.

29. Vasconcellos, "Message from John Vasconellos," in *Toward a State of Esteem,* ix. Also see Garry Trudeau, *Calling Dr. Whoopee!* (New York: Holt, 1986).

30. Harry H.L. Kitano, "Alcohol and Drug Use and Self-esteem: A Sociocultural Perspective," in Andrew Mecca et al., eds., *The Social Importance of Self-esteem* (Berkeley: University of California Press, 1989), 294.

31. Ibid., 303.

32. Ibid., 305.

33. Ibid., 320.

34. Leonard Schneiderman, Walter M. Furman, and Joseph Weber, "Self-esteem and Chronic Welfare Dependency," in *Social Importance of Self-esteem*, 223.

35. Ibid.

36. Thomas J. Scheff, Suzanne M. Retzinger, and Michael T. Ryan, "Crime, Violence, and Self-esteem," in *Social Importance of Self-esteem*, 177.

37. Ibid.

38. Ibid.

39. Martin V. Covington, "Self-esteem and Failure in School," in *Social Importance of Self-esteem*, 79.

40. Ibid.

41. Ibid., 79–80.

42. Ibid., 83.

43. Ibid., 79.

44. California Task Force on Self-esteem, *Toward a State of Esteem: The Final Report of the California Task Force on Self-esteem* (Sacramento: California State Department of Education, 1990), 43.

45. Ibid.

46. Ibid.

47. Ibid.

48. Ibid., 44.

49. Neil J. Smelser, "Self-esteem and Social Problems," in *Social Importance of Self-esteem*, 8.

50. Ibid., 7–8.

51. John Vasconcellos, preface to *Social Importance of Self-Esteem*, xx.

52. John Vasconcellos, "Politics for Growing Humans," audiotape, listed in California State Department of Education, *Appendixes to Toward a State of Esteem* (Sacramento: California State Department of Education, 1990), 72.

53. See, for example, Marcia Invernizzi, Mary Abouzeid, and J. Thomas Gill, "Using Students' Invented Spellings as a Guide for Spelling Instruction That Emphasizes Word Study," *Elementary School Journal* 95, no. 2 (1994).

54. Duke Helfand, "Teaching the Basics, Finally," *Los Angeles Times,* 11 February 1999, 1.

55. Richard Lee Colvin and Richard T. Cooper, "Reading Moves to the Front of the Class," *Los Angeles Times,* 27 September 1998, A24.

56. Nick Anderson and Duke Helfand, "A Long Road Back from Reading Crisis," *Los Angeles Times,* 13 September 1998, A1.

57. Ibid., A36.

58. Kathleen Kennedy Manzo, "Drilling in Texas," *Education Week,* 10 June 1998, 32.

59. "National Push for Reading," *Los Angeles Times,* 27 September 1998, M4.

60. Kathleen Kennedy Manzo, "A Glimpse at the States with Big NAEP Gains," *Education Week,* 10 March 1999, 13.

61. Peter Kingston, "Atlantic Crossing for Early Learning Scheme," *Manchester Guardian Weekly,* 26 May 1996, 19.

62. Duke Helfand, "Phonics Spells Business for Entrepreneurs," *Los Angeles Times,* 29 November 1998, Sunday final, 1.

63. Kathleen Kennedy Manzo, "British Government Urges Phonics-Based Reading Strategy," *Education Week,* 16 September 1998, 6.

64. Richard Lee Colvin, "Trouble in the Mecca of Reading," *Los Angeles Times,* 4 May 1997, A1.

65. Ibid.

66. Ibid.

67. Ibid.

68. John Leo, "More Feel-Good Theory in Academia: Grammar Just Don't Matter," *Las Vegas Review-Journal and Las Vegas Sun,* 13 April 1997, 4D.

69. Theresa Perry, "'I'on Know Why They Be Trippin': Reflections on the Ebonics Debate," in Theresa Perry and Lisa Delpit, eds., *The Real Ebonics Debate: Power, Language, and the Education of African-American Children* (Boston: Beacon, 1998), 3.

70. Ibid., 4.

71. "Resolution of the Board of Education Adopting the Report and Recommendations of the African-American Task Force," quoted in *Real Ebonics Debate,* 143.

72. Ibid., 143–144.

73. Perry, "I'on Know," 5.

74. Ibid., 6–9.

75. Jesse Jackson, quoted in Michelle Locke, "Black English Fit for Classroom, Board Says," *Globe and Mail* (Toronto), 23 December 1996, A7.

76. Lynn Schnaiberg, "Anti-Ebonics Ad Was Mistake, Head Start Group Says," *Education Week,* 28 October 1998, 3.

77. Ibid.

78. Lynn Schnaiberg, "Oakland Board Revises 'Ebonics' Resolution," *Education Week,* 22 January 1997, 3.

79. Ibid.

80. Shelby Steele, "Indoctrination Isn't Teaching," *Education Week,* 29 January 1997, 48.

Chapter 6

1. Winston Churchill, quoted in James Charlton, ed., *A Little Learning Is a Dangerous Thing: A Treasury of Wise and Witty Observations for Students, Teachers, and Other Survivors of Higher Education* (New York: St. Martin's, 1994), 96.

2. Gloria Steinem, *Revolution from Within: A Book of Self-esteem* (Boston: Little, Brown, 1992), 31.

3. Ibid., 32.

4. Verne Faust, *Self-esteem in the Classroom* (San Diego, Calif.: Thomas Paine, 1980), 119.

5. Beth Teolis, *Ready to Use Self-esteem and Conflict-Solving Activities for Grades 4–8* (West Nyack, N.Y.: Center for Applied Research in Education, 1996), xiii.

6. V. Alex Kehayan, Ed.D., *SAGE Self-awareness Growth Experiences: Strategies That Promote Positive Self-esteem for Grades 7–12* (Rolling Hills Estates, Calif.: Jalmar, 1990), 1.

7. Teolis, *Self-esteem,* xiii.

8. Ibid., 82.

9. Ibid.,177.

10. Ibid., 181.

11. Michele Borba, *Esteem Builders: A K–8 Self-esteem Curriculum for Improving Student Achievement, Behavior, and School Climate* (Torrance, Calif.: Jalmar, 1989), 139.

12. Ibid., 228–229.

13. Peter N. Berger, "Portfolio Folly," *Education Week,* 14 January 1998, 76.

14. Ibid.

15. Ibid.

16. Margaret M. Clifford, "Students Need Challenge, Not Easy Success," *Educational Psychology 94/95* (Guilford, Conn.: Dushkin, 1995), 182.

17. Jessica Portner, "Today's Lesson: Self-esteem," *Education Week,* 9 December 1998, 25.

18. Clifford, "Students Need Challenge," 184.

19. Ibid., 184–185.

20. Faust, *Self-esteem,* 141.

21. Borba, *Esteem Builders,* 278.

22. Ibid.

23. Kehayan, *SAGE,* 104.

24. Debra Viadero, "Boston Swaps Flunking for 'Transition' Grades," *Education Week,* 17 March 1999, 3.

25. Don Dinkmeyer and Rudolf Dreikurs, *Encouraging Children to Learn: The Encouragement Process* (Englewood Cliffs, N.J.: Prentice-Hall, 1963), 13.

26. Ibid., 75.

27. Michael W. Kirst, "Bridging the Remediation Gap: Why We Must (and How We Can) Align K–12 Standards with College Placement," *Education Week,* 9 September 1998, 76.

28. Jeanne Ponessa, "Chain of Blame," *Education Week,* 22 May 1996, 30.

29. Ibid.

30. John Chandler, "Remedial Ed Among CSU Freshmen Shows Slight Increase," *@csun.edu,* 31 March 1997, 6.

31. Patrick Healy, "CUNY's Four-Year Colleges Ordered to Phase Out Remedial Education," *Chronicle of Higher Education,* 5 June 1998, A26.

32. Charles W. Lindahl, *Memorandum to Presidents of the California State University System,* 27 May 1997, 1.

33. Robert C. Johnston, "Calif. Targets K–12 'Social Promotions,'" *Education Week,* 9 September 1998, 1, 33.

34. Healy, "CUNY's 4-Year Colleges" A26.

35. Jeanne Ponessa, "Chain of Blame," *Education Week,* 22 May 1996, 32–33.

36. John Vasconcellos, foreword to Jack Canfield and Harold C. Wells, *100 Ways to Enhance Self-concept in the Classroom* (Englewood Cliffs, N.J.: Prentice-Hall, 1976), xii.

37. Ibid.

38. Ibid.

39. Canfield and Wells, *100 Ways*, 6.

40. Kim Murphy, "General's Mission: Shape Up the Schools," *Los Angeles Times*, 6 October 1996, A3.

41. Teolis, *Self-esteem*, 2.

42. James G. Henderson, *The Study of Your Constructivist Practices*, 2d ed. (Englewood Cliffs, N.J.: Prentice-Hall, 1996), 8.

43. Faust, *Self-esteem*, 112.

44. Jane Nelsen, Lynn Lott, and H. Stephen Glenn, *Positive Discipline in the Classroom: How to Effectively Use Class Meetings and Other Positive Discipline Strategies* (Rocklin, Calif.: Prima, 1993), x–xi.

45. Canfield and Wells, *100 Ways*, 43.

46. Ibid., 45.

47. Nelsen, Lott, and Glenn, *Positive Discipline*, 82–83.

48. Ibid., 83.

49. Ibid.

50. Noel McInnis, *Association for Humanistic Psychology Newsletter*, quoted in *100 Ways to Enhance Self-concept*, 83.

51. Ibid.

52. Ibid.

53. Ibid.

54. Elaine Woo, "Taming Those Exam Jitters," *Los Angeles Times*, 21 September 1995, B2.

55. Ibid.

56. Canfield and Wells, *100 Ways*, 143.

57. Ibid., 180.

58. Ibid.

59. Ruben Navarrette Jr., "My Special Education: Spare the Rod and Discard the Student," *Los Angeles Times*, 2 February 1997, M6.

60. Ibid.

61. Edward A. Wynne and Kevin Ryan, *Reclaiming Our Schools: Teaching Character, Academics, and Discipline*, 2d ed. (Upper Saddle River, N.J.: Prentice-Hall/Simon & Schuster, 1997), 98.

62. University Counseling Services, California State University, Northridge, *A Faculty/Staff Guide: Toward Enhancing Communication with Students and Helping the Emotionally Distressed Student* (Northridge, Calif.: University Counseling Services, 1986), 5.

63. Ibid.

64. Tara Fitzgerald, "Illiteracy a Matter of Life and Death, Unicef Study Finds," *Globe and Mail* (Toronto), 8 December 1998, A15.

Chapter 7

1. Orson Welles, quoted in James Charlton, ed., *A Little Learning Is a Dangerous Thing: A Treasury of Wise and Witty Observations for Students, Teachers, and Other Survivors of Higher Education* (New York: St. Martin's, 1994), 15.

2. Adolf Hitler, quoted in *A Little Learning*, 73–74.

3. Lilian G. Katz, "All About Me: Are We Developing Our Children's Self-esteem or Their Narcissism?" in Kathleen M. Cauley et al., eds., *Educational Psychology 94/95* (Guilford, Conn.: Dushkin, 1995), 37.

4. Ibid., 38.

5. Jessica Portner, "Today's Lesson: Self-esteem," *Education Week,* 9 December 1998, 27.

6. Hillary Rodham Clinton, *It Takes a Village to Raise a Child and Other Lessons Children Teach Us* (New York: Simon & Schuster, 1996), 13.

7. Ibid.

8. Neil Postman, *Technopoly: The Surrender of Culture to Technology* (New York: Vintage Books/Random House, 1993), 70.

9. Organization of American Historians, quoted in Karen Winkler, "Organization of American Historians Back Teaching of Non-Western Culture and Diversity in Schools," *Chronicle of Higher Education,* 6 February 1991, A5.

10. For the complete exchange on ethnic studies and multiculturalism, see Molefi Kete Asante and Diane Ravitch, "Multiculturalism: An Exchange," *American Scholar* 60 (Spring 1991).

11. David Bromwich, *Politics by Other Means: Higher Education and Group Thinking* (New Haven: Yale University Press, 1992), 231.

12. Lynn Schnaiberg, "In Questioning Bilingual Ed., Hispanic Parents Join Backlash," *Education Week,* 28 February 1996, 11.

13. Lynn Schnaiberg, "Parents Worry Bilingual Ed. Hurts Students," *Education Week,* 28 February 1996, 11.

14. John H. Lee, "UC Meets LA," *LA Weekly,* 18–24 June 1993, 17.

15. See, for example, Gloria Steinem, *Revolution from Within: A Book of Self-esteem* (Boston: Little, Brown, 1992).

16. Carol Gilligan, Nona P. Lyons, and Trudy J. Hammer, eds., *Making Connections: The Relational Worlds of Adolescent Girls at Emma Willard School* (Cambridge: Harvard University Press, 1990), 4.

17. Carol Gilligan, *In a Different Voice: Psychological Theory and Women's Development* (Cambridge: Harvard University Press, 1982), 173.

18. Lani Guinier, Michelle Fine, and Jane Balin, *Becoming Gentlemen: Women, Law School, and Institutional Change* (Boston: Beacon, 1997), 2.

19. Katherine S. Mangan, "Lani Guinier Starts Campaign to Curb Use of the Socratic Method," *Chronicle of Higher Education,* 11 April 1997, A12.

20. Christina Hoff Sommers, "Pathological Social Science: Carol Gilligan and the Incredible Shrinking Girl," in Paul R. Gross, Norman Levitt, and Martin W. Lewis, eds., *The Flight from Science and Reason* (New York: New York Academy of Sciences/Johns Hopkins University Press, 1996), 370.

21. Ibid., 374–378.

22. Beith Reinhard, "Report Casts Doubt on the Value of Single-Sex Schooling," *Education Week,* 18 March 1998, 8.

23. Ibid.

24. Debra Viadero, "For Better or Worse, Girls Catching Up to Boys," *Education Week,* 24 June 1998, 5.

25. Barbara Vobejda and Linda Perlstein, "Teenagers Closing Gap Between Sexes," *Washington Post/Manchester Guardian Weekly,* 28 June 1998, 15.

26. Viadero, "Girls Catching Up to Boys," 5.

27. Ibid.

28. Vobejda and Perlstein, "Teenagers Closing Gap," 15.

29. Ibid.

30. Patricia Chisholm, "Bad Girls," *MacLean's*, 8 December 1997, 10.

31. "Teen Convicted in Virk Death to Serve Sentence in Adult Jail," *Globe and Mail*, 19 June 1999, A6.

32. Chisholm, "Bad Girls," 13.

33. Sibylle Artz, quoted by Chisholm, "Bad Girls," 16.

34. Colin L. Powell, "Recreating the Civil Society One Child at a Time," in E. J. Dionne Jr., ed., *Community Works: The Revival of Civil Society in America* (Washington, D.C.: Brookings Institution, 1998), 72.

35. Ibid.

36. Michael Walzer, "The Idea of Civil Society: A Path to Social Reconstruction," in *Community Works*, 140.

Chapter 8

1. Nancy Astor, quoted in James Charlton, ed., *A Little Learning Is a Dangerous Thing: A Treasury of Wise and Witty Observations for Students, Teachers, and Other Survivors of Higher Education* (New York: St. Martin's, 1994), 67.

2. Mary Ann Zehr, "District Might Let Students Pick Teachers," *Education Week*, 19 November 1997, 1.

3. Ibid., 9.

4. Ibid.

5. Ibid.

6. "Former Law Student Stages Hunger Strike," *Chronicle of Higher Education*, 23 January 1998, A8.

7. "Student Claiming Anxiety Sues School for Bias," *Chronicle of Higher Education*, 19 January 1996, A6.

8. Nathaniel Branden, *The Six Pillars of Self-esteem* (New York: Bantam, 1995), 203.

9. Thomas Armstrong, Ph.D., *The Myth of the A.D.D. Child: Fifty Ways to Improve Your Child's Behavior and Attention Span Without Drugs, Labels, or Coercion* (New York: Plume, 1997), 9.

10. Pat Wingert and Barbara Kantrowitz, "Why Andy Couldn't Read," *Newsweek*, 27 October 1997, 58.

11. Ibid.

12. Armstrong, *Myth*, 4–5.

13. Ibid., 8.

14. Ibid., 8–9.

15. Ibid., 8–11.

16. Nancy Gibbs, "The Age of Ritalin," *Time*, 30 November 1998, 90.

17. Ibid., 94.

18. Ibid., 92.

19. William Damon, *Greater Expectations: Overcoming the Culture of Indulgence in America's Homes and Schools* (New York: Free Press, 1995), 80.

20. Elaine Showalter, "Taming the Rampant Incivility in Academe," *Chronicle of Higher Education*, 15 January 1999, B4.

21. Ibid.

22. Ibid.

23. Ibid.

24. Ibid., B5.

25. Alison Schneider, "Insubordination and Intimidation Signal the End of Decorum in Many Classrooms," *Chronicle of Higher Education*, 27 March 1998, A12.

26. Ibid.

27. Ibid.

28. Ibid., A13.

29. See "Why Professors Don't Do More to Stop Students Who Cheat," *Chronicle of Higher Education*, 22 January 1999, A8.

30. William Damon, "The Path to a Civil Society Goes Through the University," *Chronicle of Higher Education*, 16 October 1998, B4–5.

31. Michael Lerner, *The Politics of Meaning: Restoring Hope and Possibility in an Age of Cynicism* (Reading, Mass.: Addison-Wesley, 1997), 10.

32. "BA Cracks Down on 'Air Rage,'" *Los Angeles Times*, 30 August 1998, L3.

33. Ibid.

34. Jack Aubry, "Canada Leads Fight Against Air Rage," *Vancouver Sun*, 5 June 1999, A8.

35. Julie Cart and Tere Petersen, "Group Offers Rewards to Counter Skiers' Deadly 'Road Rage,'" *Los Angeles Times*, 14 February 1999, A3.

36. Don Dinkmeyer and Rudolf Dreikurs, *Encouraging Children to Learn: The Encouragement Process* (Englewood Cliffs, N.J.: Prentice-Hall, 1963), 25.

37. Gertrude Himmelfarb, *The De-Moralization of Society: From Victorian Virtues to Modern Values* (New York: Knopf, 1995), 9.

38. Louis E. Raths, Merrill Harmin, and Sidney B. Simon, *Values and Teaching: Working with Values in the Classroom*, 2d ed. (Columbus, Ohio: Merrill, 1978), 137–139.

39. William Kilpatrick, *Why Johnny Can't Tell Right from Wrong and What We Can Do About It* (New York: Touchstone/Simon & Schuster, 1992), 94.

40. Stanley Elam and Lowell C. Rose, "The Twenty-seventh Annual Phi Delta Kappa/Gallup Poll of the Public's Attitudes Toward the Public Schools," *Phi Delta Kappan*, September 1995, 50–51.

41. Lowell C. Rose and Alec M. Gallup, "The Thirtieth Annual Phi Delta Kappa/Gallup Poll of the Public's Attitudes Toward the Public Schools," *Phi Delta Kappan*, September 1998, 51.

42. Elam and Rose, "Twenty-seventh Annual," 51.

43. Ibid.

44. Stanley Elam and Lowell C. Rose, "The Twenty-fifth Annual Phi Delta Kappa/Gallup Poll," *Phi Delta Kappan*, October 1993, 145.

45. Ibid.

46. Elam and Rose, "Twenty-seventh Annual," 54.

47. Alfie Kohn, "How Not to Teach Values: A Critical Look at Character Education," *Phi Delta Kappan*, February 1997, 432.

48. Ibid.

49. Ibid.

50. Kay Haugaard, "Suspending Moral Judgment: Students Who Refuse to Condemn the Unthinkable—A Result of Too Much Tolerance?" *Chronicle of Higher Education*, 27 June 1997, B4–5.

51. William Kilpatrick, *Why Johnny Can't Tell Right from Wrong and What We Can Do About It* (New York: Touchstone/Simon & Schuster, 1992), 93–94.

52. Ibid., 94.

Chapter 9

1. Eric Hobsbawm, *Age of Extremes: The Short Twentieth Century, 1914–1991* (London: Abacus, 1995), 149.

2. Ibid.

3. Jacques Ellul, *Propaganda: The Formation of Men's Attitudes* (New York: Vintage, 1973), 57.

4. Ibid., 59.

5. Ibid., 25.

6. Ibid.

7. Stephen Hawking, *A Brief History of Time: From the Big Bang to Black Holes* (New York: Bantam, 1990), 13.

8. Michael Guista, letter to the editor, *Chronicle of Higher Education*, 12 March 1999, B10.

9. Dr. David Dutton, quoted in David Cohen, "It's a Mystery to Me," *Guardian Weekly/BBC World Service*, 24 January 1999, 7.

10. Neil Postman, *Technopoly: The Surrender of Culture to Technology* (New York: Vintage, 1993), 148.

11. Ibid., 145–147.

12. Ibid., 150.

13. Ibid.

14. Diane Ravitch, "What If Research Really Mattered?" *Chronicle of Higher Education*, 16 December 1998, 33.

15. Ibid.

16. Ibid.

17. Ibid., 34.

18. Ibid.

19. Postman, *Technopoly*, 157.

20. Alan G. Gross, *The Rhetoric of Science* (Cambridge: Harvard University Press, 1990), 7.

21. Ibid., 15.

22. Steven Ward, "Filling the World with Self-esteem: A Social History of Truth-Making," *Canadian Journal of Sociology* 21, no. 1 (1996): 1.

23. Ibid., 8.

24. Ibid., 9–10.

25. Ibid., 10.

26. Ibid., 11.

27. Ibid., 12.

28. Ibid., 10–11.

29. Ibid., 3.

30. Ibid.

31. Joseph Kahne, "The Politics of Self-esteem," *American Educational Research Journal* 33, no. 1 (1996): 12.

32. John P. Hewitt, *The Myth of Self-esteem: Finding Happiness and Solving Problems in America* (New York: St. Martin's, 1998), 49.

33. Ibid., 50.

34. Ibid.

35. Oliver James, "Who Needs a Degree? Discuss," *Manchester Guardian Weekly,* 20 June 1999, 23.

36. John Vasconcellos, quoted in Richard Lee Colvin, "Losing Faith in Self-esteem Movement," *Los Angeles Times,* 25 January 1999, A14.

37. Robin Wilson, "A Challenge to the Veracity of a Multicultural Icon," *Chronicle of Higher Education,* 15 January 1999, A14–15.

38. Ibid., A16.

39. Ward, "Filling the World," 3.

40. Ibid., 1.

41. Ibid., 17.

42. Marcia Angell, M.D., *Science on Trial: The Clash of Medical Evidence and the Law in the Breast Implant Case* (New York: Norton, 1996), 19–22.

43. Ibid., 19–31.

44. Ibid., 189.

45. Ibid.

46. Christina Hoff Sommers, "Pathological Social Science: Carol Gilligan and the Incredible Shrinking Girl," in Paul R. Gross, Norman Levitt, and Martin W. Lewis, eds., *The Flight from Science and Reason* (New York: New York Academy of Sciences; Baltimore: Johns Hopkins University Press, 1996), 378.

47. William Damon, *Greater Expectations: Overcoming the Culture of Indulgence in America's Homes and Schools* (New York: Free Press, 1995), 81.

48. Denis Diderot, quoted in *James Charlton, ed., A Little Learning Is a Dangerous Thing: A Treasury of Wise and Witty Observations for Students, Teachers, and Other Survivors of Higher Education* (New York: St. Martin's, 1994), 100.

49. Jessica Portner, "After Anti-Smoking Effort, Fla. Youths Light Up Less," *Education Week,* 14 April 1999, 12.

50. Mike Clary, "A Disney You Can Go Home To," *Los Angeles Times,* 27 September 1996, A15.

51. Ibid.

52. Thomas Kuhn, *The Structure of Scientific Revolutions,* 2d ed. (Chicago: University of Chicago Press, 1972), 19.

53. Benjamin Barber, *An Aristocracy of Everyone: The Politics of Education and the Future of America* (New York: Oxford University Press, 1992), 267.

54. Ibid.

Epilogue

1. See Christopher Lasch, *The Culture of Narcissism: American Life in an Age of Diminishing Expectations* (New York: Norton, 1978).

2. See Eric Hobsbawm, *Age of Extremes: The Short Twentieth Century, 1914–1991* (London: Abacus/Little, Brown), 1994.

3. Clive Ponting, *Progress and Barbarism: The World in the Twentieth Century* (London: Chatto and Windus, 1998), 536.

4. Ibid., 546.

5. Ibid., 541.

6. David Tyack, "Needed: More Educational Conservationists," *Education Week*, 23 June 1999, 68.

7. Marian Wright Edelman, quoted in James Charlton, ed., *A Little Learning Is a Dangerous Thing: A Treasury of Wise and Witty Observations for Students, Teachers, and Other Survivors of Higher Education* (New York: St. Martin's, 1994), 5.

Index